Phonograph Record Libraries

THE INTERNATIONAL ASSOCIATION OF MUSIC
LIBRARIES – UNITED KINGDOM BRANCH

Phonograph Record Libraries

Their organisation and practice: 2nd edition

Edited by
HENRY F. J. CURRALL, FLA
Head of the Music Division, Westminster City Libraries

With a Preface by
A. HYATT KING, M.A.
Superintendent, The Music Room, British Museum

ARCHON BOOKS
HAMDEN, CONNECTICUT

PHONOGRAPH RECORD LIBRARIES. Published in the
U.S.A. by Archon Books, The Shoe String Press Inc.,
and published in Great Britain as
GRAMOPHONE RECORD LIBRARIES.
© 1970 CROSBY LOCKWOOD & SON LTD
First Published 1963
2nd edition 1970 published by
Crosby Lockwood & Son Ltd
26 Old Brompton Road London SW7

ISBN 0.208.00381.9

Typeset by Academic Services Ltd., Dublin
and printed in Great Britain by
Clarke, Doble & Brendon Ltd., Plymouth.

ACKNOWLEDGEMENTS

The Editor wishes to make grateful acknowledgement to the following:
   The Decca Record Company for use of illustrations on groove and stylus wear
   Philips Records Ltd. for use of illustrations of gramophone record manufacture
   Cecil E. Watts, Esq. for the illustration of perfect LP microgrooves
   The Year Book of Education, for permission to reprint Mr. Saul's article
      "Museums of Sound – History and Principles of Operation"
   Barnet Borough Council for the illustration of the Gramophone Record Library
   La Discothèque Nationale de Belgique for illustrations of the "Discobus"
   Alec Hyatt King, Esq., M.A., for helpful criticism and advice
   Margaret Judges for typing and much help.

Contents

v

List of illustrations

Editorial

In the years that have passed since the publication of the first edition of *Gramophone Record Libraries* in 1963, there has been much expansion and development both in Britain and elsewhere. I have taken advantage of this new edition to explore the subject more thoroughly, and to make the coverage, at least for Britain, as comprehensive as possible, except, perhaps, in the case of tape recordings.

At the time of writing (March 1969), tape recordings and cassettes are not used to any considerable extent in public gramophone record libraries in this country, but I imagine that the editor of a future edition of this work, should there be one, will of necessity ask his contributors to discuss them more widely because of their increased use in libraries. Video tape, and in fact all forms of audio-visual material will probably be more used in a few years' time than we imagine possible now.

A comparison of the contents table of the first and second editions of *Gramophone Record Libraries* will show how much new material has been added since 1963. Record selection is fully covered, and the cataloguing of gramophone records in the average public library collection is dealt with, as well as the much fuller treatment necessary in a collection such as the BBC Gramophone Record Library.

Commercial record library procedures, both in this country and across the Channel are described by Ivan March, who demonstrates the various ways in which these services differ from those offered by public libraries sometimes to the disadvantage of the latter.

The reader will note these and other additions to the contents of the first edition, but he should also realise that the material which is common to both editions has in fact been thoroughly revised, or in many cases completely rewritten for the second edition, which is virtually a new book.

Every effort has been made to be as up to date as possible at the time of going to print (Winter 1969). Some contributors have completely revised or rewritten their articles within the last few months to ensure this, and I am most grateful to them for doing so.

Preface

by ALEC HYATT KING, M.A.
The Music Room, The British Museum

In the six years since the first edition of this book appeared, the provision of gramophone records throughout the United Kingdom has expanded to keep pace with demand. Statistics show that in rate-supported libraries alone the number has risen by nearly fifty per cent. If figures were available for university and college libraries, a comparable increase would doubtless be found. Another aspect of this activity is seen in the Sound Recordings Group of the Library Association, which has steadily expanded since its foundation in 1964 and has organised some successful courses for students.

While most of this growth has to do with music, it should be remembered that students of the spoken word are relying more and more on records. Whether on disc or tape, recorded sound should be regarded, not as a poor relation of books and (in music) of scores, but as an essential partner to them, imposing on the librarian its own peculiar and exacting discipline.

If in the next decade or so there lie ahead technical developments as rapid and far-reaching as those of the long-playing and stereo period, the record librarian is faced with a challenge as big as anything the printed word is likely to offer. Professional expertise, in procurement, processing and servicing, will become more essential that ever. Because small collections may expand far more rapidly than is expected, the more he can learn about larger collections the better.

This book deals primarily with the work of British libraries at many different levels. At first sight the small local branch library or county library may not seem to have much in common with the huge collections of the BBC or of the British Institute of Recorded Sound, but all in fact need a basis of rules and regulations, and problems of processing, storage, staff-training and so on are common ground.

In this edition some space is rightly allotted to developments outside Britain. It is, for instance, most instructive to be able to compare the work of the BBC and BIRS with their counterparts in France. Any survey of some part of the vast, complex and rapidly changing scene in the USA can hardly fail to offer stimulating and challenging ideas. Again, a comparison between British Commercial record libraries and some of those in Europe shows illuminating parallels and divergencies.

The reader who wishes to pursue the subject on the widest possible basis will find not a few entries in the bibliography which reflect the intense and multifarious activity in other countries.

I am delighted with the range and variety of contributions which Mr. Currall has skilfully and patiently assembled and I confidently hope that the book will be as useful as its predecessor, and to an even wider public.

The International Association of Music Libraries

by J. H. DAVIES, MBE, FLA
Vice President, IAML; President, United Kingdom Branch, IAML

The Association was conceived in Florence, 1949, and, after gestation in Lüneburg 1950, was born in Paris 1951 (with UNESCO as *accoucheur*). By 1952 it had its constitution and its first President (the late Richard Hill, of Washington). Since then under King, Lindberg, and Jurres and with Fedorov as an *éminence grise* throughout, IAML has steadily expanded and consolidated as far as its present membership of over 1,000 in more than 40 countries. Domestic committees include those for academic, public and broadcasting libraries and for sound recordings, cataloguing, music information centres and the dating of music. To these must be added the Commission Mixte (IAML and the International Musicological Society) first for the *International Repertory of Music Sources*, (RISM) and latterly for the *Abstracts of Musical Literature*, (RILM). Progress in all these activities is currently described in the Association's journal *Fontes Artis Musicae*.

Co-operation with other bodies such as that quoted above has become a characteristic feature, e.g. with IFLA and IFD (Brussels, 1955), the Galpin Society (Cambridge 1959) and the International Music Council (New York and Washington, 1968).

The pattern of full congress every third year, interspersed with annual meetings of the various working parties, has established itself as practical, and has been rewarded by a steady increase in the number of delegates.

IAML's publications-list (below) points to a consistent effort to realise its objective: *viz*. the co-ordinated development of the music collections of the world and the systematic stimulation of music librarianship everywhere. Through its central offices, working commissions, and national branches, the Association now occupies a strategic position in the fields of music and libraries, which formerly pursued their courses all too independently.

The United Kingdom Branch, with over 200 members, is one of the largest, and is the only one to issue its own journal.

PRINCIPAL IAML PUBLICATIONS

Second World Congress of Music Libraries Lüneburg.	Bärenreiter, 1950
Documenta musicologica. Erste Reihe: Druckschriften-Faksimiles. *In progress*	Bärenreiter, 1953
Fontes artis musicae. *In progress*	Bärenreiter, 1954
Code international de catalogage de la musique. *In progress*	Peters, 1957
International congress of libraries and documentation centres, Brussels, 1955. Proceedings (jointly with the International Federation of Library Associations and the International Federation of Documentation). 3 vols.	Nijhoff, 1958
Catalogue of rare (orchestral) materials. *In progress under the auspices of the European Broadcasting Union*	Radio Commission, IAML, 1959
Music, libraries and instruments, Papers: (Joint congress, Cambridge, 1959, with the Galpin Society).	Hinrichsen, 1961
Répertoire International des sources musicales. *In progress*	Henle, 1960
Catalogus Musicus. *In progress*	IAML, 1963
Brio: journal of the U.K. Branch	IAML (U.K.) 1964
Directory of music research libraries. *In progress* part 1: Canada and USA.	University of Iowa, 1967
RILM Abstracts of musical literature. *In progress*	IAML, 1968
Polyglot Wörterbuch. *In preparation*	

The Sound Recordings Group of the Library Association

by J. W. HOWES, FLA
Hon. Secretary 1964–6

During the many meetings which preceded the first issue of this book the contributors became very much aware of the need for some permanent professional group dealing with Gramophone Record Libraries. After preliminary work by a steering committee, the Library Association was approached, and approval for the establishment of a new group of the Library Association was given in May 1964.

On 17th September 1964 a meeting of the Group was held at Chaucer House. The Constitution was approved and first Committee elected. Soon after this date the majority of the members of the Committee found themselves involved in the "amalgamation" of the London Boroughs. The problems resulting from this prevented as much attention being given to the newly formed Group as many of the Committee would have wished. It is perhaps a tribute to this first Committee that during the first two years of office a well supported course was arranged by the North-Western Polytechnic in collaboration with the Group, a working party on minimum standards established and relationships with the record industry improved. The Group was also approached on several technical matters from Libraries both in Great Britain and overseas, and held several interesting meetings.

As the number of Gramophone Record Libraries grows the number of staff able to deal with this more recent "special material" grows as well. The Sound Recordings Group is most interested in assisting the professional education of all concerned with Gramophone Records, which alone can help to establish a high standard of service to the public, who in growing numbers are using (or demanding the establishment of) Gramophone Record Libraries.

The Gramophone Record Library is no longer a novelty, and the Sound Recordings Group would seem to have been established at the right moment to enable this no longer novel service to be incorporated into standard Public Library Practice.

Policy in the Provision of Public Gramophone Record Libraries

by L. G. LOVELL, FLA
Chief Librarian, Rotherham Public Libraries

The Need for Public Gramophone Record Libraries

It has generally been assumed that one of the happier results of the last war was an improvement (particularly among younger people) in standards of musical appreciation, evidenced in a greater willingness to listen to serious music, albeit within a rather limited range. Be that as it may, there has not been any substantial increase in the facilities available in this country for attendance upon "live" musical performances. In London, there is more opera than before the war and a greater number of orchestral concerts, but the latter is probably balanced by a decline in chamber music and, more particularly, solo recitals (1*). In the provinces, opera is probably sparser than ever before, and certainly less in amount than in any other area of comparable population in Europe except Spain: what little there is is also concentrated more heavily than ever before in a very few centres, whole counties being completely deprived of it. Before the First World War several opera companies toured continuously, visiting even quite small towns. Between the wars there was the Carl Rosa company and (never since in the provinces approached in range of works presented or, so those who remember say, quality of performance) Beecham's BNOC. In the early post-war years the Carl Rosa was supplemented by some Sadler's Wells and Covent Garden touring. Now Covent Garden very rarely appears outside London, the Carl Rosa is gone, Sadler's Wells's thirty weeks touring a year largely repeats the same few stock works in ever fewer places, and the Glyndebourne Touring Opera (commenced 1968) visits only three or four places a year. The new Scottish Opera is producing quality but hardly quantity. Sheffield had its last visit from Sadler's Wells in 1965, when this city of half a million population heard *Flying Dutchman, Figaro, Butterfly* and *Orpheus in the Underworld.* In 1964 it got *Tosca, Barber of Seville, Attila* (wonder of wonders) and *La Vie Parisienne;* in 1963 *Carmen, Don Pasquale, Magic Flute, Traviata* and *La Belle Helène;* in 1962 *Tosca, Bartered Bride, Rigoletto, Magic Flute* and *Iolanthe.* To take the works of one composer – Richard Strauss – only

*See references at end of essay.

4

(not an opera of his has been given in Sheffield since before the war), what hope has Hull now of seeing *Elektra* (it saw it in 1912) or Halifax of seeing *Rosenkavalier* (which it saw in 1932) (2)?

Though there are more orchestral concerts, held in a greatly increased number of towns, as a result of programmes being planned for repetition in a number of widely differing places the range of music performed outside the half-dozen great cities is small indeed. The Arts Council's policy of fostering (in a manner reminiscent, in both method and liberality*, of the nineteenth-century poor law) local chamber music societies has led to an increase in this sort of music, but the deplorable artistic immaturity of many Arts Council stipendiaries (4), coupled with the virtual disappearance of the "touring celebrity" has for ever ended the palmy days of the 20s and 30s when an ordinary provincial town might hear regularly artists of the quality of Menuhin, Tauber and Heifetz†.

It is, unfortunately, true that to lead a full musical life is not possible in Great Britain, for even in London there is not that opportunity to keep abreast of developments in all musical fields on a worldwide scale which is the feature of the greatest continental cities. Particularly is this so in the field of dramatic music. Reference has been made to the operatic situation in the provinces. In London Sadler's Wells was, prior to its removal to the Coliseum, a little more enterprising (with Janacek mostly), but very unevenly so, and now appears to have run ahead of its available vocal resources. New productions outside the well trodden repertoire at Covent Garden in the last few years amount to *Moses und Aron, Katarina Ismailova, Khovantschina*, English works by Britten and Tippett, and a couple of one-acters. In the (not untypical) 1965–6 season, for example, the most recent opera to receive a new production was first performed in 1911 (and was nothing more unusual than *Rosenkavalier*), and the next newest dated from 1857. It is salutary to compare this situation with continental cities of size similar to the larger English provincial centres. In 1965–6 new productions announced for Kiel (population 270,000) included Einem's *Dantons Tod* and Ronnefeld's *Die Ameise*, Leipzig (590,000) among other new works gave the première of *The Sugar Reapers* by the *English* composer Alan Bush; and the mouth-watering programme at Hamburg (1,850,000) included *two* premières (*Jacobowsky und der Oberst* by Klebe and *Fluchtversuch* by Blacher) apart from a new production of Richard Strauss's *Frau ohne Schatten*. Zurich (440,000) saw *Moses und Aron* eleven years earlier than London. In one week chosen at

---

*The "guarantee" basis of the grants makes it virtually impossible for a society to build up reserves in good years to tide over the bad. The actual amount offered in 1965–6 averaged £89 per society, or under £25 per concert (3).

†In Middlesborough (population then 139,000) appeared, during 1937 and 1938, Schnabel, Hubermann, Heifetz, Gigli, Menuhin, Tauber and Arrau, among others including the Czech Philharmonic Orchestra with Kubelik (5).

random Stuttgart (not much bigger than Leeds), apart from a performance of *Die Meistersinger* with soloists of European reputation, heard a modern German work of high quality, a revival of a work of the German romantic school, an Italian repertory work, and an evening of ballet consisting of a standard French work and a contemporary German one; a random week in Düsseldorf (about the size of Manchester) produced two works by Wagner and one each by Krenek, Weill, and Richard Strauss. All these works were of a quality to justify them being made available here — but how long shall we have to wait (in London let alone the provinces) for Krenek's *Karl V* or Weill's *Street Scene* (even *Die Dreigroschenoper* is a curiosity here, in the land of its setting) among modern works, and the only Lortzing heard in Great Britain for many years has been two productions (one in Edinburgh, one in London) by visiting German companies, for a handful of performances each concentrated in a couple of weeks.

The growth of the "stagione" system at Covent Garden (and also to a lesser extent at Sadler's Wells) recently, by which all the performances of a work in a season may be stuffed into a period of three weeks or less, has, incidentally, made it even more difficult than before to keep up to date with operatic events in London, particularly for the person resident in the provinces. For example, *all* the performances of Covent Garden's new (1967) production of *Die Frau ohne Schatten* took place between 14th and 29th June. This just does not happen in Germany.

Musical comedy and the efforts of no less than four orchestras (one of them a chamber ensemble known throughout the world) were also available in Stuttgart, and music is subsidised from public funds to the extent of hundreds of thousands of pounds annually. Leeds in the late 50s could spare only £18,313 (6, p. 50) to help music *and* the theatre along (and that is better than most English cities), and allowed its only local symphony orchestra to be disbanded because it was costing more than that figure (7). Frankfurt's municipal theatre employs some 600 persons (8) (the majority musicians, vocal and instrumental), which compares rather favourably with the City Organist at Birmingham and the tiny company at Manchester Library Theatre. This state of affairs applies right down the population scale: Karlsruhe and Stoke on Trent are much of a size, but the former has an opera capable of taking *Tristan* in its stride whilst the latter now has no theatre at all, so cannot even enjoy a Sadler's Wells *Vie Parisienne* once a year (6, pp. [2], 80); Heidelberg and Oxford are similar both in size and other respects, but Heidelberg has an opera which can turn out a competent *Entführung* as a matter of routine whilst Oxford has only the university amateurs; Mainz and Middlesbrough have similar numbers of inhabitants and both make chemicals, but whilst the municipal theatre and orchestra at Mainz employs 288 persons (9) professional opera (except for the Arts Council "Opera for all" sort) was last heard in Middlesbrough some forty years ago; Esslingen and Rotherham are both six miles from large cities, are approaching 90,000 population, and have civic theatres — but one doubts whether the Brecht/Weill *Happy End* will ever be seen at Rotherham's.

Admission prices, too, for such music as is available in Great Britain, are generally higher than abroad — even where, to casual tourists, this would appear to be untrue (most English music-hunters abroad confine themselves to package tours at top price festivals, La Scala or Vienna); the prevalence of reduced subscription (Abonnement and Volksbühne*) rates in Germany, scaling down of prices for repeat performances in Italy, the existence of répétitions générales, and special prices for anyone with the remotest claim to student status in most countries, makes listening to music relatively cheap for local residents. In the British towns where admission prices have been kept low (for example Sheffield) the ration of soloists of international reputation is proportionately reduced — they may be foreign, but that does not necessarily mean the same thing!

Unlike the situation in "live" music, for broadcast music Great Britain is relatively fortunate. No other country has anything like our "Music" programme, and the quiet tenacity the BBC has shown in supporting this most valuable of its services against the irresponsible attacks levelled at it from time to time must be highly commended. Not only does it make available to the remotest corners of the country a steady stream of good music, it also brings us representative broadcasts from the great European festivals, and occasionally does great work in drawing to our attention the excellences of a neglected composer, by presenting a conspectus of his works such as cannot be obtained in public performances (the awakening of interest in the then-neglected Janacek was primarily due to such a campaign, and somewhat earlier a series of programmes of the work of Schütz opened doors in musical appreciation which had been closed for well over a century).

Nevertheless, even the brilliant results achieved by the BBC do not fill the gap which exists in musical provision. True, a great deal of modern music not otherwise available in this country is performed. In this way we heard Schönberg's *Moses und Aron* years before its elephantinely protracted gestation at Covent Garden, and Liebermann's *Leonora 40/45* — but what of Reutter's *Doktor Johannes Faust* and the works of Alan Bush? Some notable revivals of little-performed or forgotten works of earlier centuries have also been given (performances of Berlioz's *Requiem* and recordings of revivals by Italian houses of operas of the bel canto school, for example, long before Beecham and Callas respectively made them fashionable), though here again there are unpredictable gaps

---

*At Hamburg and other German opera houses the author has been privileged to attend semi-private Volksbühne ("people's theatre") performances, indistinguishable in quality from ordinary ones, at less than half normal prices — at Hamburg, for example, a good stalls seat costs DM7 (12/6) against a normal DM24 or more (in a house with standards comparable with Covent Garden).

(the BBC promised *Les Huguenots* even longer than Covent Garden promised *Moses und Aron* before it appeared, and the school of Meyerbeer has been in general curiously neglected by it, as also has the amazing post-war flowering of Dutch music, and to select a case at random, composers of local repute and wider worth such as Kuhlau). Even of the works which are performed, however, only one or two performances can be given. There is no opportunity to really get to know an important new work or a revived forgotten one, short of the dubiously-legal practice of "taping" it. Furthermore, of course, as with all broadcast or "live" music, there are two insuperable difficulties – the listener cannot plan his own listening, nor can he choose his own performers or compare side-by-side the work of alternative performers. To take the latter point first, it is true that, for popular works, over a long period, one may, by broadcast performances here and live performances here and abroad, get that special insight into a work which comes from comparing the approaches and results of different performers in it, but *only* over a very long period and *only* for very popular works. The cases which have been mentioned above of gaps which exist in the range of public and broadcast musical performances – Handel's choral works and Bach's church cantatas are more examples – are absolute cases in which a listener cannot plan his own listening, but the insuperable difficulty, even in the most musically well-provided community, that it is only possible to cover the whole range of music by actual performances over a great length of time, is quite as serious.

Fortunately, however, there is one means by which all the deficiencies so far enumerated (absence of live performances in Great Britain, gaps in the range of broadcast performances, lack of possibility of individual planning of listening, and impossibility of comparative listening) can be greatly minimised – by the use of gramophone records. Anyone with access to a comprehensive collection of gramophone records, built up over a long period (this it must be, as the available recorded repertoire changes quickly in these days of transition from monaural to stereophonic discs), is able to plan his listening to suit any objective, be it recreational or instructional*, and in the case of the established repertoire to do an

---

*For example, of Richard Strauss's fifteen operas, of which only six have been performed in Great Britain in recent years, at least eight have been recorded complete, together with considerable excerpts from others. All Bruckner's and Mahler's symphonies are available on record. Eighty-eight of Bach's church cantatas are in the current British catalogue, and ninety-four works by Telemann – how long would we have to wait to hear all of these in public or broadcast performances? Of Smetana's operas all we see here is *The Bartered Bride* – four more are available on record. Two of the greatest works of the twentieth century – Schönberg's *Moses und Aron* and Berg's *Lulu* – were available here on record for years before they were (briefly) put on live show (10).

endless amount of comparative listening to different performances of the same work*.

So much for the usefulness of records – they are demonstrably a most valuable, and indeed indispensable, element in the overall provision of musical facilities for any community. Now what are the means by which, in the twentieth-century world, community facilities are provided? Certain amenities any normally-privileged individual provides for himself – for example, by private contract with commercial firms, he provides his own furniture and clothing, and in general food and housing.

At this point, however, another factor appears. Of very recent years the community as a corporate entity has taken upon itself certain aspects of food provision (subsidised foods and orange juice for infants, and cheap restaurants where such are not available through private enterprise) and for many years the community has regarded it as a corporate duty to make available adequate housing for the under-privileged. Corporate provision of libraries and educational facilities, like municipal housing, started as a service for the under-privileged, but more recently two new elements have intruded themselves into social theory. The first is corporate provision of services as a means of redistribution of income (for example, the National Health Service, financing, mainly out of taxation based on income, a service equally available to all). The second is the corporate provision of services as a means of economical management of them. A situation whereby each individual provided his own water, sanitation and roads was found inefficient centuries ago, and one whereby each manufactured his own electricity and gas is even more inconceivable on sheerly technical grounds.

Public libraries are no longer a service for the under-privileged but an integral element of a welfare state in a technological society: *all* classes now use the public library. indeed in many cases the under-privileged – such as now exists of it – is the hardest class to attract. The growth of specialisation has led to such a proliferation in the amount and a variety in the forms taken by recorded knowledge that a new specialisation – call it librarianship or documentation – has arisen to orientate knowledge so that it may be used for further technological expansion. Gramophone records are one of the new forms taken by recorded knowledge, and like the other forms (microforms, automatic data processing by computers and punched

*For example, one can compare the Don Giovanni of Brownlee (pre-war) with that of Siepi (two versions), Fischer-Dieskau, Waechter, London, Ghiaurov and Taddei. Of Ponchielli's *La Gioconda* (about which there appears to be a conspiracy among English opera promoters to deprive us of a live hearing) there are three recorded versions available in England, and no less than six versions of many popular operas. There are about seventeen versions available of the Brahms violin concerto, *twenty-nine* of Beethoven's *Eroica* symphony and seventeen of his *Choral*. Of such relatively rarely-performed works as the Janacek Sinfonietta and Mahler's *Resurrection* symphony there are four and five versions available respectively (10).

cards, photographic reproduction and so on) the case for their provision by the community as a body rests on two propositions – firstly that they are an element in the production of some amenity which will lead to a fuller life for the community, or a significant part of it, and secondly that it is impossible for each individual to make full provision personally for his own needs in the field involved.

That music is such an amenity none can deny. That it has been regarded as worthy of community support from early times is indisputable: from the days when culture was an ecclesiastical monopoly to be used for the service of God, through the days when culture was accessible only to a minority with nobility and wealth, to today when, as a result of growth in social enlightenment, it is within the grasp of all who require it – by means of almsgiving, private patronage, and now financing from local or national taxation, music has been at least partly supported from funds provided by others than its direct users. This patronage of music has, it is true, as demonstrated above, been less generous in Great Britain than in many other countries, but the *principle* is firmly established, nationally by government financing of the Arts Council and locally by local authority assistance for concert provision in their areas (the Leeds example quoted above is far from unique – most large cities and many smaller places now make possible at least a few orchestral or smaller concerts annually in their areas). Furthermore, musical education, in schools and universities and through adult education, is now general.

On the evidence given here, it is submitted that gramophone records are an essential feature in musical provision and appreciation, without which no full musical life is possible. It is submitted that, though an individual may build up a library of records for himself (as he may of books), unless he is possessed of quite abnormal wealth (and house room!) he will not be able to purchase for himself (even if they were available when he wished to purchase them, which – again as with books – is far from being the case) all he needs. Therefore, as with books, there is an irrefutable case for their provision by some public authority, which will both purchase and, by the ministrations of specialist technicians (in this case librarians), make them available to the public as a whole (11). The basis of finance of such publicly formed collections should be such that the collection is made available to the public.

Social services are provided, in general, on one of two financial bases: either the providing body may bear from corporate funds the *whole* cost of the service, making it available free of charge (as is the case at present with book provision in public libraries), or the providing body may make what it considers reasonable charges for the service (such charges as will not deter the user, *not* "economic" charges, which often *will* deter the user), bearing from corporate funds the sum by which the cost of the service exceeds income from such charges (examples of this method are common in public music-provision – it is the method used by the Arts Council, and also by continental cities financing opera houses and British local authorities providing concerts). It would seem to be only common sense to use one of these two methods in financing publicly provided record collections as these are the two methods used in the social services most nearly allied to public provision of gramophone records.

With the coming into force of the Public Libraries and Museums Act, 1964, the battle to establish the legitimacy of the record collection as an integral part of the public library service was won. Though they were not made an obligatory provision, library authorities must "have regard to the desirability" of providing "facilities . . . for the borrowing of, or reference to . . . gramophone records . . . sufficient in number, range and quality to meet the general . . . and any special requirements of adults and children . . ." (12) What we have to do now is to bring home to library authorities (and, alas, still to some librarians) that record provision *is* desirable, and that it should be provided on the same generous lines as regards quality and quantity as is the bookstock, and not treated merely as a minor sideline of about the same importance as the newsroom. We must also consider the exact nature of what we ought to provide.

What Record Libraries should Provide

From what has been said above, it is obvious that gramophone record libraries are envisaged primarily as a force in musical appreciation. It therefore follows that the foundation of the collection should be the standard musical repertoire together with non-established works of serious intent, both old and new. It is, however, necessary to consider what else should be provided. So far as music is concerned, there are two classes to consider – "light" music and "ephemeral" music. "Light" music connotes such work as that of Sullivan, Lehar, the Vienna Strausses, and even such modern musical comedies as would seem to have some likelihood of extended life (*Oklahoma* and *West Side Story* are two such examples). There is also now a long enough history behind us in the field of jazz for it to be apparent that this form, too, has its standard works which have stood the test of time, and the recent flowering of interest in folk music, confused as it is by non-musical humanist and political undertones, and (like jazz) shading at one end imperceptibly into the "pop music" (or ephemeral) field, must not be overlooked (public demand will hardly permit us to do so, anyway). "Ephemeral" music includes so-called "dance" music in all its weird varities (ranging from foxtrot to "beat"), and the modern equivalent of the Victorian popular ballad. A feature of this latter type is that single items rarely occupy more than one side of a 7 in. 45 RPM disc. The larger (33 RPM) discs of this sort of music are always of the "recital" type, including a number of short works on one side. The costs involved in private purchase of this type are therefore much lower than of multi-sided "serious" works (13; 14, pp. 19–20, 26).

Here, again, it is suggested that invaluable lessons can be learned from parallels in public financial support of "live" music and from the established practices of public libraries. Except in holiday resorts, in this country publicly financed music is usually of the "standard-repertoire" type, though the Sadler's Wells opera now follows the practice of continental cities, where a rather broader policy has long been pursued. On the two nights following the set of performances listed above as having been given at Stuttgart, the opera there presented two operettas – *Das Opernball* and *Die lustige Witwe* – and at least one of the works of our national operettist, Sullivan (*The Gondoliers*), has been given in a German state-financed house (15). Sadler's Wells is now following suit with a liberal diet of Sullivan, Lehar and Offenbach – though, as yet, for reasons not explained, no Lortzing or Suppé – to provide a sorbet between the heavier but more nourishing courses of Rossini and Puccini. So far as is known, however, except as a "sprat to catch a mackerel" in holiday resorts, or on a profit-making basis to keep public halls employed, nowhere in Great Britain or elsewhere does the *ephemeral* type of music receive public sponsorship.

Public libraries, with few exceptions, have pursued a less well-defined "quality" policy in their book selection. Most of them, nowadays, are providing everything from technical documentation at the top of the scale to love stories and science fiction at the bottom. This dissipation of effort over a wide field, combined with a dualism of purpose between instruction and recreation, has not been to public libraries' advantage (in particular it has militated against "specialist bibliographical" training of staff), and it is no exaggeration to say that in the past the reason money was not available in most places for gramophone records was because it was spent on ephemeral novels. Public libraries with gramophone record collections have generally seen the danger of casting the net too wide (16), and if anything the tendency so far has perhaps been to place the bar too high, with a resultant limitation in the potential number of users. This is probably justified in the inaugural stages, in which many existing collections still are. However, it is vital, now that record libraries are becoming standard provision, that principles as to the nature of material bought should be firmly established.

It is not economical to provide ephemera from public funds. This applies as firmly to records as to books. There are overheads inherent in public enterprise (a hierarchical establishment, a costly building, the apparatus of democracy) which are not present in private enterprise of the type with which we are concerned (record and paperback-plus-greeting-card shops). In the case of records there is the additional factor that whereas ephemeral novels usually wear themselves out in use, the ephemeral record dies in popularity so quickly that there may well be a problem of obsolescence to add to that of the wastefulness of subjecting such records to all the necessary processes of a public record collection — accessioning, cataloguing, issuing, discharging and so on. It is therefore submitted that, on economic grounds and also on the ground that they are of no value in the furthering of musical appreciation, records of purely ephemeral music should not be included, except in the unlikely event of a library authority deliberately making separate financial provision for them. In such a case, the processes of accessioning, cataloguing, etc. should be reviewed critically and cut to the irreducible minimum — as many public libraries now do with their fiction stocks.

Not all records are of music, and a definite policy regarding the types of non-musical record is as important as for those of music. Recordings of poetry and drama would seem to be subject to much the same considerations as music — it is the quality of the item recorded which should be the criterion, and, whilst the line should be drawn against providing recitals by television personalities of verse of the type tucked away in odd corners of popular newspapers or recordings of "light programme" feature shows, the librarian should aim at providing not only Shakespeare and Milton but also T. S. Eliot and Arthur Miller. A particularly valuable feature would seem to be recordings in the original language of important foreign plays (unfortunately, however, only French plays are at all easy to get in this country at the moment). Apart from the intrinsic usefulness of these non-musical records (which are highly popular when available in reasonable numbers (17)), their provision is important from a policy point of view in that they widen considerably the circle of intelligent people interested in the record collection, which otherwise is limited to the musically conscious part of the population. The advantages of as many people as possible supporting the record library are (particularly when money is required) too obvious to need elaboration.

This consideration also applies to another class of non-musical records, language teaching sets (16). These consist of "long" courses of a number of discs accompanied by printed manuals (issued mainly by Assimil, Berlitz and Linguaphone), and "short" courses of one or two discs (issued by a number of bodies, notably Conversaphone which provides courses in languages not otherwise available on record). "Long" courses are best embarked upon only by people who already have a smattering of some foreign language (not necessarily the one to be learnt), including a little grammar, or alternatively who have already worked through a "short" course in the language concerned. More libraries provide these than any other non-musical type. Nevertheless, despite their popularity when provided, objection to their provision has been made on the ground that the wear and tear on them is excessive and that the "long" courses, consisting as they do of a series of records, may be covered more rapidly by one user than another, and thus one user may be held up by the slow progress of another (14, p. 21). The answer to this latter point would seem to be a generous degree of duplication, which will be justified anyway by the use made of them. This is made easier if for each language only one brand of "long" course is provided, and a "consumer survey" to establish the most suitable for our purpose is badly needed (one is available for "short" courses (18)). The provision of these courses would seem to be a natural corollary of providing language textbooks, which brings up another point – the use of records to supplement public libraries' reference collections. A collection of gramophone records (together, of course, with a player) can serve many purposes in a reference library. The most obvious of these is to illustrate the library's stock on musical history (19) (the various musical archive collections and histories of recorded sound are of especial use in this connection), but other purposes, perhaps less obvious, are a collection of bird songs and sounds of musical instruments. The use of a record player in the reference library is, surely, no more unorthodox than the use of a microfilm reader. The use of a tape recorder to record voices of personalities and locally important events for the local history collection is, perhaps, rather off the subject of gramophone record libraries, but it must never be forgotten that a good many commercially produced recordings are of local history interest somewhere – for instance, the two discs of Thurston Dart performing on the organ of Rotherham parish church (20), find a natural home in the Rotherham Public Library's local history collection. At least one library (Manchester) provides languages courses on tape in its reference library (21).

The only other class of records needing consideration is sound effects. So far as these record *specific* sounds (e.g., Big Ben, the bells of a specific church, the Bruges carillon, or an Amsterdam street organ) they may, like bird songs, have their uses in a reference library. It is far more doubtful, however, whether libraries should provide the *general* type of sound effects (train whistle, waves on rocky shore, aeroplane diving, and so on) used for theatrical performances. So small a proportion of the costs of even an amateur production do they account for, and so heavy is the wear and tear they receive, that it would seem desirable for dramatic societies to provide their own sound effects. When a play does require a "specific" sound there seems to be no reason (other than performing rights, which may in this connection perhaps be safely ignored in some cases) why it should not be re-recorded on tape from the reference collection. Nothing, incidentally, will stop borrowers quite illegally re-recording on tape musical and other performances from library records, but needless to say this practice should *never* be officially countenanced, the library's rules should prohibit it, discs should bear an appropriate label (these are available free from the copyright societies), and borrowers who remark that they are in the practice of doing it should be warned of its illegality.

The Extent of Provision and Use

Having disposed of considerations of the nature of the records to be provided, we must now proceed to the policy to be implemented regarding coverage of the field decided upon. Two factors are involved here: the *physical form* of records to be stocked and the *number* of records needed. There is, of course, now no case for the provision of SP (78 RPM) discs; libraries which possess stocks of them now find them virtually completely unused, and most have disposed of them. What was once of use for historical purposes on SP has now mostly been transcribed on to LP (33 RPM). LP discs will form the great bulk of any record library, and form the whole of many existing collections (22, pp. 218–19), but despite the objections to them expressed by some (23) there seems no valid reason for rigidly excluding 45 RPM (EP) discs, and substantial advantages are to be gained from including a small proportion of them, the most notable of which are the availability of certain material on EP which is not available on LP (for example, one of the two discs by Thurston Dart mentioned above (20)) and the possibility of reducing casual wear on the popular sections of LP "recital" discs, which sections are often duplicated on EP.

A far more difficult problem is the policy to be adopted regarding the balance of monaural and stereophonic discs. In keeping with their usual reaction to new ideas, many librarians for as long as possible stuck their heads in the sand to hide from the obvious conclusion that once stereo arrived it would, within a few years, become the standard and universal form (long after the arrival of LP many were still trying to stem the inevitable tide by continuing to purchase SP!) (23). The decision of EMI to cease the production of new mono classical titles from July 1967 (24) has forced us to formulate a policy instead of continuing to temporise. At present at least half of our users have stereophonic equipment. Gramophone record libraries, if they are to avoid having dead stock left on their hands, need to have a wary eye for future trends. For a new record library half and half monaural and stereophonic would now seem to be sensible, the popular (for example, Beethoven and Tchaikovsky), which will wear out quickly, on monaural, and the less popular, which will be with us for a long time, on stereo. There will be a proportion of potential users who will not join unless reasonable stereo coverage is provided; this applies also to persons requiring tapes, and this type too should eventually be available (both mono and stereo), albeit in much smaller quantities than discs. That language courses should be stocked on tape is particularly important, despite the risk (greater by far, due to techniques of use of language courses, than with music tapes) of accidental deletion of sections by users: many potential users of language courses have tape recorders but (not being interested in music) do not possess disc record players. Reasonable eventual proportions, in a stock of 3,000 say, might at the present time be 45 per cent mono discs, 45 per cent stereo discs, 6 per cent mono tapes, 4 per cent stereo tapes, but it seems likely that by 1970 we shall be thinking in terms of stereo-only record libraries, except perhaps for tapes. Hence the importance of not now buying in mono anything which will not have worn out in use within a couple of years.

We must also decide what the irreducible unit of size amounts to, if the library is to be able to operate usefully and reasonably independently, except for non-standard items, of outside assistance. That a library should be able to operate efficiently on the basis of its *own* resources, rather than those available in *other* libraries, is perhaps more important for records than for books, for whereas there exists for books an extensive (and highly costly) system of interlending between libraries, little of the sort yet exists for records, and in view of the paucity (as compared with books) of the items involved and the lessons we have learned on such matters as the cost of maintaining union catalogues (25), it seems unlikely that there will ever be interlending between libraries of records comparable with that existing of books. The time has now arrived, however, when some outcome ought to be discernible from the deliberations on the subject of interlending records which have been taking place during the last few years. There seems no reason (other than organisational problems which are simple compared with those involving books) why an interlending system covering all records (other than those currently purchasable in Great Britain) should not be instituted – there is no case at all for interlending records which can be bought, and this should not be countenanced.

It must never be forgotten that musical taste does not stand still, and the record library should aim at always being a little ahead of musical fashion rather than behind it. It really needed little prescience by anyone familiar with musical trends on the continent to forecast the breakthrough of Schönberg, Bruckner and Mahler into popular esteem in the last decade – exactly the same thing happened with Stravinsky immediately after the last war. Yet how many record librarians, indoctrinated in their student days by the English musical press, now find themselves, as a result of basing their selection only on demand over the *previous* few years, cluttered with unused Vaughan Williams and over-duplicated Sibelius. Nobody familiar with the decidedly lukewarm enthusiasm for these former favourites of the English musical scene shown by the mainstream of musical opinion abroad could have so grossly over-estimated both their stature and the lasting power of their popularity. One gets the impression that not much Menotti is heard here today; in the 50s he was a dominating figure in certain circles here and in America. In Europe, Richard Strauss's post-Ariadne operas are standard fare. The only reason that they are not yet so here is that they were completely ignored until recently by both our national opera companies. More recently, their cause has hardly been widely advanced by Covent Garden treating *Die Schweigsame Frau* in a manner which reminded this author of Gilbert and Sullivan gone decadent, using *Arabella* as something for Glyndebourne-fanciers to snooze expensively through in the winter, or (as mentioned earlier) compressing the few performances of its new *Frau ohne Schatten* into an even more restrictive time-band (fifteen days from first performance to last!) than usual. Surely Sadler's Wells, if it can tackle *From the House of the Dead*, ought not to find *Intermezzo* beyond it? Despite the handicaps they have suffered in Great Britain they will eventually come into the repertoire here, as American and British musical taste *always, at a few years remove*, follows the continent so far as composers who prove their worth in the world musical scene are concerned. Similarly, the *bel canto* epidemic virtually died out abroad in 1964/5/6 – and by June 1967 for the first time even Sutherland could not fill all Covent Garden's seats for *La Fille du Regiment*. Signs are appearing of a resurrection of French grand opera – this will become a new craze, which will eventually spread to Britain and America, when the widespread current distaste for all things French (arising from political conditions in France, and paralleled by a similar revulsion against German art in the 30s) is resolved by the normal (or assisted!) processes of human mortality.

We must learn, then, to develop a world perspective in musical taste – for only through this can we learn to distinguish between popular favourites (who come and go) and composers whose works are destined to become true "basic stock". It is suggested that much the same considerations apply to determining the nature of this basic stock in records as in books. No general library worthy of the name should be lacking in works such as the plays of Shakespeare, Aeschylus and Shaw, the poems of Milton, the novels of Dostoevsky, or such modern classics as *The Seven Pillars of Wisdom* and *Ulysses*. No matter how small the readership served, somewhere in every general library system should be copies of these books; there can be no excuse for relying on interlending to supply them. Similarly, every record library should from its own stock be able to supply all Beethoven's symphonies, Mozart's six great operas, and the whole of Wagner from *Der Fliegende Holländer* onwards. It is estimated (by reference to *The Gramophone Long-playing Classical Record Catalogue*) that to provide in single copies the whole of the absolutely basic easily available repertoire would mean purchasing rather over 500 discs: this, of course, does not take into account the question of duplication of titles in monaural and stereophonic forms, or the provision of non-musical recordings of the types discussed above. It will also be necessary, even in the smallest library, to duplicate from the start a few works for which there is great public demand (*Messiah* is a notable example). No library, however, can subsist only on classics – the basic stock must be leavened by a liberal element of the popular and the new. In order to give the collection variety, to ensure that it is not too academic for use by the general public, and to keep its users' interest, it is suggested that not much more than 50 per cent of the stock should be of the "standard classical" type – the remainder will be the serious contemporary music and light music of lasting interest mentioned above. It would appear, then, that the minimum size for a public record collection, if it is to satisfy its users' reasonable requests from its own resources, will be well over 1,000 discs, making some allowance for non-musical records, which will involve an initial cost of at least £2,000 on stock alone, to which must be added a substantial figure for equipment. The cost of establishing a satisfactorily sized record library, then, would appear to be comparable with that for a small branch of a public library. It seems unlikely that public library authorities of so small a size that the establishment of a new branch library is a serious matter financially will be able to contemplate the provision of a gramophone record service on worthwhile lines. It is, furthermore, most desirable that in charge of a gramophone record library should be a librarian who possesses not only professional qualifications but also a sound knowledge of music and records – a subject specialist in fact. Subject specialists are *not* employed in small general libraries – there are too few of them even in the large city, county, and university libraries, and they just do not occur elsewhere.

So much for the minimal sized collections. Larger general libraries do not limit their bookstocks to important English books, but attempt to acquire at any rate some representation of the trends of literature and learning throughout the world. Larger record libraries will need to apply this internationalism to their record selection. This type of library should be a little ahead of public needs, and can, by providing a combination of carefully selected stocks and the specialist staffs needed to exploit them, play an important part in the formation of taste. As, by a combination of informed selection and skilled exploitation a library can introduce its German-speaking readers to Berthold Brecht and Hermann Kasack, so it can introduce its music lovers to Hermann Reutter and Gottfried von Einem.

A library service which interprets its functions so seriously as this, however, is taking on a responsibility that can only be effectively discharged if ample resources are available – resources of stock and staff, and also of *organisation* – for the selection and acquisition of foreign material, be it books or records, is largely a matter of organisation. Great city, county, and university libraries will have on their staffs not only subject specialists in music, but also in foreign bibliography, and will maintain a wide range of foreign contacts as well as relations with specialist agencies in this country. They will subscribe to the necessary foreign bibliographies, which will be used as a basis for their activities in the foreign language field. These are not without relevance to the selection of foreign *records*, as the techniques and organisation established in such libraries for the acquisition of foreign books will be an invaluable parallel upon which to build an organisation to do the same job for records, substituting, of course, the record catalogues of foreign countries for the national bibliographies. Similarly, the channels of purchase established for foreign books will serve as a model for similar channels of record supply.

A pattern begins to emerge of the structure of a national record library service. It will consist of a number of minimal, or near minimal, sized collections which, together with a small number of much more comprehensive collections, should cover the whole country.

How the Service should be Provided

The 1964 Act (12, pp. 3–6) establishes the structure of library areas for the foreseeable future – the long debate which stretched from the McColvin proposals (1942) of *ad hoc* "library units" (26, chapters 14 & 15), through a variety of subsequent attempts at establishment of standards, to the Roberts report of 1959 (27) and the report of the Minister of Education's Working Party (28) is ended, and we are committed (subject, of course, to any radical changes in structure resulting from the impending report of the Royal Commission on Local Government) to a future pattern of library authorities varying from urban districts of, or even below, 40,000 population, to cities and counties of a million or more. How does this structure align with the needs of record library service? The service points are there, and staff trained in the appropriate techniques of registration, cataloguing, and distribution. There is at least a skeleton of staff with relevant subject knowledge of music and records, and the general establishment of record libraries will lead to an increase in their number. The new (1964) Library Association examination syllabus, List C of which for the first time introduced a degree of elementary subject specialisation, for music as for other subjects, at the basic qualification level (instead of, as formerly, only at the level of qualification for Fellowship), will also help a rapid growth in the number of young librarians with some knowledge of music and records and their special library techniques. Library schools are teaching this subject well (except, at some, for an irrelevant over-emphasis on special problems of music classification), and this paper is proving one of the more popular alternatives in List C. It is a pity that a paper on *gramophone record librarianship*, as distinct from music literature, was not included in List B of the new syllabus – record libraries are far too important and complex a subject to be treated as a minor aspect of music literature. Perhaps it is still not too late for something to be done. Most important of all, public libraries in Great Britain and elsewhere made an early and substantial start in providing record collections (16; 29; 30; 14, p. 17) – 80 library authorities in Britain provided some records by 1960 (31), by late-1968 this had risen to about 170 (more than a third), and under the influence of the new Act complete coverage will be achieved within a few years. Only a minority of existing collections, however, have anything which can be called a reasonable sized stock, and no British library as yet has succeeded in applying to its record collection the standards of comprehensiveness which the largest libraries apply to their book collections, though one or two of the new Greater London Boroughs are rapidly moving this way.

Public libraries, then, are accepted as the means by which record collections are made available to potential users. This being said, we must face up to the fact that the present and proposed future British public library areas are far from ideal for the purpose of record libraries, mainly because most of them are, and will be, units far too small for providing *any* public library services beyond the limits of a popular lending library and quick-reference collection. Even a quite small area can provide a satisfactory fiction and light non-fiction service if it is prepared to levy a high rate for the purpose (there are libraries of this type operating quite efficiently, at high cost, at about 20,000 population). For other types of provision, however, (reference, technical, music and records), the fact that there are certain high and irreducible unit costs involved (certain books and other material, or our basic record stock mentioned above, that *must* be provided, together with subject-trained staff, no matter how small the area, in order to do the job efficiently) makes provision by very small authorities virtually impossible.

It should not be overlooked that in the "pioneer" period just concluded the most progressive areas in respect of gramophone record service were the non-county boroughs of reasonably large size, with counties and county boroughs lagging badly behind. There are two provable reasons for this: firstly, that the bulk of the larger non-county boroughs were concentrated in the London area, where influences very easily spread across the completely arbitrary boundaries between library areas, with the result that a service initiated experimentally in one area soon tends to become established practice in many areas in the same vicinity, and where financial conditions were in general much easier than in the provinces; and secondly that in non-county boroughs, with their more restricted range of functions, libraries tend to be relatively more important than in the counties and county boroughs, and their needs for expansion into new types of service do not get submerged under more pressing considerations, as happens all too frequently in counties and county boroughs. It will be interesting to see whether in the long term the new local government set-up in the London area, giving as it does far greater powers than previously to generally much larger "Greater London Boroughs", will react to the favour of library service in an area which is, financially at least, at present well provided for in this respect, or whether the provincial county and county borough situation of libraries being a minor service dwarfed by education and other major services will become general in the London boroughs also. They have made a good start, and the backward areas, both former small authorities and county administered, have appointed extra staff on a formidable scale – but will it continue in the light of mounting rate increases (an average rise of over 3/- in the £ over the four-year period 1965–69)?

To return to small library areas, effectiveness is, particularly when one is concerned with establishing a minimal-sized unit, very closely geared to economy. Even though the new Act specifically mentions gramophone record provision, is it certain that the smallest future library areas will all have the potential demand to make the minimal-sized record library outlined above an economical proposition? To allow of mono, stereo, and tape provision, we now have to think in terms of well over 1,000 items initially and an eventual 3,000 or so items, *with a specialist librarian in charge*. To assess if such a demand is there is not easy.

Whereas the extent of use of books does not quantitatively vary very greatly between two areas of similar size and wealth (though the *types* of books read may vary), there are indications that the extent of use of gramophone record collections does vary greatly in different areas – it appears to be the "middle class" as distinct from the "working class" type of area which makes by far the greatest use of record libraries in Great Britain (16, p. 257), particularly where "classical" music is concerned. This may not be the case in other countries (32), but anyone who observes the nature of a British concert or opera audience can have little doubt that music would have a very unprosperous time in an entirely working class community*.

Whilst, therefore, it will be economically justifiable on grounds of likely use to provide effective sized gramophone record libraries in some areas right down to the likely minimum size of future library authorities (some of the best used of existing collections were in residential areas near

---

*It is not without significance that the Hulton Readership Survey, 1955 (p. 7) revealed that only two of an extensive list of Sunday newspapers carried a certain amount of musical news (*The Observer* and *The Sunday Times*), and that these two were read by about a quarter of the "professional" classes and by not much more than 1 per cent of the "working" classes. *The Sunday Telegraph* (founded 1961), which also carries a little musical matter, also, from the nature of its general content appears to be aimed at the "middle" classes. From personal observation in Sweden, Denmark, the Netherlands, Belgium, Germany, France, Switzerland, and Italy I would say that in most European countries (Scandinavia is to some extent an exception) musical audiences tend to be of much the same classes (i.e., professional, managerial, student, and clerical) as in Great Britain.

London in this population group before the 1965 London government reorganisation), there may well be areas (probably of mining and industrial types) of that size where a collection would not get such an amount of use as would justify its provision at the minimal level of size and effectiveness outlined above. It is obvious, therefore, that considerations of the means of provision and the extent of use are closely inter-related, and the nature (particularly, alas, the social constitution) of an area is as important as its size in determining whether the likely use of a gramophone record library would justify its local provision, and if so whether at the minimal or some higher level.

All county libraries and libraries of county boroughs, or whatever equivalent to them emerges from the Royal Commission on Local Government's deliberations, which in future will surely be over 100,000 population at least and most of them substantially more (33), and London boroughs (which are all much larger) will obviously provide their own record libraries. It would be absurd to suggest that authorities charged with operating school systems and technical colleges could not efficiently administer a record library. What of the provincial urban areas below county borough size? At the bottom end of these 40,000-minus to 100,000-plus areas will be some of the "industrial" rather than the "residential" type, in which potential use may not justify the economical provision (and particularly *specialist staffing*) of a minimally effective record library. Yet they will all have a number of residents who will wish to make use of record library facilities, and should not be denied them.

It is suggested that authorities which are not prepared to appoint to their staffs a librarian with expertise in the field of gramophone records (but not necessarily *fully* engaged on record, or even general musical provision) ought not themselves to operate record libraries. With a probable maximum qualified staff of seven or less up to 40,000 and nine or ten at 60,000 (28, p. 27), it seems unlikely that a specialist music and record librarian employed as such is likely to become a feature of the staffs of libraries serving under 60,000. This population figure is envisaged as the minimum for the "most purpose" non-county boroughs and urban districts foreshadowed in the white paper on Local Government Functions (34). It might well form a convenient dividing line below which library authorities would not provide their own record libraries. Provision for the needs of people living in the areas which do not provide their own record libraries could be made by means of these smaller libraries acting as local distribution points for the collections provided by the county libraries (as is frequently done at present for sets of plays and parts for choral and orchestral societies), the smaller libraries contributing their fair share to the county libraries' costs.

In theory this should result in efficiency, as it would ensure that records were provided only by reasonably large authorities, but in practice there are two objections to it: firstly it would mean a slight complication of the rating system (in that some independent library authorities would pay two rates, one for their own service, another to the county library for the gramophone record service); secondly, as mentioned above, it is a fact that so far non-county boroughs (and in particular the former Metropolitan Boroughs) were in the forefront of gramophone record provision, whilst counties and county boroughs have, with few exceptions, shown less enthusiasm for the subject. Nevertheless, this possibility should not be too lightly dismissed, as it is likely to be the *only* means of obtaining sizeable areas for the purpose. The alternative could be a proliferation of tiny, incomplete collections lacking the trained staff necessary for proper choice and effective use; there are already signs that this is happening in small authorities desperately fighting to justify retention of independent library powers.

The trained subject specialist librarian who should always be in charge of a gramophone record library should always be acknowledged as a responsible department head, and paid as such (that is, his special qualifications and responsibilities should ensure that his post is regarded as above the level of "professional duties normally expected of a qualified librarian" (35) and that he is always graded above the basic scale for chartered librarians). It seems common sense to amalgamate the record library with the music library where a music library already exists, and to use the record library as an opportunity to establish a special department for records and music where there is no existing special music department: gramophone record provision, then, should always form part of a special music library, with a responsible music librarian in charge, directly accountable to whoever the other department heads (such as the reference librarian) are accountable to (usually chief and deputy librarians), and not to any other department head. In smaller libraries certain other functions might conveniently be managed by the music and records librarian: services which fit in well with music librarianship are picture loan collections and the organisational work connected with extension activities.

This is not the place to embark on consideration of extension activities in general — they are admirably covered elsewhere anyway (36) — but one valuable form of such activities is directly in our field — gramophone record recitals. These were provided by a number of libraries long before they started record-lending libraries (several of these have in fact, grown out of collections bought for recital purposes). Such libraries have realised that they have a responsibility for actually encouraging and furthering the spread of musical appreciation through records and that the main method of doing this is the sponsorship of recitals. The incursion of libraries into this field raises the wider question of relations with local gramophone societies, which exist in most towns of such size as to have a record library.

The best of such societies are genuine public societies with properly planned and presented programmes – some even sponsor such additional activities as university extra-mural lectures or live recitals. The less good are small, semi-private cliques, with completely haphazard programmes and poor equipment, having no worthwhile impact on the musical life of their areas. The librarian's duty in this respect is clear. Where the existing society is a good one he should limit himself to lending it records, providing its members with information about the library, and rendering any other ancillary help in his power. Where the librarian is not satisfied that the local society is all that it might be, he should, if premises and equipment suitable for the purpose can be found (and that the premises must have a music licence must not be overlooked), provide regular series of recitals aimed both at popularising the record collection and providing a valuable addition to the public music provision (37). He should, however, aim at the eventual formation of a society with proper aims and resources to take over this activity when the time is ripe. He should be careful, also, to distinguish between societies which exist for *musical appreciation* purposes (which are relevant to the work of the record library) and societies primarily of "hi-fi" enthusiasts, which are often little concerned with music as such.

A more orthodox way in which the record library can foster musical appreciation and broaden public taste is by organising record libraries on open-access rather than "indicator" lines, at least so far as the record "sleeves" are concerned. The coming of the pictorial sleeve with the LP record entirely changed the situation in this respect – with the fragile and bulky SP disc, with no descriptive cover, there were no advantages at all in open access, and many disadvantages. Whether the discs are left inside the sleeves which are put on open access, or issued from store to borrowers bringing the sleeves to the counter, is immaterial in this respect. Open access to discs as well as sleeves greatly reduces routine work, but some nasty shocks have been experienced regarding theft, which tends to develop suddenly on a large scale after a long period with little stolen. Some libraries have found evidence of systematic depredation of records of a certain type perpetrated by single thieves – for example, all the records (opera, recital and other) including the voice of a certain singer may be found to be missing, having obviously been stolen by one of his admirers. What *is* important is that borrowers allowed to browse among the sleeves will take out a very much wider range of music than if they are left to choose their existing favourites from a catalogue – in the author's library Vivaldi, Telemann, Nielsen, and Copland go out nearly as well as Bach, Mozart, Sibelius, and Britten by being thrust into public view (but not, alas, Bartok, whose name is too well known to be taken – and enjoyed – by mistake or ignorance!).

We do not even need to consider whether record collections may be made available only to organised groups. All collections should be made available to all those members of the public, individuals as well as groups, who can satisfy the librarian's reasonable requirements regarding the safety and proper use of his records (and the public will take a lot in the way of safeguards, if properly explained – in Rotherham they all quite happily buy diamond styli and submit them for examination when required). There can be no justification for any librarian barring persons who can fulfil these requirements, on the ground that he only serves groups or societies – the librarian's job is to *disseminate* culture, not to *limit* its dissemination.

It must not be forgotten, however, that a library *must* sometimes actually discourage use of its gramophone record collection, by insistence on a satisfactory standard of playing equipment. Time (and the advent of stereophonic discs) has completely solved the problem of the dangerous botched conversion to LP of cheap SP players, and LP itself has removed the menace of the steel needle, but questions such as how to ensure that styli are replaced before they are so worn as to damage the grooves, and how to ensure that records are properly handled and stored would seem to admit of only one solution – to lend them only to those whose private collections are such as to indicate that they have some respect for records. Experience in this country does not seem to support that of Wilmette Public Library, Illinois, USA, where damage to records became a serious problem, with Gilbert and Sullivan singled out for especially vicious treatment. (38)

How to get the Service Started

Having demonstrated the need for record libraries, and examined the means and necessary extent of such provision in relation to the community to be served, we must finally examine the actual process of starting them, now that they have the firm blessing of, but are not made explicitly obligatory by, legislation. The establishment of record libraries will, for a few years yet, be the result of individual librarians inspiring their committees with the idea, or the musically conscious public inspiring librarians with the idea: if the history of other developments in library service can be taken as a parallel the former is more likely. The mere existence of the hortatory legislation in the 1964 Act will not suddenly persuade every library authority to immediately start record (or picture loan or film) services, particularly in the prevailing climate of financial stringency and governmental exhortations to delay the development of less urgent services. The government circulars sent to local authorities during the summer 1965 sterling crises permitted employment of extra teachers – explicitly mentioned as important – but not librarians, and library building was halted but not schools, and matters got worse in the 1966 and 1967 crises. The areas lacking record libraries are now, in general, those which are in most respects cultural and artistic backwaters – areas with any substantial musical life now mostly have them. These will be the hard nuts to crack, not only with regard to the actual inauguration of a service but, perhaps more important now that we are beyond the pioneering days, also with regard to provision of reasonably generous funds to put it on a viable financial footing.

Whilst the Minister of Education's Working Party standards (28, pp. 18–19) have been, in the Act itself and the subsequent departmental circular (39, pp. 4 & 9–15), largely accepted as minima for *book* service, we have no such numerical standards for records. Many so-called record libraries are still in a state of development, and a condition of financial starvation, reminiscent of some of the blacker pictures of book service in the McColvin Report of 1942 (26, chapters 3 & 4).

There being no governmentally approved standards for record provision on the lines of those available for books, it is obviously essential for us to formulate them.

It is suggested that, to make adequate provision of all the types of record with which we are concerned (standard music, lighter music, non-musical records and language courses), in the several forms involved (discs and tapes, both in mono and stereo), libraries should aim at an eventual stock, within five years of opening, of 50 items per 1,000 population (excluding any removed to secondary collections because of obsolescence, or in the case of deleted works irreplaceable but in too bad condition for general use), divided between the forms as mentioned earlier, and with a minimum total of 3,000. Where day population greatly exceeds resident population, the higher figure should be used as a basis. Annual additions need to be 15 per 1,000 population where issues are normal, with a proportionately higher figure where annual issues exceed 375 per 1,000 population. Staff should be at least one per 60,000 population, with the first staff member and every third one thereafter qualified: this staff will cover all work in the musical field, not only records – more will be needed where issues are unusually high. There should be a measure of decentralisation where the distance of the central library is more than about three miles – not to every branch library but to convenient centres, on a regularly exchanged deposit collection basis. In cities these deposit collections should be well over 1,000 discs but in counties they may have to be as small as 500. Exceptionally scattered counties will have to pool the stock for a wide area in a mobile library to achieve even this figure, rather than placing deposit collections in small branches with catchment areas inadequate to justify a reasonable sized deposit collection. Tapes should not be decentralised except in county libraries and the very largest cities, as there are unlikely to be enough to make sizeable deposit collections.

It is too much to be hoped that these standards will be accepted (as have the governmental ones for books) as quasi-holy writ by librarians (and their treasurers) uninterested in, or opposed to, record provision. It is obvious, therefore, that judicious publicity will still be an important factor in the spread of record libraries. This publicity will need to take several forms: firstly, professional opinion even now is still badly split on the question of record library provision – whilst the London area is favourably inclined, there is a hard core of opposition in the provinces. Nor is this "hard core" limited to conservative opinion (indeed, Mr. Simpson late of Coventry, whose ideas on "spoonfeeding" the public by reserving books for them are well known, was an enthusiastic supporter of record libraries, whilst his fellow-opponent of book reservation systems, Mr. Haugh of Bristol, is one of their opponents (40)). However, nobody is beyond hope of conversion, as the tardy interest shown by many public libraries in technical services for industry demonstrates, and in the mention of gramophone records in the new Act we have at least a foot available to put in the office door, to prevent unmusical chief librarians slamming it in our faces – the responsibility to provide record libraries is firmly placed on the *public library* if the locality concerned can be proved to need one *at all*. How then can we prove that all localities *do* need them and need them provided on a generous scale, not merely as a poverty-stricken appendage to a generally prosperous book service?

Probably the most likely way of achieving our purpose would be a bringing to bear of pressure from musical opinion generally. The most dangerous argument flaunted by the conservative school against the provision by public libraries of technical library service for industry was that "industry doesn't want it". Had industry demonstrated firmly that it *did* want it, and, what is more, expected it from public libraries, the way to achieving decent technical provision throughout the public library service would have been easier. Similarly, a vocally expressed demand for proper-scale gramophone record library service from the musical public (and, human nature being what it is, from the famous and popular figures of the musical world) would both help the enthusiastic librarian in obtaining the necessary funds, and form correctly the ideas of those librarians as yet uninterested or inclined to fob off with a sub-standard level of provision those who want records.

A third direction for publicity to take presents itself: action by the official and semi-official bodies which nowadays have so much power and influence. Widespread publicity is given each year to the annual reports of the Arts Council. For years now, each of these reports has stressed a line – "Partners in patronage" (the Arts Council and the local authorities) in the 1960–61 report is an example. Would not one with the theme "Music in the home" do inestimable good to the cause of gramophone record libraries, particularly now that it is the policy of the Arts Council to do the bulk of its work in the provinces through independent bodies? The Arts Council has shown itself none too friendly to date towards public libraries, having on occasions hardly disguised its opinion that public libraries are a waste of public money (41). Could it be that the provision of effective record libraries would lead to a change in this regrettable attitude?

How to achieve all this publicity, with the end in view of securing a favourable climate of opinion for the spread of record libraries as complete in their fields as public libraries now generally are in the field of books, is outside the scope of this review, but that steps should be taken to achieve this climate cannot be too strongly stressed.

Not all the librarians who delay or starve gramophone record provision at the moment do so on ideological grounds. Too many public libraries are dissipating inadequate funds (and even less adequate trained staff) over too wide a field. Some libraries which make a great show of "extension activities" and other non-book services are among those whose financing (and particularly staffing) is still basically unsatisfactory. No library should embark on widening its activities until it is doing properly what it is already attempting – extending the field of a service badly inadequate in its existing provision cannot in any circumstances be commended. It is, therefore, obvious that those in favour of the establishment of healthy gramophone record libraries should also favour the raising to proper high standards of the more basic aspects of a library service – gramophone record libraries may, if the widespread need for them is brought home forcibly by proper publicity, prosper in a generally prosperous library service; they will never prosper as a limb of a body which is ailing or starved. In the next few years we may see a great many libraries (particularly very small ones trying to preserve their independence in the light of the requirements of the new Act) rushing in all directions at once, frantically trying to establish at least the facade of a modern public library service in miniature, and this at a time of national financial stringency aggravated by a present shortage of qualified librarians (which, before it rights itself, will pass through a transitional period of libraries being flooded with immature, recently qualified people in the lower professional ranks – adequate to carry on existing services but not experienced enough to be trusted with properly inaugurating new ones).

Only one more matter of policy remains to be considered – the user's part in the financing of the service. Free provision (except for such minor charges as reservation fees) has always been so much a basic tenet in public librarianship that there is, perhaps, a tendency on the part of librarians (themselves an impoverished part of the community) to take for granted that what was undoubtedly justified in the days when a great part of the population was living on or below a bare subsistence level may not be so when, as is the case today, television aerials sprout in slum areas and the lack of garages in municipal houses is a source of annoyance to their (rent subsidised!) tenants. Surely, in the provision of a gramophone record library, which is only of use anyway to people in such a financial position as to be able to purchase (or, at least, hire purchase!) a fairly costly playing apparatus, the possibility of the users bearing some part of the cost directly should be considered, particularly in view of the fact that such an arrangement might well help to dispose in their favour people who object to the provision of a service for what is alleged to be a small minority. Sensibly, the new Act (which, equally sensibly, outlaws charges for book service) provides for this.

It would be unwise to suggest that the service should be made entirely self-supporting. It is, perhaps, not without relevance that the only British public gramophone record library known to have closed for "lack of support" was the only one which, from the start, deliberately set out to make itself self-supporting by means of charges for the service. On the other hand, another library (Coventry) has levied charges which are a substantial element in the cost of provision, providing in 1957–8 all but £360 of the £2,386 spent on new records (42), and its record library is one of the most thriving in the country. On the basis of the standards outlined above, it is likely that a charge of about 6d per disc per week would produce about half the desirable record fund, leaving the library authority to provide the other half and the administrative costs, which seems a fair division.

Such, then are our objectives. We must achieve a favourable climate of opinion professionally, locally and nationally – for gramophone record libraries as an equal and integral part of the library service. We must have a library service of such satisfactory general level that it can safely embark on the new activity of a record library. We must work out an equitable distribution of the cost between taxation and the library's potential users. We must do what we can to ensure that the authorities which are to provide the service are of such size and resources that they can do it properly and economically, by co-operation where necessary rather than by vain local striving after unattainable ends. Only by proper attention to all these considerations can we ensure that gramophone record libraries will become a vital force in the communities they serve.

Conclusions

1. That in the interests of a widespread improvement in the level of musical appreciation in Great Britain, particularly in view of the lack, outside London, of a planned programme of performances of musical masterworks of all ages and countries, public provision of gramophone record libraries, available (subject to reasonable safeguards) to

individuals, should be made available everywhere, through the public library authorities charged with this duty by the Public Libraries and Museums Act, 1964.

2. That there is no intrinsic objection to reasonable charges being made for the use of such services, but they should not be expected to be self-supporting.

3. That, though such collections should attract such government grants as are now, or may in the future be, available for public library services, the absence of such grants should not preclude the provision of such services on a proper scale.

4. That the smaller libraries in particular should consider the extent to which, in the provision of record libraries, organised co-operation with other library authorities could produce high levels of service at reasonable cost.

5. That publicity should be inaugurated for their establishment on an adequate scale by:
   (a) Influencing library professional opinion in their favour.
   (b) Influencing, through the medium of the musical press and the intelligent newspapers, musically active individuals and local societies to bring pressure to bear at local level to this end.
   (c) Obtaining moral support for them from national bodies (the Arts Council is one) and nationally known individuals (popular musical figures and eminent critics, for example), and that means of influencing such bodies and persons in their favour should be considered.

November, 1968

REFERENCES

(1) *The Times*: concert and theatre announcements in Saturday issues – 1939 as compared with 1968.

(2) Jefferson, A. *The Operas of Richard Strauss in Britain, 1910–1963*. 1963, pp. 9–15.

(3) Arts Council. Twenty-first annual report, 1965–6. p. 58.

(4) Arts Council. Seventh annual report, 1951–2, p. 30 ("Auditions").

(5) Corbett celebrity concerts, Middlesbrough. [Programmes].

(6) Arts Council. *Housing the Arts in Great Britain*. Part II. 1961, p. 50.

(7) *Yorkshire Post*. 1955. *passim*.

(8) Frankfurt-am-Main. Städtische Bühnen. *Abseits vom Rampenlicht*. [1955]. p. XXI.

(9) Chaput de Saintonge, R. A. A. *Public Administration in Germany*. 1961. p. 204.

(10) *Gramophone*. Long playing classical record catalogue. March 1966 issue and June 1967 supplement.

(11) *Bogens Verden*. 36(7). Oct. 1954. pp. 297–304. (per *Library Science Abstracts* 4103).

(12) Great Britain. *Statutes*. Public libraries and museums Act 1964.
(13) *Library journal* Vol. 76. 1951. pp. 1779–80.
(14) Overton, C. D. *Gramophone Record Library*. 1951.
(15) *Opera*. 5(10). Oct. 1954. p. 628.
(16) *Library Association Record*. 56(7). July 1954. pp. 251–9.
(17) *Ontario library review*. 38(3). Aug. 1954. p. 252f.
(18) *Which*. June. 1964. pp. 187–92.
(19) *Librarian*. XLI (4). Apr. 1952. pp. 81–5.
(20) EMI Records Limited ("His Master's Voice") – 7ep7051 *and* CLP 1212 (both 1958).
(21) *Library Association Record*. 68(5). May. 1966. pp. 161–5.
(22) Bryant, E.T. *Music Librarianship*. 1959.
(23) *Library world*. 60(705), March 1959. pp. 176–8; 60(707), May. 1959. pp. 248–50; 61(709), July 1959. pp. 21–3.
(24) *Library Association Record*. 69(6). June 1967. pp. 205–8.
(25) Vollans, R. F. *Library Co-operation in Great Britain*. 1952. pp. 99–103, 137(table).
(26) McColvin, L. R. *Public Library system of Great Britain*. 1942.
(27) Ministry of Education. *The Structure of the Public Library Service*. (Cmnd. 660). 1959.
(28) Ministry of Education. *Standards of Public Library Service*. 1962.
(29) *New Zealand Libraries*. XIII(8). Sep. 1950. pp. 181–5.
(30) Leigh, R. D. *Public Library in the United States*. 1950. pp. 84–7.
(31) UNESCO bulletin for libraries. XIV(5). Sep.–Oct. 1960. p. 197.
(32) *Illinois libraries*. 33(10). Dec. 1951. p. 450.
(33) Ministry of Housing and Local Government. *Areas and Status of Local Authorities*. (Cmnd. 9831). 1956. p. 8.
(34) Ministry of Housing and Local Government *and* Home Office. *Local Government Functions*. (Cmnd. 161). 1957. pp. 2–3.
(35) National Joint Council for Local Authorities' Administrative, Professional, Technical and Clerical Services. *Scheme of Conditions of Service*: Sixth edition. 1967.
(36) Jolliffe, H. *Public Library Extension Activities*. 1962. *Especially* pp. 262–5.
(37) *Library Association Record*. 53(10). Oct. 1951. pp. 320–22.
(38) *Illinois Libraries*. 38(10). Dec. 1956. pp. 303–4.
(39) Department of Education and Science, Circular 4/65 (March 27th 1965).
(40) Library Association. *Proceedings of the Annual Conference, Southport, 1955*. pp. 41–2.
(41) Arts Council. Thirteenth annual report. 1957–8. pp. 6–7.
(42) Coventry: City Libraries, *Books and Readers*. 1868–1958.

The New Record Library: Establishment and Maintenance

by FRANCIS R. WEBB, ALA
Music Librarian, Porchester Road District Library,
Westminister City Libraries

One danger inherent in the setting out of statistics, particularly of those relating to costs and expenditure, is that of presenting them without due regard for the prevailing circumstances that make them relevant. This contribution is to deal with the establishment and maintenance of one particular gramophone record library in one particular set of circumstances, which may or may not be "typical" and which will certainly not be applicable in all cases. So I propose briefly to fill in the background history, then to set out in detail as far as possible first the initial costs and then the present running costs; the result will, I hope, be of some interest and even of some practical value.

The Library

Before April 1965, there had seemed little hope for a record library in the Metropolitan Borough of Paddington, solely for reasons of lack of space. However, on amalgamation with St. Marylebone and Westminster — each with its own large and well established collection — such a service became not only even more desirable but, at long last, feasible. Two former offices in the Central Library (now the Porchester Road District Library) were now vacant, and it was agreed that although the amount of space involved was not lavish, a library of gramophone records could be housed there. Open to the public since February, 1966, the new library occupies an area 20 ft X 15 ft in one corner of the lending library, and operates full time with a staff of three. It is the third record library in the City of Westminster, and though available to borrowers throughout the City, serves especially the area of former Paddington (pre-amalgamation population 115,000). It is very similar to a new branch library, in that it both provides a service to an area where previously there was none and, at the same time, is an extension of the same sort of service provided over a larger area as a whole. Various techniques and standards common to Westminster were adopted, and this would naturally have some bearing on the costs.

Statistics of Initial Costs

INITIAL STOCK.   On February 4th 1966 (Opening day), there was an initial stock of 2,150 records which cost £3,244. On March 31st 1966, the total stock was 2,856 records costing £4,274.

INITIAL FURNITURE.   Counter, £178. Record shelving, £80, consisting of two units: for the counter area a record press in two sections, 6 ft 6 in × 3 ft and 6 ft 6 in × 5 ft 6 in, with 80 compartments 13 in deep, capable of holding up to 2,000 records; also a storage cupboard for the workroom, 6 ft 6 in × 3 ft 6 in, with 35 compartments for up to 875 records. Work bench (for workroom), £120. Tubular swivel stool, £5. 9. 0. Anglepoise lamp, £5. Provision for a microscope, £10. Four-drawer catalogue cabinet, £10. 13. 0.

INDICATOR.   245 Strafoplan panels and equipment, £52. Wooden frame and backing, £47. Notice "Gramophone Records Available", red on grey, 30 in × 3 in, £3. 3. 6. 3,225 plastic tickets at 20/— per hundred, £32. 5. 0. (3 $\frac{3}{8}$in × 2 $\frac{3}{8}$in, of 20/1000 mm thickness, cut to specification).

GRAMOPHONE.   Deccalion Mark IV, £41. Headphones, £8. Socket adjustment, £3.

STATIONERY – FOR RECORDS.   3,914 polythene bags at £8. 2. 0. per thousand, £31. 14. 0. Processing of pictorial sleeves: 2,500 at approx. 1/1d each, £135. 2,500 plain inner cases at 1/5d each, £177. 3,500 printed outer cases at 1/— each, £175. 2,000 date labels (for carrying boxes), £4.

STATIONERY – OTHER.   Membership vouchers, £10. Borrowers' tickets, £4. 10. 0. Overdue stationery, £10. Reservation cards, £27. Stock cards, £12. 10. 0. Renewal cards, £22.

MISCELLANEOUS.   Imperial 76 Typewriter, £55. Issue trays, date and fines guides, £12. Fines boxes and equipment, £41. Visible index panels and wall bracket, £3. Structural alterations, approx. £200 (these included removing former partitions and ceiling, installing power points and new lighting, etc.). Notice "Music Library", red on grey, 2 ft 11 in × 12 in, £3. 5. 0. Introductory leaflets, rubber date stamps, stamp pads, and a few minor items came from the general fund.

Comments

STOCK.   A basic stock of 2,000 records was envisaged, and the expenditure necessary to cover this and later additions up to the end of March was £4,274. The advantage of having been able to start off with a large and, what is more, a varied collection is obvious. There are relatively few gaps to fill, and the borrowers' choice is wide, so speech recordings, stereo and jazz (none of which were included in the basic stock) have been or are being added much earlier than might otherwise have been the case.

FURNITURE.   No special comment is called for here, except that the counter, record presses, cupboard, and work desk were made to specification by Libraco; the workroom referred to adjoins the library area and is shared with the Lending Department.

INDICATOR.   This shows records IN, not the entire stock, which is shown in the card catalogue. Plastic tickets representing records IN are inserted in the slots of the indicator and the borrower selects the ticket for the record he requires and hands it to the staff. The Strafoplan panels link together thirty-five across and seven deep, and are secured with metal rods to the wooden backing and frame. The whole indicator measures 7 ft 5 in × 3 ft 7 in and is mounted on the wall facing the counter; each panel has ten slots, so the total capacity of the board is 2,450 tickets.

Because of the small amount of floor space available, the library was committed from the start to closed access. Other librarians may be in a better position and thus able to consider open access. I am indebted to Mr. John Morgan, Head of Music Services, Camden, for the information in the following paragraph.

Camden Libraries use three-tier stands or browser boxes, of which each compartment can hold sixty-six 12 in records comfortably, being 1 ft 6 in deep from front to back. An average cost can be calculated on the basis of £15 per compartment. Now, it is reasonable to assume that, of a library's record stock, 45 per cent should be the very most available at one time, the remaining 55 per cent being out on loan. In many cases the first figure would be considered far too high; but if this can at least be taken as a possible figure, then it follows that every 1,000 records will require browser box space for 450. That is, seven compartments 1 ft 6 in deep and, allowing a width of 14½ in to each, a total frontage of approximately 8 ft 6 in. Cost: £105. This is an estimate only, and should be treated with due caution; however, it is suggested that a reasonable calculation of expenditure on browser boxes can be made on the basis of £100–120 per 1,000 records.

GRAMOPHONE.   This was bought for record testing. Owing to the proximity of the workroom to public departments and offices, it was considered advisable to adapt the player so that it could be used with headphones.

STATIONERY. Before issue to the borrower, each record is provided with three protective wrappings. First, the polyphene bag 12 in X 13¾ in — anything of this nature supplied with the record is often inadequate and is discarded; secondly, the picture sleeve, strengthened, slit down one side, and with a full scale damage chart hinged to the top edge — this work is sent out; records without picture sleeves, such as those in boxed sets, are given a plain inner sleeve with the damage chart attached; thirdly, a strong outer case printed with date labels, hours of opening and other information. Carrying boxes are also provided for sets of records; the initial supply came from the general stock of the music libraries, but later supplies have been bought from the library grant.

TOTAL COST OF ESTABLISHMENT. Approximately £5,800. Between three- and four-fifths of this was taken by the record grant; the other main items of expenditure were on record stationery, £527, furniture, £388, alterations to site, £200, indicator and equipment, £134.

Present Running Costs (1966–7)

STAFF SALARIES (LONDON WEIGHTING NOT INCLUDED). Music Librarian APT IV £1,340. Assistant G.D. £750. Assistant G.D. £725.

RECORD GRANT. £1,750 for 1,000 records.

STATIONERY AND OTHER ITEMS. Processing of 1,000 pictorial record sleeves, £54. 1,000 printed outer covers, £50. 100 carrying boxes, £4. 2,000 plastic record tickets, £20. Other minor items of stationery are met from the libraries' general fund and are inconsiderable.

Issues and Membership

	REGISTRATION	RECORDS ISSUED
On 4. 2. 66 (Opening day)	43	52
On 5. 2. 66 (Saturday)	92	143
Total at end of February	688	1,904
Total at end of March	966	4,409
Total registration at end of September	1,753	
Total issues April to September inclusive		12,775

Staff

The record department is part of a complete Music Library; the Librarian, an ALA, is responsible for the selection of music books, scores, and gramophone records, also for the music stock of the two former Paddington branch libraries. As far as the records are concerned, ordering and much of the cataloguing is centralised, but some cataloguing and the complete processing are carried out by the department. The staff of three has been found adequate enough in normal times and self-sufficient, but at holiday periods or in times of sickness relief staff may have to be called upon.

Stress has been laid from time to time on the desirability of record library staff having a good knowledge of music and records. Not so much seems to have been said of the advantage of a good general library experience. This is equally important (it might even be argued *more* important), particularly in a library where the Librarian only is qualified. He cannot be available all the time, so his assistants must be capable of taking that much more responsibility. One Librarian, at least, has been fortunate in his staff.

Other Items

Other expenditure is largely self-explanatory; a good store of stationery had been provided for the library's opening, much of which will last the current year, some even the next (1967–8). The cost of records, salaries and stationery can be considered to give a reasonably accurate figure for one year's expenditure.

Membership

Membership is open to all from the age of 15 upwards who reside, work or study in the City of Westminster; no separate figure has been kept for non-resident borrowers, but the proportion is small, probably no more than 10 per cent. Members are given one ticket on which they may borrow one record or one set of records at a time. The period of loan is two weeks.

In Conclusion

The Library has, at the time of writing, been open less than a year, so it would obviously be unwise to pontificate too much on any conclusions to be drawn or lessons to be learnt. The service has, on the whole, been well received, if without the mad stampede of would-be borrowers forecast in ,moments of fancy. Membership, as the figures above show, has risen steadily from the beginning, but this has not been altogether matched by a corresponding rise in issues; for this, the intervention of summer is probably responsible; the oncoming winter could well see an increase in traffic.

As indicated in the introductory paragraphs, the area of the library is small – 20 ft X 15 ft, and this includes the counter, the catalogues and much of the music shelving. So far, this has seemed adequate; but busy periods, where borrowers returning records mingle with others selecting from the indicator, while yet others attempt to consult the catalogues or the music shelves, have shown that space is, in fact, in short supply. Should the amount of activity increase considerably, then the problem may well become acute. Mr. Currall, in his contribution to the first edition, stated 15 ft X 15 ft as the very minimum area for a record library, and though the smaller area may be possible up to a point, I would consider that this still holds good.

The policy as regards record provision has been to offer a large and reasonably well varied collection for whatever the borrowing potential, rather than to begin in a small way and to build up according to demand. In consequence, from the day of opening there has always been a wide choice of records available to the borrower. It would have been possible to have opened with a basic stock of 1,000 records, probably the absolute minimum for a library service in an area of this size; yet every advantage rests with beginning with as large and comprehensive a stock as reasonably possible. As Pooh-Bah said, "Don't stint yourself. Do it well" – back-handed advice in its original context, but good counsel in this.

Note: Language tuition records are now available in certain languages, as well as speech recordings and jazz. Stereo records are purchased as a matter of course. Record Expenditure is now over £1,900 per annum.

Records are now protected by a printed inner sleeve, polythene lined (cost £29.15.0 per 1,000), inserted in the picture sleeve which is permanently sealed in a PVC cover (cost of processing the picture sleeves, including the cost of the PVC cover, £7.16.4 per 100).

Records are now issued on tokens (one token for one record, two tokens for two records or a set of records). Editor, April 1970.

Personnel and Training

by MIRIAM H. MILLER, LRAM, FLA
Lecturer, School of Librarianship, North-Western Polytechnic

The recent rise in the number of collections of gramophone records in libraries, either for loan or reference purposes, has given rise to a demand for staff to administer such collections, but advertisements in the professional press show a marked uneveness in the salaries offered, and the responsibilities to be undertaken. A gramophone record library may be created in one of three ways: either a well-established music library will have recorded music added to its stock, or the decision to make gramophone records available may be accompanied by a decision to collect all existing music stock together and to house it, with the discs, in a new departmental library, or a collection which has been built up somewhat haphazardly, with only nominal supervision, will become so large as to require professional attention in its own right. All three methods have their advantages and disadvantages as far as the library's staff are concerned.

In the first case — where there is already a music library — the gramophone record stock may be expected to fit into the existing service with as little upheaval as possible, the recorded music being an extension of the printed variety, but with two very important provisos. First, sufficient space should be available for the two services to run amicably, and second, extra staff should be added to the library's complement to cope with the new service. It is unfortunate that these two conditions have not always been met. In some libraries the gramophone record collection has had to be housed at some distance from the central music library, and the two services have to function as two autonomous units. This is not the best way to run a music service, but the failure to provide extra staff is much more serious. There have been instances of gramophone records being added to a music library without any corresponding increase of staff or any increase whatever being made in the salary of the music librarian to compensate for the extra responsibilty involved. This is an iniquitous situation, but it does exist and hardly reflects to the credit of the employing authority. The second method — where a library authority decides to create a music and gramophone record service at the same time — is usually met with in a library system which serves a wide area by means of several branches. In such a situation, all printed music and books on music will be called in from branches and then used to form the nucleus of the new department, a circumstance which an intelligent librarian can use to advantage, because, although the stock from the branches can usefully fill the shelves for a while, one is virtually starting both services from scratch, and one can thus ensure that they complement each other successfully. The disadvantages are that, again, not sufficient staff may be available for two services, or, that the new music librarian may find that while he or she may have a free hand to spend that portion of the library's budget which has been allocated to the purchase of gramophone records, the right to purchase all printed material is jealously guarded by the accessions department and the music librarian is expected to act in an advisory capacity only. Diplomacy can achieve much in such a situation, which is fairly common in public library services, the music librarian's salary being on a par with that of the children's librarian in the same system, but, occasionally, less than that of the Reference Librarian. The third method — that of coping with a collection which has "just growed" — is met with when the discs have been purchased individually, with no one purpose in mind, for use, perhaps, in a library's extension activities or as illustrations to a series of lectures, or even a loan collection that has been started rather tentatively with a donation from the local music appreciation society. In such a situation, the librarian may find that the discs are in rather poor condition due to bad handling or complete lack of any checking for damage after loan, and it may be difficult to train staff and public to treat the stock with the proper amount of care. The salary offered will vary according to whether the employing authority regards the responsibility for such a collection as being deserving of departmental status, or whether the gramophone records are administered by one particular assistant among several with supervision by a senior librarian.

Discrepancies in salary and status are partly due to the relative unfamiliarity of the gramophone record as library stock. Many collections were started in the nature of an experiment and some are still regarded as such, however successful they may be. There is, too, a wide divergence in the relative importance each library system attaches to its gramophone record stock, and, obviously, a system which places its gramophone records in the care of a suitably qualified librarian, must think that stock more important than does a system which employs a part-time general assistant for the same purpose. There is no doubt that any gramophone record library will benefit from being administered by a qualified person from the beginning, as anyone who has been faced with the "just growed" type of situation will agree, and extra staff must be made available when the gramophone records are added to any library as an extension of the existing service. Gramophone records take much longer to charge and discharge than books, particularly when they are checked for damage. In a time-and-motion study carried out by the author, the results proved that the average counter assistant takes four times as long to discharge a gramophone record as to discharge a book. There is an art in the handling of gramophone records, whose fragility is notorious and one of the reasons why library authorities are reluctant to house them, but, with the correct training of staff and public, a gramophone record can last as long as some classes of book and give as much satisfaction to the borrower. It follows, then, that a gramophone record library should be administered by a person interested enough to have given some study to the special problems of discs in libraries, and, if the library is to be run on standard lines, that person may be expected to be a qualified librarian.

We are here faced with the problem of defining exactly what is meant by the phrase "qualified librarian", and it is no longer possible to do this by means of a straight comparison between the syllabus of the University of London School of Librarianship and Archives and that of the Library Association. Post-graduate diplomas in librarianship are currently being offered at other universities, and the prospect of degree courses in librarianship being more widely available in the near future must alter the whole business of education for librarianship in this country, and makes it impossible accurately to forecast with what degree of importance the gramophone record will be regarded as library material in any of these courses, even allowing that, next to periodicals, they are the most common non-book materials in use in libraries today. Only one prediction can be made with any certainty, namely, that gramophone records may be expected to be a subject of study in any course devoted to music librarianship, since the bulk of available recorded material is still recorded music. However, the growing number of non-musical recordings, both private and commercial, that is being produced in this country, and the increasing use of the sound recording as a means of supplementing the printed word in fields such as speech therapy, ornithology, and ethnology, as well as history, would seem to indicate that libraries other than those devoted to music must be prepared to house them in the near future.

Many of the subjects studied as part of a course in librarianship can be of great assistance in administering a collection of discs, but, as with all special materials, they have particular problems of their own, and some library schools have found it advantageous to offer short specialist courses on gramophone record librarianship as a separate study, but acquiring the practical experience to back up such a course of study is not always easy. Although there is a steadily growing number of gramophone record collections in libraries in the British Isles, those libraries which do have them are still in a minority, and the geographic grouping is such as to place the majority of them in or around Greater London. Again, the majority of known collections of gramophone records are housed in public libraries, so that a librarian wishing to work with such a collection may not only have to change his residence, but also change the type of library he or she works in, and neither change is always welcome. It is not always easy to acquire actual training in such a library, because so many of the posts advertised require the successful applicant to take charge of a new library, and habitually specify that experience in working with gramophone records is one of the qualities necessary for the post. It is for this reason that so many aspiring gramophone record librarians become discouraged, but it is as well to remember that many appointments committees, although habitually well-disposed towards candidates with practical experience, are sometimes impressed by personal enthusiasm, and that several excellent gramophone record libraries were set up by librarians with very little else to guide them.

If a librarian is fortunate enough to work in a library system which has a gramophone record library, there should be little difficulty in acquiring the necessary experience, although chances of a transfer to such a department may be determined by the staff situation, in that if it is customary for only junior staff to assist the librarian in charge, then a senior assistant from another department of the system may find himself debarred by his own seniority. A librarian who is faced with such a difficulty, or one who works in a library system which has no gramophone records, will have to accept the necessity of moving to another library system, and probably to a public library system, for there is no doubt that it is still the public library authorities who offer more opportunities of work with gramophone records than any other, especially since general administrative changes, such as the amalgamation of London boroughs have created larger authorities which can afford more service points. There has been considerable development among the universities and colleges of the British Isles in recent years, but it is still the prevailing system in such institutions to leave the selection, purchase, and administration of gramophone records in the hands of the staff of their Music departments. It must be admitted that this system works very well in meeting the requirements of staff and students, since the discs are generally intended to illustrate lectures, and any loans are restricted to the department. There is nowhere in this country any loan service to students on a par with those to be found in American universities. Certain university departments, particularly those concerned with the study of language, have their own collections of original recordings of dialects, and so on, but these are not always in the care of the university or department librarian. Gramophone record libraries of all kinds are on the increase, but it is still necessary to look for them.

A mastery of the technique of handling gramophone records is not, however, sufficient to make a good gramophone record librarian. Although not all gramophone record libraries are exclusively concerned with music, the vast majority of records in libraries are there because of their musical content, and it follows that musical knowledge is a necessary attribute of anyone in charge of them. This is one of the reasons why a gramophone record collection benefits from being administered by a music librarian. No one can be expected to build up a collection of the world's recorded music "blind", but the fact remains that an astonishing number of people, both inside the library profession and without, are ignorant as to what musical knowledge entails and how that knowledge can best be applied to gramophone record stock. In a library which serves a musical community, e.g. a music college, the gramophone records will be purchased at the request of the teaching staff, but if the librarian is to have any standing with staff and students alike, he or she must have the musical knowledge to select records on his or her own account, for requests may not always be particular or very well expressed, and one cannot always reach for the *History of Music in Sound*. Musical knowledge is even more necessary in a public library where there is no higher musical intelligence to refer to, and especially where the music librarian is responsible for public recitals of recorded music. This raises the vexed question of extension activities, and how deeply the music librarian can become involved in them. The phrase "extension activities" can cover many different aspects of a library's service but may generally be taken to mean anything other than the loan and reference services. Many librarians are enthusiastic about this part of their work and regard their library's extension activities as the most important part of its service, but the gradual transformation of a music and record librarian into a sort of unofficial entertainments officer is not unknown, and cannot always be said to be in the library's best interest, quite apart from the fact that there are some librarians who find themselves to be definitely antipathetic towards extension work, however valuable the resultant publicity may be. The amount of extension activities to be undertaken and the designation of staff are problems to be settled by the individual library system, but such activities invariably call for the provision of music at some stage and that inevitably involves the music and record library, so that a librarian accepting a post involving work with music and gramophone records should consider whether or not he is likely to find this aspect of the work congenial.

The training of an assistant in a gramophone record library will, in the main, follow the same lines as training in any other type of library, so we shall consider here only those details peculiar to work with gramophone records. Since the greater part of an assistant's day is spent at the issue counter, that assistant must be made thoroughly familiar with the library's rules and regulations regarding the procedure of charging and discharging. In a book library, this is straightforward, but gramophone record librarians have shown themselves to be so adept at surrounding themselves with so many rules, generally of their own invention, and varying from library to library, that it is essential that an assistant should understand fully those rules which he has to uphold. Most libraries are concerned about damage to records and practise some form of checking discs both before and after loan. The system should be explained to a new assistant, and a few examples of what to look for in the way of groove-marks, fingernail scratches, grazes, and pick-up digs pointed out with a brief explanation as to possible causes. Many libraries require proof that an intending borrower's equipment is satisfactory and others ask their borrowers to produce evidence that the stylus on their record player is renewed after a given number of issues. All of this, on top of the normal duties of a busy issue counter, places a heavy responsibility on the shoulders of the young and inexperienced assistant, and many find it so distasteful that they prefer not to work in a gramophone record department. We are, as a profession, divided on this point, as the sporadic outbursts in the correspondence columns of our professional press show, and it is therefore wise, when explaining these details to a trainee, to explain also the library's reasons for making such rules and regulations and to give some advice on how best to tell a borrower that a record will need testing for damage. Tactful handling of one's public is the most valuable attribute of any librarian, and is more than ever necessary under such circumstances, for the legal and other implications of an unguarded remark are enormous.

It is, however, the experience of most librarians working with gramophone records that the public is remarkably co-operative about such matters and trouble can be expected in only a few cases. The new assistant will learn early the importance of handling discs with care, for it is useless to exhort the borrowing public to do this unless we ourselves show them a good example. Although it is not always possible in a busy department, the gradual "drawing-out" of a borrower on his opinions about particular composers and their work can yield much valuable information as well as covering the inevitable and sometimes agonising wait while the record is examined. This practice not only helps with record selection, but also builds up the borrower's confidence in the library staff and encourages him to ask for advice on his own personal choice of music, for not all members are aware of the intellectual resources available in a library and have to be apprised of them by devious means. There has grown up recently in library circles the belief that any member of a library staff who spends the greater part of his working day at the issue-desk must necessarily be inferior to one who works "inside". Nowhere is this belief proved to be more erroneous than in a gramophone record library, where the service must be a personal one, and it is a measure of the public's appreciation of such a service that they are so co-operative with regard to charges for damage and complicated rules and regulations.

Efficient use of the catalogue is important in any library, but it is particularly so in one which houses gramophone records. Music has many special problems for the cataloguer which are scarcely lessened when it is recorded. What the assistant should learn is intelligent interpretation of the catalogue entries. Again, personal musical intelligence helps enormously, but there are gaps in everyone's knowledge, and a thorough grounding in the library's cataloguing policy can go a long way towards filling up these gaps. All explanations should be as simple as possible, not only because simplicity is less likely to confuse an unfamiliar assistant, but also because the assistant will have to pass on this information to new members of the library, for, since staffs of special departments are always relatively small, even the most junior and inexperienced assistant will be left alone and in charge at some time. He or she should be prepared for this and instructed in the various resources of the library so that there shall be as little falling-off as possible in the standard of the service. When reliefs must come from the central library pool, it is advisable to use always the same reliefs, for there is no doubt that people who borrow gramophone records prefer to be attended by the same assistant each time. This is, of course, not always possible, especially in a public library where the opening hours necessitate shift-work, but the benefits are sufficient to outweigh any juggling with the timetable.

Once the catalogues have been thoroughly understood, the assistant should be introduced to the various bibliographical and commercial guides which deal with gramophone records. These vary from library to library both in quantity and importance, but are most useful in tracking down the answers to odd queries and they do answer some questions that the catalogue may not, indeed some of the more important commercial guides can be used to supplement the main catalogue in much the same way that the *British National Bibliography* is used for bookwork. It is not wise, however, to rely entirely on reference works which deal exclusively with gramophone records, for the amount of recorded music is so infinitesimally small compared with that which has not yet been recorded, and the present system of deletions is so ruthless, that it is as well to have some standard musical reference work to hand. It is better to tell an enquirer that no gramophone record is available than to say that no information can be found. (This does not apply, of course, in an existing music library.) Most libraries hold sets of one or more of the currently available periodicals devoted to record reviews, and the assistant should be shown how perusal of these reviews can help the librarian to decide which of the many available versions of Beethoven's Fifth Symphony (there are 34) should be purchased for inclusion in the library's stock. Some libraries have very definite policies on such matters. A small budget may compel a librarian to buy only bargain issues, or the library's stock may be limited to stereophonic recordings, jazz is expressly excluded from some libraries, and so on. The assistant may very well have played no part in the forming of such policies, but should at least be given the chance to defend them against the criticism of the public.

In conclusion, it may be said that although gramophone record libraries are still in a minority in this country, they are by now well out of the experimental category into which so many library authorities would place them. The gramophone record is now being accepted as library stock and as collections grow not only in number but also in size, so staff will be needed to administer them. Work with gramophone records can be difficult and is always exacting, but it is also immensely rewarding to any librarian who is interested in presenting music in its various forms to an ever-growing, and, on the whole, grateful public.

Rules and Regulations

by JEAN C. HITCHON, FLA
Music Librarian, Barnet Public Libraries

Library rules and regulations are formulated within the framework of the Authority's byelaws, and under the appropriate section of the current Public Libraries and Museums Act, at present that of 1964.

A revised set of model byelaws has recently been issued by the Department of Education and Science, working in conjunction with the Library Association; and authorities of the newly formed London boroughs, which came into being in April, 1965, have been awaiting the arrival of this document before finalising rules and regulations, including those governing library services.* It thus happens that up-to-date printed regulations for many large and important record libraries were not available while this chapter was in preparation. However, it is not anticipated that any significant changes in the general form of record library rules and regulations is likely to emerge.

In Section 1 (f) of the new model byelaws, the definition "book" includes, among other materials, the gramophone record. Apart from this they have no direct bearing on gramophone record collections. In fact, byelaws appear to be mainly concerned with persons intent on maliciously causing damage or disturbance, lying or sleeping on the floor or furniture, eating, smoking and unlawfully parking dogs, bicycles, and perambulators on the premises. Rules and regulations are often expressed in cumbersome, legal phraseology, or have an *Alice through the Looking Glass* kind of logic. I quote from Section 1, paragraph (i), of the general library regulations of one of the larger pre-amalgamation London boroughs. "Words importing the masculine gender shall include the feminine and where appropriate the singular shall include the plural."

Nevertheless, in considering a gramophone records collection, well thought-out and clearly-phrased regulations provide a good blue print of the service, which may be set out in outline only or in considerable detail. Sets of regulations studied have yielded examples of both types. Where

*These model byelaws are now available – Ed.

regulations are set out in great detail they have the disadvantage that, as points of administration and conditions of borrowing change from time to time in a growing service, they must be revised and reprinted. Thus, such a phrase as "the number of records which may be borrowed at any one time will be decided by the Library Authority from time to time, as this is required", may be preferable, in the printed regulations, to a more specific statement, which can be kept for an introductory leaflet or handout.

On the other hand, detailed regulations, particularly concerning damage, playing equipment and styli, provide support for the staff in situations where disputes or disagreements with members of the public may arise.

Fig. 1.   *The Music Library contains records, scores and literature.*

For the purpose of discussion, gramophone record library regulations can be divided most conveniently into three sections, under the headings "General: Conditions of Borrowing", "Care of Records and Responsibility for Damage", and "Copyright".

General: Conditions of Borrowing

ELIGIBILITY FOR MEMBERSHIP.   Membership is usually limited to residents of the borough or town concerned, and non-residents who employ, are employed, or attend school or college therein. Some regulations specify that students can only be accepted if they are "full-time", no doubt because part-time students and those attending evening classes are a shifting population and tend to disappear without trace.

A guarantee, usually involving liability of two or three pounds, or a recommendation, from a local government elector, is almost invariably required for applicants for membership under twenty-one, or, for some other reason, not on the electoral register. Presumably proof of being a ratepayer of the borough concerned must always be accepted even though the applicant is not on the register. The term "ratepayer" does not often appear in regulations, although occasionally it is included with the term "elector". In the more recently formulated regulations studied a recommender, without financial liability, rather than a guarantor, is asked to vouch for any person not on the electoral register.

The age of eligibility for membership varies between fifteen and eighteen years.

SOCIETY MEMBERSHIP.   In nearly all sets of regulations society membership is granted. It generally applies to schools and colleges, and to music and similar societies which hold meetings in the borough. Extra records, the number usually unspecified, can be borrowed for recitals. The application form must be signed by one or two responsible members or officers of the society, or head teacher of the school, and, in some cases, it is stipulated that not more than two representatives must be nominated to borrow the records. In some regulations a loan period shorter than the normal one is specified for societies.

SUBSCRIPTIONS AND DEPOSITS.   In the sets of rules studied most authorities do not now demand a deposit from record library members. Where deposits are still asked for, they vary from one to three pounds.

A few libraries charge an annual subscription to all members, usually of one guinea, and, in a very few cases, subscribing membership is open to anyone living outside the borough and without employment or student qualifications. Two libraries are known to make a small charge per issue, in one case one shilling, and, in the other, sixpence, and there may, of course, be others who do so.

As far as deposits are concerned, experience has shown that, for the sake of the comparatively few cases where borrowers who have damaged records have refused to pay for them, they are not worth the time, trouble, and expense involved in collection and repayment.

The needs of subscribing borrowers should eventually be partly catered for by general interavailability of record library tickets, but, for the foreseeable future, there are likely to be boroughs not providing a record library service. It is to be hoped that the larger boroughs may be willing to open their doors to the unfortunate residents of such places, either on a subscription or some other basis.

HOURS OF OPENING – PERIOD OF LOAN – TICKETS – FINES. Regulations governing these aspects of the service require only a passing mention. Hours of opening usually correspond to those in the main lending departments, but some libraries include a regulation whereby records may not be exchanged, or, in some cases, returned, after a period varying from fifteen to thirty minutes before closing time. The single-handed record library assistant is grateful for such a regulation, and there is also the consideration that the last-minute borrower has not time to examine his records for damage.

One record ticket per borrower is the usual allowance, although a few libraries now allow two. One 12 in long player, a complete set of any number, or two or three 10 or 7 in discs is the normal allocation per ticket.

In the early days of record libraries, one week was the most general loan period, due to limited stocks, but the tendency now is to make loan and renewal periods correspond to those for books. Reservation fees and fines on gramophone records are as varied and idiosyncratic as they are on books.

SUSPENSION OF TICKETS. Finally, a safeguard is usually included in the general regulations whereby the librarian or his representative has the right to refuse an application for membership or to suspend use of a borrower's ticket. These clauses have a special application to gramophone record libraries, where questions of damage and liability for faulty equipment have to be dealt with.

Care of Records and Responsibility for Damage

INSPECTION: CARE OF RECORDS. The rules formulated under this heading are of vital importance to the record librarian and record users. They are usually detailed and specific, and the original intention was to protect records from damage in the early closed-access libraries where stock and funds were very limited, and eyebrows were still being raised at the idea of lending such material to the public.

This attitude has been modified, but most libraries retain the clauses concerning inspection and care of records, as well as safeguards against damage, not so much to guard valuable material from harm as to impress on borrowers the need to treat records carefully, in order to obtain the maximum pleasure from playing them.

Regulations usually specify that examination of records by the borrower before leaving the library indicates his acceptance of these records as being free from visible damage, apart from that already clearly marked in whatever manner of indicating damage is in use. Further, he is deemed fully responsible for any damage not so marked which may be found by the librarian who examines the record when it is returned to the library. A typically worded regulation runs as follows:

> Borrowers will be held responsible for the safe keeping of records issued to them, and for returning them in good condition. All records must be examined by borrowers before acceptance, and any damage other than that already noted must be pointed out to the assistant in charge. Borrowers will be held responsible for damage not pointed out at the time of issue.

In some regulations a further proviso is made as follows:

> The acceptance of records by the librarian on return from loan shall not preclude the Library Authority from claiming for damage occasioned to a record whilst such record was in the possession of the borrower, but which damage is not apparent at the time of return.

This is important, as damage caused by a worn stylus is not always visible when the record is examined, and is only discovered, in the form of distortion and background noise, at the next playing. If this type of damage is reported by a borrower after the first playing on his gramo-phone, the stylus of the previous borrower, should the system provide means of tracing him, can be called in for inspection, and, under the wording of the regulation, he may be liable to pay for the damage.

Rules for the care of records usually stipulate that they should be handled only by the edges, that they should be cleaned before and after every playing with a special record cleaning cloth or slightly damp sponge, that they should be stored upright and away from sources of heat and damp, and always kept in their containers when not in use. Other clauses are sometimes included to the effect that no part of a work shall be played more frequently than another (this was particularly applicable to sets of 78 RPM discs), that the pick-up arm shall not be raised or lowered part-way through a side, and that records shall be transported to and from the library either in suitable carrying cases, or in the carrying cases provided.

RESPONSIBILITY FOR THE CARE AND USE OF RECORD PLAYING EQUIPMENT.   A general regulation usually states that long-playing records should be played only on equipment specifically designed for them. Among the sets of regulations examined only one made any separate provision for stereo records, and this was under the heading of "Styli".

Styli: Rules vary greatly as to the amount of detail included under this heading. In some cases the only stipulation is that the stylus should be in good condition, in others a maximum number of sides to be played is recommended, varying from 50–100 for a sapphire, and 1000–3000 for a diamond, or else a similar calculation is made in playing hours.

Although some librarians make a regular routine examination of all styli, no specific rule about this was found. One library, however, has a regulation stating that a monaural stylus should be examined under a microscope after one year's wear, and a stereo diamond stylus after six months' wear, while, to quote from yet another set of regulations, "Any borrower may be required to provide proof, from time to time, that a new stylus has been fitted to the machine upon which library records are played".

Auto Changers: Nearly all sets of regulations include a clause demanding that only one record at a time shall be loaded onto an auto changer. The danger of damage from faulty changer mechanism and stiffness of the pick-up arm mounting – a frequent cause of groove-stripping – was not mentioned in the rules studied, but, with various other causes of damage, this is probably better relegated to an introductory leaflet or handout.

Inspection of Equipment: Several libraries have a rule giving them the right to inspect borrowers' equipment. Many of the early record libraries did not lend to individuals, but only to societies, and the record librarian was expected to go the society's premises and inspect the record-playing equipment before an application for membership was accepted. A typical regulation in this connection is worded: "A representative of the library authority shall have the right to inspect the instrument to be used for playing records and/or to attend recitals at which they are being played". Now that eligibility for membership is mainly unrestricted, this type of rule has fallen into disuse.

Borrower's Responsibility for his own Equipment: Only a few libraries include a regulation which stipulates that a borrower shall play library records only on his own equipment, his assent to comply with the regulations on his application for membership being deemed to imply personal possession of equipment and responsibility for its maintenance in good condition. To quote from one of the few regulations dealing with this matter: " . . . proof of the personal ownership of suitable playing equipment should be provided. The right is reserved not to issue records should the equipment be regarded as unsuitable by the library authority". In the same connection, two or three libraries include a regulation that a record may only be used by the registered borrower to whom it is issued.

The lack of rules on both these points in most sets of regulations is, in the writer's view, a grave omission. Records are undoubtedly damaged through being lent by borrowers to non-library users and people who may be ignorant of the effects of bad handling and worn styli. A warning against thoughtlessness on this score could well bear fruit. More positive and important, however, is a rule making the borrower personally responsible for playing equipment, which he should vouch for as being his own or his family's. Most assistants will have had the experience of having to allow a person, eligible by age and residential or other qualifications, to join the record library, although he has no equipment, but intends to play the records on a gramophone belonging to a friend. All information regarding styli and so on is gleaned secondhand, so to speak, and the nebulous friend never appears in person.

CHARGES FOR DAMAGE.   The regulations governing damage allow such charges to be made as shall be assessed by the librarian after he has ascertained the extent of the damage. The borrower is usually made liable up to a total sum not exceeding the original cost of the record, with the proviso that, where a record from a set cannot be replaced individually, the borrower is liable for the cost of the complete set. In a few cases the regulations go even further, specifying that, if a lost or ruined record is unobtainable, or cannot, at the time, be obtained through the normal supply channels, twice the original cost of the record can be claimed. As more and more imported records are becoming available, often for a limited time only, and deletions continue to mount, this rule may be of significance, but, to the writer, it seems unnecessarily vindictive, and is not recommended. It is usual for the person paying the replacement cost of a record to be able to claim the damaged record if he wishes to do so.

Copyright

A regulation absolving the library from all responsibility for any infringement of copyright by persons borrowing records must always be included. Some years ago a reminder on this score was sent out by the Library Association to authorities with record libraries, and wording for such a regulation was recommended as follows:

> No charge shall be made for admittance to any performance of records borrowed from the Library without the previous consent of the librarian. The use of any record which is the property of the Library Authority shall not confer upon the borrower any right or licence in respect of copyright or public performance. Any borrower proposing to use such records for public performance shall inform the librarian beforehand, and shall give a written undertaking indemnifying the Library Authority against any claim which may be made against them on this account in respect of any record borrowed from the Library.

The copyright clause in this rule, will, of course, cover the library with regard to any infringement of copyright due to tape recording the library's records.

Conclusion

To sum up: library regulations are drafted mainly for the purposes of giving legal protection to the library authority in the actions taken on its behalf, to ensure the running and maintenance of the service in good order, and without abuse, and of setting out clearly, for library users, their rights, responsibilities and liabilities in using and borrowing from the library.

In the case of gramophone records, it is clear that rules must, of necessity, be fairly complex and detailed. All borrowers, on joining the record library, should either be given a printed copy of the regulations, or a printed leaflet summarising and clarifying them. Even where printed copies of the regulations, as they stand, are issued to new members, an introductory leaflet to the service should still be included. The all-important rules on the care, handling, and playing of records can be set out in more detail, and often expressed more directly, than in the formal regulations.

Draft for a Suggested Set of Record Library Regulations

1. *Membership and Tickets.* Subject to these regulations, gramophone records (herein referred to as "records") may, at the discretion of the Library Authority, be borrowed by:

(a) any person who is either
    (i) a resident in the Borough of ——,
    (ii) a non-resident employer or employee working in the Borough; or
    (iii) a non-resident full-time student attending an educational institution in the Borough;
    and who is over — years of age, or
(b) a music society, school or other educational or cultural organisation whose meetings are normally held in the Borough.

Provided that any person under 21 years of age, and all non-residents, shall furnish a recommendation from a local government elector for the said borough.

2. A person referred to in Regulation 1 (a) hereof shall complete the prescribed form of application and present it to the librarian. The signing of the form of application shall be deemed to be an assent by the person signing it to be bound by these Regulations.

3. Records will be issued only to those borrowers who possess, and who sign an undertaking to use, the appropriate type of record-playing

equipment, including a light-weight pick-up with a sapphire or diamond stylus. Records may be played only by the borrower to whom they are issued, and on the equipment specified by him on his enrollment form. Stereo records will be issued only to borrowers possessing stereophonic equipment, details of which must be supplied on the borrower's enrolment form.

4. A society, school, or other organisation referred to in Regulation 1 (b) hereof shall complete the prescribed form of application, and it shall be presented to the librarian by their secretary, accredited representative, or headmaster or headmistress or teacher acting on their behalf, in the name of such society, school, or organisation, as the case may be. If the signatory to the form of application during the currency of the registration shall cease to hold the office or position held when the application form was signed, such person shall notify the Librarian and a fresh form of application shall be submitted on behalf of such society, school or organisation, provided that, until such notification is received by the Librarian, such person shall continue to be responsible for any breach of these Regulations and for any loss or damage which may be incurred whilst a record is in the possession of the society, school or organisation concerned.

5. A borrower's ticket for records shall be issued to a person or society whose application is approved. Such tickets shall remain in force for such period as the Library Authority shall determine from time to time.

6. Tickets shall be issued at the discretion of the Librarian who may, if he considers it in the interests of the Library Authority, refuse to issue a ticket or a record to any person. The Librarian shall also be entitled to cancel or suspend tickets following any breach of these Regulations.

CONDITIONS OF ISSUE AND USE OF RECORDS

7. *Loss or Damage to Records.*

(i) A borrower shall be responsible for the care of records whilst in his possession, and shall make good any loss, damage or breakage of records occurring between the time of their issue and their return to the library. The borrower must examine records at the time of loan and report any damage or blemish to the Librarian. The borrower will be held responsible for any damage not so reported. Records shall be examined in the presence of the borrower on return, but the acceptance of records by the Librarian on return from loan shall not preclude the Library Authority from claiming for damage occasioned to a record whilst such record was in the possession of the borrower, but which damage is not apparent at the time of return. The cost to make good any damage shall be assessed by the Librarian.

(ii) If the damaged record is one of a set it may be necessary to buy a complete new set. In such a case the borrower paying for or supplying the new set shall be entitled to retain such part of it as is not required to replace damaged records, unless the new set is a different recording, in which case the Librarian shall retain the whole of the new set, the borrower being entitled to claim the old.

(iii) A borrower shall be entitled to retain any damaged record he may replace or pay for except in the case of a record published by a society or otherwise specially published, where such record must be returned to the publishers as a condition of supplying a new one.

(iv) The charge to the borrower for replacement of a record shall not exceed the original cost of the record when new.

8. The number of records which shall be borrowed at any one time will be decided by the Library Authority from time to time, as this is required.

9. A society or school shall be entitled to borrow a complete programme of records provided that due notice is given. The number of records which may be borrowed is entirely at the discretion of the Librarian.

10. Any record or set of records in the stock of the library may be reserved by the same procedure as for the reservation of books.

11. Borrowers shall take all possible care of records lent to them and shall safeguard them against loss, damage and unnecessary wear. All records shall be kept in the containers provided, stored in an upright position and sufficiently closely packed to prevent warping. They should be handled only by their edges, and should be wiped carefully before and after each playing with a record cleaning cloth or a special record sponge, which should be clean and only slightly damp. Records shall be protected from heat and damp. Records shall be transported to and from the library in the carrying cases provided or in similar suitable carrying cases.

12. Sapphire styli shall be changed after 40–45 playing hours (approximately 100 long-playing sides played) for monaural records, after 25–30 playing hours (approximately 50 long-playing sides played) for stereo records. Diamond styli shall be checked under a microscope after twelve months' use in the case of a monaural stylus, after six months' use in the case of a stereo stylus.

13. Any person borrowing a record or set of records from the library shall not be entitled to retain the same after the expiration of the period of loan in force at the time following the date of the borrowing thereof, unless, during the said period, the Librarian has received a verbal or written application from the borrower for an extension, and, being satisfied that the record or records are not otherwise required, grants the said application. The borrower may then retain the record or records until the expiration of the period of loan following the receipt of the said application by the Librarian.

14. Any person who, having borrowed a record from the library, fails to return it within the period prescribed by Regulation 8, shall pay to the Library Authority a charge as determined by the Library Authority under (the appropriate) byelaw.

15. All records issued on one borrower's ticket shall be returned together.

16. Borrowers shall be held responsible for any records which may be taken out in their names, and shall take every reasonable precaution against the loss of their borrower's ticket.

17. *Performance of Records.*

(i) No charge shall be made for any performance of loaned records without the previous consent of the Librarian.

(ii) The use of any record which is the property of the Library Authority shall not confer upon the borrower any right or licence in respect of copyright or public performance, and every borrower proposing to use such records publicly shall inform the Librarian beforehand, and give an undertaking in writing indemnifying the Library Authority against all claims which may be made against them on this account in respect of any records borrowed from the library.

BBC Gramophone Library Cataloguing Practice

by DEREK GRAFTON

Assistant Gramophone Librarian, BBC Gramophone Library

Cataloguing practice in the BBC Gramophone Library was dealt with at some length and in considerable detail by my predecessor, Mr. R. G. Angel in the last edition of *Gramophone Record Libraries*. That was in 1963. The intervening years have seen numerous changes in the pattern of broadcasting – the introduction of extended hours (including the Music Programme on the Third Network), the setting up of a chain of Local Radio Stations throughout the country, and Radio 1 with floods of discs devoted entirely to the output of Light Entertainment. Colour at the BBC is no longer confined to TV. It is also provided by purple-suited, pink shirted disc jockeys with insatiable appetites for "pop" records.

The Cataloguing Section of the BBC Gramophone Library has always had to deal with the documentation of any form of record, ranging from "Pop" to Plainchant, from Jazz to Jewish Religious Music. Within recent years, however, the field has expanded enormously. It seems only twenty years or so ago, when the addition of a Vivaldi concerto to the catalogue was regarded as something of a novelty. Nowadays, one tends to look upon the delivery of yet another volume of Vivaldi concertos as almost commonplace, no longer a task fraught with difficulties for the cataloguer. His problems however, have increased in recent years with the marketing, amongst other things, of volumes of obscure mediaeval dances, madrigals, masses, to say nothing of a flood of foreign folk music and other material.

The hard-worked cataloguing team at Broadcasting House is now riding high on a flood tide of "pop" discs. Naturally, it is just as important for these to be catalogued correctly as it is for their more classical cousins; added to which is the demand nowadays for speed. The newest 45 "pop" single which arrives on Friday may be "on the air" the same evening. It will have been delivered in company with perhaps twenty or thirty other "pop" discs, all of which have to be put through the cataloguing process as quickly as possible. But the need for swift cataloguing is not only confined to "popular" records. A classical record may have been ordered from abroad for a particular programme and arrives just in the nick of time. It is desirable that it is catalogued before transmission. Having been heard on the air, enquiries may follow and the necessary information must be available from the Catalogue.

To achieve speed in our work, it is essential that the basic construction of cataloguing should be as simple as possible. It is also advisable for our cataloguers to be trained typists, with a good eye for layout, so that the relevant entries may be easily looked up and read.

My predecessor explained in his article that a card catalogue system is in use, divided into three parts, with cards of a different colour for each part – title (white), composer (yellow), artist (blue) – each of which is complete in itself. An important alteration has recently been made in the case of the composer catalogue, which formerly included writers, such as authors, poets, playwrights and translators. These have now been removed to form an "Author" Catalogue, a process which took place not without difficulty. What does one do in the cases of Noël Coward, Ivor Novello, and other men of the theatre, who are equally at home in both words and music? Some titles, inevitably, must appear in both composer and author catalogue, – *Bitter Sweet, Conversation Piece*, and many more. Boïto provided an easy case. In the new author catalogue he appears as the librettist of a handful of operas, including his own and the two great Shakespearian masterpieces of Verdi's old age, *Otello* and *Falstaff*. Naturally, he also appears in the composer catalogue.

Those interested in statistics may like to know that the BBC Gramophone Library Catalogue now contains more than two million entries. It is being added to at the rate of not less than 10,000 entries each month. The work, all of which is checked, is spread amongst a team of ten cataloguers. I am often asked what qualifications are required for this task. Whilst it is obvious that the cataloguer should have a wide knowledge of music and records and real interest in his work, the need for languages is becoming more and more important. A cataloguer is of limited use if he is unable to decipher the sleeves and labels of the numerous foreign discs purchased by the BBC. These may be printed in the less common European languages, in Cyrillic characters, and in some cases, in African or Asiatic languages. Few individuals will be able to supply all the demands required, but a vital quality – almost more important than any other – is the necessity for common sense and clear thinking. And a cataloguer, no matter how impressive his qualifications, is useless to us if he is not strictly accurate in his work.

In the last edition, examples were given of cards in the catalogue. These were of operas, symphonies, lieder, together with their associated composer and artist cards.

At this stage, the reader may wish to study a further, wider range of examples. Let us tune in to Radio 1 and begin with the ubiquitous "pop" music. The piece chosen is the Beatles' number *Yellow Submarine*, all versions of which, including those sung in foreign languages, are catalogued under this title. Further information includes the name of the publisher (which appears in red directly underneath the title), and the date of issue of the records in the UK. The absence of a date indicates that the record has been obtained from abroad.

YELLOW SUBMARINE (Northern Songs)		LENNON: McCARTNEY		
The Beatles (vocal & instrumental) (Aug. '66)	PARLOPHONE		R	5493
			PMC	7009
			PMC	7016
The She Trinity (vocal & instrumental) (Aug. '66)	COLUMBIA		DB	7992
Maurice Chevalier (vocal) with Caravelli and his	HMV		POP	1562
Orchestra (Nov. '66)			EGF	940
(In French "Le sous-marin vert")				
Los Bulldogs (vocal & instrumental)	RCA VICTOR		31A	0952
(In Spanish "El submarino amarillo")				
Simo Salminen and Spede (vocal) with Chorus and	SCANDIA		KS	664
Orchestra conducted by Lahiran Nikkolaivasto				
(In Finnish "Keltainen Jäänsärkijä")				

Cross-reference cards are always made for the foreign language titles:

(LE) SOUS-MARIN VERT	LENNON: McCARTNEY

SEE: YELLOW SUBMARINE

The artist card for one of the Beatles' records containing the above number is shown as follows:

(THE) BEATLES	Vocal & Instrumental

PARLOPHONE
PMC 7009
    Revolver
    Love you to (with Anil Bhagwat, tabla)
    For no one (with Alan Civil, horn)
    Got to get you into my life
    Eleanor Rigby
    Taxman
    I'm only sleeping
    Here, there and everywhere
    Yellow submarine
    She said she said
    Good day sunshine
    And your bird can sing
    Dr. Robert
    I want to tell you
    Tomorrow never knows

It will be seen that this artist card also includes a "sleeve title", "Revolver" which is underlined. Records are sometimes requested by their "sleeve titles"; it is therefore necessary for this information to appear in the title catalogue. The card gives the briefest details, merely names of artists and record make and number.

REVOLVER – Sleeve Title

The Beatles (Vocal & instrumental)	PARLOPHONE PMC 7009

Artist cards have been made for Anil Bhagwat (tabla) and Alan Civil (horn), who are accompanying the Beatles in two of their numbers on this disc. These cards are merely cross-references.

The widespread interest in foreign travel which has sprung up within the last twenty years or so has produced a great demand for Continental popular music. An important example, shown below, is "Flamenco", a section for which has been built up in recent years within the main title catalogue. Here is an extract from one of the cards:

FLAMENCO

Songs and Dances of Spain, Vol. 3	WESTMINSTER	W 9804
Various flamenco groups		
Flamenco Fever	HMV	CLP 3613
Sabicas (guitar)		CSD 3613s

More detailed information of recordings of the various songs, dances and instrumental pieces collectively known as "Flamenco" should be looked up under their individual titles. Let us take our example from the section devoted to "Bulerias":

BULERIAS		VARIOUS MELODIES	
Pili, Carbonero and Juana Morales	WESTMINSTER		W 9804
(vocal) with flamenco group			
(three versions)			
Sabicas (guitar)	HMV	CLP	3613
"Jardin Sevillano"		CSD	3613s
Manitas Plata (vocal & guitar)	PHILIPS	P	70361 L
with José Reyes (vocal)		BL	7786
"Bulerias de Plata"			
Male vocalist with guitar	DECCA	LK	4762
(arr. Pena)		PFS	4091s

Not only must our catalogue be kept up-to-date but it should also provide for the demands and fashions of the day. Indian classical music, it is hoped, will always be in demand in the West; just now it is also fashionable. The following extract is from a section recently added to the title catalogue:

INDIAN MUSIC – CLASSICAL

Music of India, Vol. 2	HMV	ALP 1988
Ustad Vilayat Khan (Sitar), Ustad Imrat Khan (Surbahar), Pandit Shanta Prasad (Tabla) Raga "Suha Sugrai": Thumree piloo		
The Music of Southern India	NONESUCH	H 2003
S. Balachander (Vina) with Sivaraman (mridangam)	BOUNTY	BY 6027
Classical Ragas from India	PHILIPS	BL 7716
Various instrumentalists Ragas from Bhairavi: Raga Paraj: Raga Sari (from Kathakali dance-drama): Raga Madhuvanti: Religious Song.		

Another recent addition to the catalogue is a section listing unusual instruments, such as those mentioned above. The cards are mostly cross-references containing anything from an accordion solo to a zampogna.

The year 1967 saw the quartercentenary celebrations of the birth of Claudio Monteverdi, to which a whole issue of *Music Magazine* was devoted. The cataloguer responsible for choral and liturgical music was kept busy as new records of works by the great Italian master, together with those devoted to his pupil, Cavalli, and other madrigalists, were received "hot from the press". She is unlikely to forget one particular issue, catalogued as a rush job for inclusion in the above-mentioned *Music Magazine*. The following examples are of the Title, Composer and Author cards for the Madrigal *Baci soavi e cari*:

BACI SOAVI E CARI (5 part madrigal, Book 1, 1587) (Words by Guarini)		MONTEVERDI
Golden Age Singers conducted by Margaret Field-Hyde	WESTMINSTER	XWN 18765
Roger Wagner Madrigal Singers conducted by Roger Wagner	LYRICHORD	LL 43

MONTEVERDI (Claudio)

Baci soavi e cari (5 part madrigal, Book 1, 1587) (Words by Guarini)		
Golden Age Singers conducted by Margaret Field-Hyde	WESTMINSTER	XWN 18765
Roger Wagner Madrigal Singers conducted by Roger Wagner	LYRICHORD	LL 43

GUARINI (Giovanni Battista)   Poet

SETTINGS BY MONTEVERDI
Ch'io t'ami
Cruda Amarilli   (Words taken from the play 'Il Pastor Fido")
O Mirtillo
A un giro sol
Baci soavi e cari
Dolcissimo uscignolo
Cor mio mentre vi miro

For some time now, the desirability of providing details of collections of recordings of a composer's works has been considered necessary. It is especially useful to producers entrusted with the job of providing a number of programmes for some particular occasion or anniversary, such as the Monteverdi Quatercentenary. These cards for "Collections" are filed in the composer catalogue as an "Appendix". They are another, more recent addition to the composer catalogue, and, as yet, are in the early stages, being compiled as time permits, and when the occasion demands. Here is part of the section devoted to collections of Monteverdi madrigals:

MONTEVERDI (Claudio)

COLLECTIONS OF MADRIGALS

Prague Madrigal Singers	SUPRAPHON	SUA 10434
Rodolfo Farolfi and Karla Schlean	AMADEO	AVRS 5023
Golden Age Singers	WESTMINSTER	XWN 18765
conducted by Margaret Field-Hyde		
Roger Wagner Madrigal Singers	LYRICHORD	LL 43
conducted by Roger Wagner		
Rome Polyphonic Ensemble	RCA VICTOR	LM 7035
conducted by Nino Antonellini	(2 records)	

Mention has been made earlier in this article of the difficulty of cataloguing recent editions of volumes of obscure mediaeval music. One member of our team is never happier than when engrossed in scores and puzzling over records of Passepieds, Estampies, Galliards, Gigues, Voltas, and the like. The following title cards provide two examples of his cataloguing of anonymous 13th and 14th Century "Estampies" (or "Estampidas"):

ESTAMPIE   ANONYMOUS
                                                                          13th Cent.
(from Oxford, Bodleian Library, Douce MS.139)

Gaston Crunelle (Piccolo) with Clayette (Drum)	ANTHOLOGIE SONORE	16
("English Dance")		
Pro Musica Antiqua	EMS	201
conducted by Safford Cape		
("Stantipes")		

Monique Rollin Ensemble ("Danse anglaise")	LONDON	W 91116
Krefeld Collegium Musicum conducted by Robert Haass ("Spielmannstanz")	VOX	PL 8110
Studio der frühen Musik, Munich (Recorder, fiddle, lute and percussion)	TELEFUNKEN	AWT 9432 SAWT 9432s

ESTAMPIE ("Rectrove" or "Petrone")   ANONYMOUS
                                                                            14th Cent.

(from British Museum, Add. MS.28550 — Robertsbridge Codex)

Thurston Dart (Snetzler Organ) ("Petrone" — Punctus 1 only)	OISEAU-LYRE	OL 50075
Pierre Froidebise (Organ of St. Trond Abbey) ("Organ estampie" — Puncta 1, 4, & 5)	DUCRETET THOMSON	320 C 131
Aimée van de Wiele (Harpsichord) (Puncta 1, 4 & 5)	CRITÈRE	CRD 130÷
Portative organ of Jaye Consort (Puncta 1 & 4)	PYE	GGC 4092 GSGC 14092s
E. Power Biggs (organ of Notre Dame de Valère Church, Sion, Switzerland) ("Organ estampie" — Puncta 1, 4 & 5)	CBS	BRG 72601 SBRG 72601s

÷ Booklet available

A more sober section of the catalogue is that devoted to hymns. Each hymn is catalogued under its title, with a mention of the tune to which it is sung and to whom the words are ascribed. A cross-reference card is also made for the tune title. The hymn *Come, Holy Ghost* (words ascribed to Rabanus Maurus) and sung to the tune "Tallis's Ordinal" appears as follows in the title catalogue:

COME, HOLY GHOST   TALLIS
                                                        Tune: Tallis's Ordinal

(Words ascribed to Rabanus Maurus)

St. Gabriel Singers with Margaret Caton (Contralto), Kennedy Ryan (Bass) and Nicholas Danby (Organ), directed by John Hoban	PYE	CCL 40003

TALLIS'S ORDINAL — Hymn Tune   TALLIS

SEE: O HOLY SPIRIT, LORD OF GRACE (English Hymnal No. 453)
          HOW LOVELY ARE THY DWELLINGS FAIR (Cambridge Hymnal No. 46)
          COME, HOLY GHOST (Westminster Hymnal No. 62)

Further entries appear in the composer catalogue under Thomas Tallis, and in the author catalogue under Rabanus Maurus. These are in the nature of cross-references to the title catalogue.

The preceding examples will, I hope, give the reader some slight indication of the range of work undertaken in the Cataloguing Section of the BBC Gramophone Library. And now, Leporello-like, I am still left with a list for which no examples have been given. Ballet music (the cataloguer is warned to skate carefully over the *Swan Lake*), musical comedy, operetta, film scores, plays (including Japanese Noh plays), poems, sketches, documentaries, masses, animal noises, birds (unhelpful commentaries in Swedish and Russian) &c. &c. The list is inexhaustible, the work of the cataloguer stimulating and enthralling.

In conclusion, gramophiles curious for statistics may be interested to learn the actual number of different recordings in the BBC Gramophone Library of a few titles taken at random from the catalogue. The number held appears after the composer's name:

Rigoletto (Verdi), 16 complete or near complete recordings.
Symphony No. 5 in C minor (Beethoven), 70.
Smoke gets in your eyes (Jerome Kern), 210.
The Blue Danube (Johann Strauss II), 299.

The Cataloguing of Gramophone Records in Public Libraries

by E. T. BRYANT, FLA
Borough Librarian, Widnes

The methods of cataloguing gramophone records used by the British Broadcasting Corporation, (see p.57) are of considerable interest to other librarians. At the same time, the BBC's method of making a main entry under the title of the work to be catalogued is not generally regarded as acceptable for public libraries. There are several reasons for this. The principal objection is that such libraries normally work to a recognised cataloguing code under which sheet music and scores are entered under the name of the composer. It is sensible to follow the same rules, as far as is possible, with recordings of music. Secondly, few public libraries imitate the BBC practice of buying recordings of ephemeral music. Such discs almost invariably raise problems as to which of the several names usually shown on the record label is that of the composer, which the name of the lyricist, and which the arranger. For "pop" music, entry under title is probably essential if a disc is to be traced via the catalogue, but few users of public library catalogues are likely to be happy with main entries under titles for classical works (particularly for standard forms such as symphonies and concertos), although added title entries are often extremely valuable.

When open access is adopted, a minority of libraries arrange their discs in a classified sequence divided into fairly broad headings. My personal view is that this scheme is much less satisfactory for discs than for scores, since experience suggests that interest in recorded music is more likely to centre around the composer or the performer in preference to the type of music. Entries for both composers and performers may be regarded as equally attractive, since both lines of approach may be expected from our users. Main entry under title presents numerous problems, particularly as many discs do not contain complete works but only excerpts from longer works, and to find such excerpts, particularly from operas, is likely to be much more difficult using the title method of approach than with search under the composer, if necessary working through the cards under his name until the required extract is discovered.

British librarians have almost invariably acted on the basis that the number of catalogue entries for any disc should be kept to the minimum, though this unwillingness is less noticeable when unit cards are available. Even then, subject entries are likely to be omitted. Main entries in British catalogues are likely to be considerably shorter than those for the same recordings that are available through the printed catalogue card service of the Library of Congress. There is a case for excluding less important items of information, though this may sometimes result in the omission of valuable details. In comparison with British librarians, their American counterparts are likely to catalogue much more fully, providing all the entries needed for a good dictionary catalogue. There would seem to be three main reasons for this. British librarians keep their catalogue entries in a separate set of trays or sheafs, usually displayed as near the collection of discs as possible; Americans often insert cards for discs in the main catalogue – a practice that almost enforces as detailed cataloguing of gramophone records as of books. Secondly, American librarians have the tremendous advantage that they can purchase well printed sets of catalogue cards for nearly all the works issued in that country by the major manufacturers. As mentioned above, these cards are produced by the Library of Congress and give full (though by no means exhaustive) main entries, while additional cards are available for subject, title and performer added entries. American librarians often arrange their gramophone record collections in exact classified order, a practice that is most uncommon in Britain.

The provision of LC printed catalogue cards must have improved the general standard of gramophone record cataloguing in the USA at least as much as the sale by the British National Bibliography of duplicated cards for books has improved the catalogues in very many British libraries. The need for a similar service here for discs is very apparent, and it will be interesting to see if commercial specialist library suppliers' attempts to fill the gap in this country prove successful, or if they will die from lack of support, probably from those very librarians who stand to benefit most from such a service.

Any cataloguer can find useful guidance in the American Library Association's publication *Code for cataloguing music and phonorecords*, issued in 1958. The work was produced under the joint auspices of the [American] Music Library Association and the Division of Cataloguing and Classification of the ALA. Every British library with a gramophone record collection (indeed, with any music in stock) should have a copy of this helpful code. Its third chapter deals with the cataloguing of "phonorecords" (a word coined to include such related items as discs, tape recordings, and player-piano rolls) and is virtually Chapter 9a of the Library of Congress *Rules for descriptive cataloguing*. This means that LC cards are based on the same rules as those used by most good American music libraries.

The simplest type of disc to catalogue is probably one which contains but a single work, so that this makes the obvious starting point for the practical suggestions which follow. One may choose, as example, the complete *Daphnis et Chloé* ballet by Ravel, recorded by Decca (monophonic LXT 5536; stereophonic SXL 2164) with the London Symphony Orchestra, together with the chorus of the Royal Opera House, Covent Garden, whose chorus master (named on the back of the sleeve) is Douglas Robinson. The whole performance is conducted by Pierre Monteux. There should be no difficulty in deciding that "Ravel" is the heading, with *Daphnis et Chloé*: [ballet] as title. Since it is assumed that this entry will not be interfiled with those for books and scores, there is no need to add *Phonodisc* as is recommended in the MLA code. Those rules suggest that the imprint consists of the trade name of the publisher (i.e., the name on the label; hence Columbia or Capitol rather than EMI), the record number(s) as listed in the manufacturer's catalogue, and the date of release, when this is available from the copy being catalogued. This last proposal seems of doubtful value, though the year in which a record was first published in Britain has usually been shown, either on the disc or the sleeve, as a result of the Copyright Act of 1956. It can, of course, be extremely misleading, as date of recording and issue may show a difference of several years. The review date quoted in the quarterly catalogue published by *The Gramophone* is an alternative source for discs generally available in Britain. However, all that seems necessary in our example, and assuming that the library has the stereo copy, is "Decca SXL 2164". If the collection includes both versions, then both catalogue numbers will be shown.

The code recommends that the collation should consist of the number of sides devoted to the work being catalogued, the diameter of the discs, the playing speed and the word "microgroove" where applicable. The last term may be omitted unless the library has 78 RPM shellac discs as well as their modern successors. Much more important is the indication of the type of recording, unless, again, the library has only monophonic discs. Even then, it could be useful to add the appropriate note if there is any possibility of stereo discs being added to stock at a later date. The collection that has neither 10 in nor 7 in discs included may also omit the details of size and speed; the borrower would understand that all the library discs were of 12 in diameter with a playing speed of $33\frac{1}{3}$ RPM. A series note may be added where thought desirable, but British discs are not often issued as part of a named series. The practice seems to be much more common in the USA.

The cataloguer has now given details of the work recorded on the disc and of the latter's format; a gap of one or two lines should be left and the performers then listed. The MLA code requires the name of the performer or group to be followed by a comma and the medium of performance, unless this is obvious from the name of the group (such as Amadeus String Quartet). Soloists' names are followed by that of accompanist or orchestra, with the conductor's name (where applicable) entered as the final item. Each of these parts – soloist, accompanist, conductor – is separated by means of a semicolon. British cataloguers may not wish to follow this procedure in detail, but it is recommended that the proposed order of soloist, orchestra, and conductor be maintained. It aids consistency and is also the order adopted in nearly all discographies and similar guides to gramophone records, and so has become a standard that is generally accepted by those interested in the subject.

How many of the performers should be listed with an opera recording? This must be a matter of opinion. For the opera enthusiast, a complete list of the cast may be thought vital; for the cataloguer, time is equally important, while the need to expand the main entry on to two or three cards is not attractive. A reasonable compromise between a complete list of names and that of the conductor alone would seem to be the entry of the performers listed on the front of the sleeve or album. If there are still too many performers for the cataloguer to be willing to note them all, a selection should not be difficult since (as with films and other forms of entertainment) the most important artists are usually given priority in listing and have their names in the biggest type.

If the disc being catalogued contains more than one work, a further space is left below the name(s) of the performer(s), and brief details given of the other item(s) on the record. The code suggests that the word *With* . . .introduces the other work or works.

Using the record already quoted as our example, the suggested information to be given, and the layout of the entry would be:

> RAVEL, Maurice
> Daphnis et Chloé: [complete ballet]. Decca
> stereo SXL 2164. 2 sides.
> Royal Opera House chorus, Covent Garden; L.S.O.;
> Pierre Monteux, conductor.

The musically knowledgeable cataloguer might well vary the normal order of entry, exemplified in this layout, by listing the orchestra first. This would be because the work is basically an orchestral one, with the chorus taking part very occasionally and singing wordlessly. This perhaps illustrates the fact that good music cataloguing is unlikely to be achieved by a person with a very limited musical knowledge unless the entries can be checked by someone who does have a good grounding in the subject, even though lacking in ability to catalogue correctly. Reverting to our entry, it will be recalled that the sleeve shows "Chorus of the Royal Opera House . . .", but inversion on the catalogue card is probably useful. Indeed, some cataloguers might well choose "Covent Garden" as the first words relating to the chorus, in order to try to ensure that the hasty reader was helped to notice the important words. There seems to be limited value in including the chorus master's name in the entry, while "L.S.O." is the standard abbreviation of the orchestra's name, though some cataloguers might prefer to quote it in full, or possibly use the form "London S.O." Finally, the word "conductor" could be shortened in order to conserve space. An alternative method of entry for orchestral works is to use "conducted by . . ." instead of using the word "conductor" as in the example above. There is, in fact, plenty of room for individual preferences within the suggested framework. Having decided which particular method and layout seems best for one's own library users, it is important that it should be consistently applied in the catalogue.

As with sheet music, recorded excerpts should be catalogued under the heading adopted for the complete work. Thus, *The Flight of the Bumble Bee* should be entered as part of Rimsky-Korsakov's *Tsar Saltan*. Since, however, many of our listeners are unlikely to be aware that the piece comes from an opera or, if they do, to be sure of that opera's name, it is obviously desirable to make a reference from the title of the excerpt to that of the work under which the item is catalogued. It must always be remembered that the cataloguing of recorded music is based on the same principles that apply to music scores. The same criteria hold for arrangements. The entry should make it clear that the particular item is not recorded in its original scoring and, if the information is easily discovered, show the name of the arranger. One might instance a recording of the scherzo from Mendelssohn's incidental music to *A Midsummer Night's Dream*, arranged for solo piano by Rachmaninov. The entry would be on the following lines.

> MENDELSSOHN, Felix
> A midsummer night's dream: [incidental music to Shakespeare's play], op. 61. No. 1, Scherzo, arr. for solo pf. by Rachmaninov.

It is my view that analytical entries should be made for every item on a disc, unless the excerpts themselves are incomplete and not readily described, or if they are virtually unidentifiable without considerable trouble. An example of the former type would be the EMI record *Yehudi Menuhin at Fifty* which contains over twenty items of which only two or three are complete. It seems pointless to make analyticals in this case; indeed, one could argue that a contents note was unnecessary, but should be replaced by brief annotation explaining the purpose of the disc and mentioning that the various items are linked by a commentary spoken by Menuhin himself.

Another violinist illustrates the other exception. *The Glory of Cremona* features fifteen famous violins, all played by Ruggiero Ricci, in brief works selected to show off the virtues of each instrument. The Decca-M.C.A.

contents note includes *Larghetto* by Handel and *Adagio* by Mozart-Friedberg. The text is devoted entirely to the instruments and not to the music. The cataloguer would be wasting time trying to identify these two works unless easily available reference sources have done it for him.

For the normal "recital" record, where analytical entries are recommended, the provision of such entries will be a lengthy task. Yet, unless it *is* done, no user of the catalogue can tell with any assurance if a particular, and possibly brief, item is included in the library stock. The matter is not unimportant, for there are many short works and frequently performed excerpts that are bound to be found as "fill-ups" or as items in a recorded concert or similar anthology since, because of their very brevity, such works can never be allotted a complete LP side by a manufacturer.

It has been argued that such entries are wasteful, on the grounds that (a) these works can be traced through the medium of the quarterly *LP Classical Record Catalogue* published by *The Gramophone* and (b) the potential life of a disc is too short for such cataloguing treatment to be justified. On (a), one can only remind readers that the quarterly catalogue, invaluable as it is to all gramophone record librarians, has its own omissions and limits its contents to discs of classical music that are generally and currently available. Any public library collection is soon likely to find itself possessing discs that either no longer appear, or which have never appeared, in the publication. Commercial record libraries apparently find that there is virtually no demand for recordings once they disappear from manufacturers' lists, and so usually withdraw such discs from their library stocks. Such a policy is unlikely to be followed by public libraries, particularly where there is no alternative version to replace a deleted one. The argument advanced in (b) is only valid if inspection of records is so poor that the life of records is short and brutish. This should certainly not be the case if advice given elsewhere in this book is adopted by librarians.

For some cataloguers, the problems of cataloguing finish with the provision of a main entry and, possibly, the inclusion of added entries for excerpts. Providing that entries are made under composers' names (plus entries under titles for anonymous works with distinctive titles) the catalogue may be considered as complete — though I would regard this as a mistaken view. The difficulties of cataloguing discs of non-musical items or of jazz, and of making unit entries for "recital" discs, will be considered later in this chapter. The basic information to be given, whatever the type of record, has been suggested above. The immediate question, once a work has been located in the catalogue, is that of finding the record itself should it be available for loan at that time. The catalogue ought to provide the link between any entry and the disc to which that entry refers, yet this important information seems often to be missing.

If records are filed by manufacturers' catalogue or by library accession numbers, then these numbers must be included as part of every main and analytical entry to ensure prompt discovery. If discs are arranged in browser boxes or on the shelves in classified order, then the catalogue should give the classification symbol on every main entry. If the sleeves are arranged in alphabetical order of composer (or performer, where appropriate) then the catalogue entry must show the name of the composer or other word under which the record is filed. Further guidance will be needed if the library stocks discs of more than one size or has both mono and stereo records, as the enquirer must be directed to the correct sequence. If the collection is administered on closed access methods, with an indicator showing which discs are currently available for choice, then the catalogue should refer to the correct heading or number on the indicator to enable the borrower to check if the record is available for loan at the time.

At Widnes, my own authority, these problems have been solved fairly simply. The method works equally well with closed access that uses the sleeves as indicator and with open access. At the upper right-hand corner of every catalogue entry, where the classification symbol would be quoted on the author index entry for a book, is shown the filing word or name used for the gramophone record to which that catalogue entry is related. For the ballet music record used as an example earlier, the filing word would be "Ravel". In the case of the *Shakespeare Festivities March* by Smetana, which occupies about two-thirds of an LP side as a fill-up to Dvořak's Fifth Symphony, the catalogue card for the march quotes "Dvořak" in the top right-hand corner, since the record is filed under that composer's name.

To ensure correct filing and to assist the easy discovery of discs, the top edge of the record cover (the sleeve itself originally; the protective jacket now that open-access methods are used) is strengthened with a linen adhesive tape on which is stencilled the disc's number at the centre and the filing word on the left. On many sleeves the composer's name is not prominent or may well be shown on the lower half of the design. This may be unimportant when the whole face of the cover is visible but if, as is usual, only the top section is visible in the cabinet, then both finding and filing are likely to be retarded. This stencilled name obviates this difficulty.

Since it is important that would-be borrowers look in the correct sequence for a disc, the size of the record is shown on the catalogue card by means of a large stamp with an open 7, 10, or 12 overprint, made with a rubber stamp. Some libraries use different coloured card for entries for stereo discs; we think it easier to use another rubber stamp to print an equally large open "S" before the size of the record. If this stamp is not used, the borrower correctly infers that the record is a monophonic recording.

Reverting momentarily to the Smetana march, the borrower notes that the work is on a 12 in mono disc, filed under "Dvořak" and has the manufacturer's number SUA 10153. Our patron has now only to find the Dvořak discs in the mono sequence, check the top edge of each for the catalogue number and know, at once, if the disc is there. There is no need to inspect each disc to see if it contains Dvořak's Fifth Symphony. Nor is there any fear that an ignorant assistant will file the disc under the wrong heading, since the operative word is clearly visible on the top edge of the protective sleeve.

At this stage, it is perhaps best to consider cataloguing methods for discs that contain more than one work, as with the Dvořak and Smetana example just quoted. In many cases, such records will couple works that conveniently fill a complete side each. Often the composer is the same for both works, but that does not affect the suggested method. Here is an example:

MOZART, Wolfgang Amadeus
    Piano concerto no. 23, in A major, K.488. DGG SLPM 138645.
        1 side. Stereo.
        Kempff (pf), Bamberg S.O., cond. Leitner.
    Other side: Mozart – Piano concerto 24

Several points need comment. First, a decision will be needed for concertos so that all are entered consistently. The choice rests between "Piano concerto . . ." or "Concerto for piano . . .". One may follow the MLA system (exemplified on the LC printed cards) of using a conventional or filing title, quoted in brackets, to be followed by the title as shown on the sleeve or label of the disc. For the above example, the LC card shows: [Concerto, piano, K.488, A major] *Phonodisc*, and this appears immediately under the composer's name, the heading on the card.

Secondly, the identification should include the number of the work if the composer has written more than one in that musical form and if there is also an agreed numbering system. Not all Mozartians are unanimous about the numbering of the composer's keyboard concertos. It may be noted that the filing title of the LC entry omits mention of "no. 23". However, there is a widely accepted standard here, and that has been used by the manufacturer of the discs and quoted in the specimen entry two paragraphs above. The identification should also, where appropriate, include both the key in which the work is written and the opus number (or its equivalent for composers such as Bach, Mozart, or Vivaldi). If the work has a nickname, authorised or added without the composer's consent, that deserves mention if the name is used in standard sources. It may be shown before or after the opus number – a matter of choice for the cataloguer but one that should be applied consistently. Thus, Beethoven's *Moonlight Sonata* (an unauthorised title, but one now universally known and used) can be listed as *Piano sonata no. 14, in C sharp minor ("Moonlight"), op. 27, no. 2* or *Piano sonata no. 14, in C sharp minor, op. 27, no. 2 ("Moonlight")*. Full identification is always desirable. To describe the Mozart work as *Piano concerto in A major* or *Piano concerto no. 23* is not adequate. *Piano concerto, K.488* is better, but is unlikely to be sufficiently helpful for the majority of users.

In this same Mozart example, the details of the performers are quoted in a somewhat different manner from those in the Ravel work. This is done deliberately to illustrate, once again, something of the scope for individual choice mentioned earlier in the chapter. As a further example, *Other side* may be thought preferable to the MLA's *With . . .*; the librarian should make his choice and adhere to it for all other similar items in the collection.

The same system can be used for a disc containing two works but by different composers. Slightly more complex is the record that allots more than one side, but less than two, for the major work and which has one or more "fill-ups" provided by the manufacturer to persuade potential customers that they are getting, in quantity if not necessarily in quality, fair value for their money in terms of the disc's playing time. It seems unnecessary to work out arithmetically just how much of the side is allotted to each item. To do this properly would need the disc to be played and the cataloguer to use a watch. Instead, it is simpler to accept the limitations of the average typewriter and show the approximate proportion taken on the second side by the major work as a quarter, half or three-quarters of a side. Even this may be no more than vaguely accurate, so that the simplest solution is to adopt "1½ sides" as a standard to indicate that the work takes more than one side but less than two. The shorter work or works on the disc can simply be described as "part side", whether the item lasts for two minutes or twenty-two. Such a method saves cataloguing time and is soon understood by library users.

The so-called "recital", "concert", or "anthology" disc introduces further complications for the cataloguer. However described, they are alike in having a number of items on the disc, usually by a variety of composers. Some cataloguers make main entry for such works under the general heading "Collections" or "Concerts" and file the record itself under the same word. This seems as unsatisfactory as entries for books, still found in some library catalogues, listed under "Various". To me, it would seem that the cataloguer has four choices. If music by a single composer takes a total of two-thirds or more of a side, i.e., approximately one-third of the total playing time of the disc (or whatever other arbitrary proportion the cataloguer cares to select), then entry should be made under that composer's name and the record filed under it.

Analytical entries would be made for the other items on the disc, with the MLA code's *With . . .* slightly amended so that only the composer's name and first work are quoted, an *etc.* indicating that there are other works on the same disc. The interested enquirer would then need to check the main entry to learn the complete contents. An example may help to make this clear. On HMV ALP 1949 (stereo, ASD 500) is, on the first side, an arrangement for violin and oboe, accompanied by a small string orchestra, of a Bach double keyboard concerto. The rest of the side is devoted to a Vivaldi concerto. On the reverse are three oboe concertos by Handel. The sleeve baldly declares "Concertos by Bach, Vivaldi, Handel". Although Bach is the first-named, preference may well be given to Handel whose music fills a complete side. If this is done, the entries for the Bach and Vivaldi items would conclude with the note "*With*: HANDEL – Oboe concertos". This would save the time and trouble of making full references under each composer. As different forces are used for each work, the saving is appreciable.

The second choice of heading is the name of the artist, orchestra, or conductor. With vocal works, the key point of the disc is almost certainly the singer's name, under which many users of the catalogue probably expect to find the entry. The same consideration applies to instrumental discs also, but (and I recognise and admit the inconsistency) thought might be given to making the main entry under the name of the instrument, particularly if it is not a common one. One could then enter solos by pianists, organists, and violinists (the actual choice would be determined by the cataloguer) under the name of the soloist, but others under the name of the solo instrument, with a reference from the soloist's name to the chosen heading. One might quote the American "Epic" disc, issued in Britain by Columbia, and entitled *Music for a Golden Flute*. Main entry would be made under *Flute*, with a reference from Maurice Sharp, the name of the soloist.

For singers and instrumentalists of international fame, some cataloguers prefer entry and filing under the name of the soloist rather than that of the composer. By this system, *Joan Sutherland sings Verdi* would be entered under the soprano, even though all the recorded items on the disc are by a single composer. The implication here is that potential borrowers are much more interested in the singer than in the music that she sings and, since one would catalogue an operatic recital by the same singer with excerpts from operas by different composers under "Sutherland", there is a case for treating the Verdi disc similarly. Consistency, indeed, is most difficult to achieve because of the range and variety of the records themselves.

The last type of anthology to be considered is that which not only contains a variety of works by different composers but has varied recording artists also. The Archive disc of *Intradas and Sonatas* contains music by three composers not mentioned in *Grove* together with some anonymous items; all are played by German instrumentalists whose names are probably unknown to English listeners. Here, "Intradas" would seem to be the best entry word, although it is admitted that it is not one that music lovers will know well. (A friend has suggested that the music is basically for two organs, and that this might provide a better approach for the cataloguer.) *Masters of the Guitar* (RCA) contains recordings by a guitar duo and other items for solo guitar played by two different soloists. Here, "Guitar" would help easy discovery. In short, the cataloguer could well work on the basis of entering under the highest common factor. Where there is a conflict of claims, the cataloguer must make a decision and follow it, as far as is practicable, in other similar cases. For example, the Philips disc *Great Music by French Composers* is a collection of orchestral works performed by the Detroit Symphony Orchestra conducted by Paul Paray. This could be entered under the manufacturer's title, under "Detroit", "Paray" or "France".

Entry under the disc's title is not recommended, since not all enquirers will know the correct title of the collection. If the library makes the main entry under performer, the cataloguer should have a rule to enter either under the orchestra or the conductor. There are arguments on both sides, though my own preference is for conductor, not least because his name is usually printed in large letters and the orchestra's name is displayed much less conspicuously. If entry under performer is not considered best for orchestral works, then "France" is the natural alternative. "French" would be better used for an anthology of spoken word items in that language. The HMV *History of Music in Sound* volumes would be entered under that title. There is, in fact, no golden rule to be grasped by the unmusical cataloguer. One hopes that the preceding examples have helped and not confused the reader.

When the main entry is made under the performer, the need for added entries under each composer represented on the disc is generally accepted. Other added entries are very much more arguable. Lack of subject entries seems to cause little hardship: each library must decide whether the likely demand for information as to which symphonies are included in the library stock, or which clarinet quintets, etc., is strong enough to justify the provision of subject entries. Much more likely are requests for recordings by particular artists, and it would seem that added entries for singers and solo instrumentalists are well worth making. All that is needed, using an earlier example once again, would be something like this:

KEMPFF, Wilhelm (pf)
    Mozart. Piano concertos 23, K.488; 24, K.491.
    With Bamberg S.O. (Leitner). DGG SLPM 138645. Stereo.

If abbreviations are used for instruments, as in the example above, they should be those that are generally accepted. The problem of an opera with a large cast has already been mentioned; it is paralleled by plays that need many actors. Only the keenest enthusiast is likely to be interested in every recording made by a very minor artist. However desirable it may be to provide entries for every name given on the record sleeve, such a procedure is time-consuming and bulks out the catalogue.

Added entries may be made under conductor or orchestra for purely orchestral records. When considering such discs (though in the context of concerts of works by several composers), it was suggested that the conductor's name is probably preferable. However, my own feeling is that the omission of such entries is unlikely to be more than a minor handicap, though local conditions will vary. Study of the use of the catalogue and of the type of enquiry made on it by borrowers should soon provide an answer. At Widnes, added entries are no longer made for such groups as string quartets, and there has been no indication that this policy is mistaken. On the other hand, the provision of title entries, both for complete works and for excerpts likely to be requested by title, has been considerably increased because of expressed demand. Such entries are made for operas and other works with distinctive titles, for nicknamed works (such as *Moonlight Sonata*) and for such extracts as *Walk to the Paradise garden* (from *A Village Romeo and Juliet*, by Delius) and *Entry of the Queen of Sheba*, from Handel's *Solomon*. A somewhat similar reference under the composer's name (e.g., DEBUSSY. *Clair de lune* see *Suite bergamasque, no. 3*) has proved an added insurance.

In order to answer enquiries for discs featuring particular solo instruments, the Widnes catalogue contains general references (except for piano, organ, and violin; these instruments are sufficiently well represented in the collection to make the discovery of recordings fairly simple) from names of instruments to the names of soloists. Thus, under OBOE, the entry continues "*See . . .*", and lists the names of all the solo oboe players represented in the collection. Details of the works performed by an individual artist are found under his name, by means of entries similar to that already quoted for Wilhelm Kempff. If the gramophone record section has to be staffed at times by assistants with very limited knowledge either of music or its executants, such entries can be helpful to them as well as to members of the public who use the catalogue. Similar references, which help to avoid the need for full subject entries, may usefully be made under any type of music for which it is felt that such aid will prove useful. This is probably particularly true of folk song and church music.

Folk music, performed by a solo artist or group, is likely to be entered under the name of the soloist(s). Title entries are desirable, though they may be so numerous as to be thought impracticable. The simple alternative (or addition) would be to make a reference from the general heading "Folk songs" to the names of singers and groups represented in the library's collection. If there are numerous folk songs in stock, the general heading may be limited to discs which contain songs from several countries, and subdivisions provided for individual nations. Thus, on this system, the heading "Folk songs – Greece" would be followed by a list of singers and groups performing this country's native songs.

Church music is a fairly well defined genre that may also be given similar treatment. If entries are made in the catalogue under the names of choirs, reference can be made to these names from the heading "Church music". If no artist entries of this type are included, then the references will have to be to individual composers. For those with a large output of other sorts of music, it is probably helpful to note the names of the compositions represented. A reference from "Church music" to "Haydn" is of little use when a library may have dozens of Haydn discs in stock.

Separate consideration must be given to jazz. This music is rarely composed in the accepted sense, but is often a series of improvisations upon a sequence of chords and a melody; for this reason the performer is the focus of interest. Main entry, accepting this approach, is therefore made under the name of soloist, group or band. Whether it is worth complementing such entries with added ones for the individual members of a band or smaller combination (on the analogy of opera or play recordings), for composers and for titles of tunes must be a matter of choice. The enthusiast may wish to know of every record in the library which features his favourite instrumentalist. This type of interest must be widespread, for the sleeve of every jazz record is now apparently expected to quote the exact personnel for each track of a disc and the date on which the original recording was made. It may even be argued that, if jazz is worthy of provision in a library's stock, its records should be treated as comprehensively as those of classical music. In practice, few library cataloguers make these entries for performers. Except for musicians of the calibre of Duke Ellington, most composers of jazz are not generally known by name and composer entries seem valueless. Title entries are also likely to be of very little value, particularly as a tune may have more than one title. If title entries are made, each will refer to the band or artist that has recorded that particular item.

Cataloguing principles, similar to those already detailed, apply to non-musical records. In order to distinguish these entries, cards of a different colour may be used for the spoken word items, both author and actor. A disc containing the works of a single author, poet, or dramatist is entered under that name. A miscellaneous anthology or collection of poems, dramatic or prose extracts, etc., would be catalogued under the name of the artist reading these works. When, usually to provide variety of voice, a disc has several different persons reading the poems of a number of authors, one follows the musical analogy again and enters under title or suitable catchword. This may be illustrated by the Jupiter disc *Conversation Pieces* which contains a series of duologues by nearly a score of different poets, read by a dozen artists. It would seem most sensible to make the main entry under the record's title, with perhaps a reference from "Jupiter" if it is thought that some enquiries might be made under that name.

From the foregoing, it is hoped that the reader can see the advantages (if not necessarily agreeing over the necessity) of making entries for every item on a disc of classical music, jazz, or literature. Added entries are more debatable, but should be made as generously as time permits and probable use justifies. The composer aspect is usually unimportant with jazz and popular music, but this highlights the increased need for artist and title entries in these fields.

Finally, the cataloguer should remember that sleeve notes and titles are not infallible. Unless the recording is of a well-known standard work, it is advisable to check the details in *Grove*, *WERM* or in reviews. The major specialist periodicals will often note any inaccuracies perpetrated by the manufacturer or writer of the sleeve note. Again, checking against a standard will result in systematic spelling of composers' names (so that "Zachow" on the sleeve is entered as "Xachau" in the catalogue, as this is the *Grove* form), and of the title of a particular work. The rules for titles are similar to those applied to sheet music, so that operatic excerpts (whatever the language of that particular recording) are entered under the correct title, usually the original one unless the work is Russian or east European.

Good cataloguing of gramophone records needs time, care, patience and some detective skill. In general, our standards are far too low and it is time that a more serious and professional outlook was adopted by many libraries.

The foregoing was written before publication of the *Anglo-American Cataloguing rules* in 1967; this has chapter 14 devoted to "Phonorecords", and shows a close relationship to chapter 3 of the 1958 ALA/MLA Code. There are, however, minor alterations and clarifications. Recital and anthology discs on which several composers are represented are now entered under the collective title of the disc (if the manufacturer has provided one) or under the name of the compiler. This means that, to take an example quoted earlier in this chapter, "Great music by French composers" would be entered under "Great". The rule has the great advantage of consistency but means that discs must often be entered under unhelpful headings, although this is offset if analytical entries are provided, as the rule requires. Entries under compiler are likely to be uncommon but would presumably include the two-disc set entitled "Spirituals to swing" compiled by John Hammond – although some cataloguers could well prefer to use the title of the set as the main heading. For collections issued without an omnibus title, the new code simply requires separate entry for each work, linked together in the catalogue by means of "With . . ." notes.

As in the 1958 ALA/MLA rules, the new code includes fractions of sides in the collation (252 D1), the inclusion of the edition used in the recording (252 F5) and the duration of a work (252 F7). Neither of these two items seems of major importance in a public library collection, although highly desirable in a university music department or other specialist collection.

Indicators

by JEAN C. HITCHON, FLA
Music Librarian, Barnet Public Libraries

In the pioneer record libraries, where the initial stocks were composed entirely of 78 RPM discs, a closed-access system, coupled with some type of indicator, was almost universal. There were one or two exceptions, notably that of Coventry, where complete open-access was adopted from the start, but where, also, a separate room of reasonable size was available to house the record collection.

Here, in this question of space, lay the crux of the matter in the case of most of the early record libraries. They were mainly to be found in the comparatively small library systems of the Greater London area, where space was at a premium in buildings often long overdue for extension or renewal. A dark, unused corner of the lending department, a partitioned-off section of reading room, reference library, or entrance hall — such was the type of accommodation for these early collections, and public access was out of the question. Since the appearance of the long-playing record, with its decorative and informative sleeve, the use of display units for empty sleeves, or adapted for complete open access, has been a logical outcome. Provision for some variant of this system is made in nearly all new library buildings, and many older libraries have adapted their systems to full or partial open access where enough space has been available. The pros and cons of these systems are discussed in the main body of the chapter.

Nevertheless, there are many record libraries still using indicators, from necessity, or, possibly, from choice, and new record libraries opening under conditions where space is very limited may still have to adopt this system, at least temporarily. It is interesting to note, in this connection, that one of the finest and largest of the newly built London central libraries has no provision for browser units or any kind of open access, but still has in use a Kardex wall indicator.

A brief account needs to be given, therefore, of a few types of indicator commonly in use.

Selection of the type of indicator best suited to any particular record library must depend, to some extent, on local conditions, and particularly on those governing money and space available. The main problems to be considered are, whether the indicator should show the complete library stock, thus fulfilling, in a limited way, the function of a catalogue, or whether it should simply show which records are in at any one time; whether it should serve any other purpose apart from showing what records are in stock or available for loan; and the method of arrangement of the indicator cards, by composers' names, makers' numbers, accession numbers or by any other method.

Indicators fall into two categories, which may be labelled as manufactured and specially made or home-made. Various record library indicators have been put on the market by manufacturers, but the one which seems to have been most widely and successfully used is the Kardex indicator, supplied by Remington Rand. It was used for many years at Lambeth, but is now being replaced by open access, and is in use in the new Hornsey central library in the London borough of Haringey. It is described below as in use in the record library at Fulham central library, where it is mounted on a free-standing, double-sided sloping stand. This type of stand is convenient, but takes up a considerable amount of floor space. At Hornsey the Kardex indicator is well spaced out on two walls.

Fitting in overlapping, hinged metal holders, the cards contain, on the visible strip, details of composer, title, artist, and makers' number, while the rest of the card, concealed by the overhanging flap of the holder above, may contain details of price, vendor, date of purchase, etc., and is ruled for date stamping. It is thus a combined indicator, charge and stock card, and may also be the catalogue card, where, as at Fulham, no separate catalogue is kept. At Lambeth and several other libraries which once used the Kardex indicator, separate catalogues were provided.

A small circle is cut out of the right-hand side of the visible strip of the card, and, when the borrower has been issued with his record, his ticket can be inserted behind the indicator card, on which the date can be stamped, and the coloured circle showing through the hole indicates that the record is "out". Alternatively a separate charging card can be inserted behind the indicator card, and removed by the borrower who wishes to take the record, when the card is placed, with his ticket, in sequence in a Browne issue system. Strips of different colours can be inserted to show that a record is being replaced, is reserved, temporarily out of stock, and so forth.

This indicator seems to have proved very satisfactory in the libraries where it is in use. Several disadvantages are apparent in theory where the charging system is part of the indicator, and no separate issue is kept. Some interference might be expected from members of the public, particularly with the date indicators. Congestion might be caused at busy periods, where charging and discharging is being carried out by the staff at the indicator while borrowers are choosing records. This operation of charging and discharging away from the issue counter must surely cause considerable loss of time, and keeping the indicator up-to-date must also be difficult when working at high pressure.

Nevertheless, these disadvantages can, to some extent, be overcome, and unlike some other manufactured types of indicator which have been seen in use, the Kardex is fairly flexible, and can be adapted for use in various ways, and modified where necessary.

The specially made or home-made type of indicator usually works on the principle of using a set of cards, generally normal book card size, 1¾ in X 4 in, one for each record or set of records in stock, or, possibly, one for each work where more than one appears on a disc or in a set. These cards are displayed in pockets or slots, usually on a flat board or in hinged frames. They can be attached to a stand, mounted on a wall, or arranged in free-standing single- or double-sided units of various shapes and sizes.

This type of indicator usually works on the system of showing only records available for loan, a catalogue being kept to show the complete stock and containing fuller details than the indicator cards. The borrower removes cards from the indicator for the records he requires, and these cards are then charged with his ticket and filed in the issue. When a record is returned the discharged card is replaced on the indicator.

The directness of this method cuts down the possibility of charging errors, and is quick and simple for the borrower. If the cards are arranged by composers the borrower can choose directly from the indicator without reference to the catalogue. If, however, cards are arranged by makers' or accessions numbers, borrowers must consult the catalogue before going to the indicator. Arrangement by accessions numbers has the advantage that cards for new records will appear together at one end of the indicator, and, if indicator and shelf arrangement are identical, the shelves can quickly and easily be checked against the indicator, and missing cards located and replaced. Indicator cards do, in fact, disappear from time to time, thus immobilising part of the stock.

The card indicator can be made to show "fill-up" items and separate entries for all works on a single disc, which might contain, for instance, four overtures. If this is not done, some titles in stock never appear on the indicator, but, on the other hand, a considerable amount of extra space is needed in order to carry this out. In the browser box system, of course, each record or set can have only one place. The addition of a "finding" word in the corner of the catalogue entry for each work will enable borrowers who use the catalogue to locate a required item.

Indicator cards should be as fully detailed as possible. They should show composer's name, short title, names of artists, makers' numbers, and, if required, accessions numbers. Popular names of works, *Emperor*, *Pastoral* etc., and any other aid to identification, should always be given on the card.

Cards stronger than ordinary book cards should be used on the indicator, as the latter are liable to become cracked, dog-eared, and illegible with constant handling. Very thick card or plastic should be used, and, where possible, the entries should be typed.

An excellent example of the type of indicator discussed above has recently been installed in two of the City of Westminster record libraries. It consists of slotting, made in a hard durable plastic, in units of ten slots each. These units rest on top of each other, so that they can be built up to any required height, and they are held and locked together by metal rods, which thread through holes in projecting pieces on each side of each unit. The panels so formed were seen fitted to large pieces of hardboard in wooden frames against a wall, but they could easily be adapted to fit various types of stands or arrangements of panels. On the indicator described, the slots were made to take 5 in X 3 in cards, but they are also made to take smaller cards, more or less book-card size. This plastic slotting is supplied by "Strafoplan".

The cards used are also made of plastic, with projecting shoulders which fit over the sides of the slots, leaving a visible strip deep enough to show the required details of composer, title, and artist. The ones seen were typewritten, and had a neat appearance, but the plastic had tended to get dirty and apparently could not easily be cleaned without removing the type. Different colours were used to distinguish between entries for mono and stereo records.

The choice of indicator lies between the simple type, such as the one described above, which shows only records available for loan, and where the indicator card usually performs the function of charge card, or a more complex type, like the Kardex, which shows the complete stock, and can be used to perform other functions, such as those of charging system and catalogue. It should be borne in mind that the second type of indicator is likely to take up considerably more space than the first, and that an indicator cannot properly fulfil the purposes of a catalogue. It is strongly urged that, except in the case of a very small record collection, a separate catalogue should always be maintained.

The Storage and Issue of Sound Recordings

by JOHN W. HOWES, FLA
Librarian in charge of Special Activities, Waltham Forest Libraries

Ideally all material relevant to any specific subject should be available from the same location within a library. It is unfortunate that often the physical nature of much non-book material makes this almost impossible unless unlimited shelf space is available to shelve books, films, tapes, maps, records, etc. in one place. Special collections, therefore, have to be formed of this material, housed away from the main book sequence. We would be well advised to remember this is a *physical* division of the library stock and not a *subject* division. In the case of musical recordings there is also a definite subject division, but recordings today cover far more than music so that the popular solution to the problem of setting up a "Music & Record" division of the library creates serious anomalies often leading to poetry and drama recordings being stocked with the music stock and being lost to many potential borrowers. Equally serious is the encouragement given by this separation to the growth of a "race apart" in the library profession concerned only with such non-book material, i.e., "Music and Record Librarians". Sound recordings of all types certainly need special storage and issuing techniques, but these are not so complex that they cannot be fitted into the general education of librarianship. The time will come when the self-winding tape cassette, boxed in such a way that it can be shelved alongside the appropriate books, will replace the present LP. When that time comes the material that follows will be of use only to the student of library history, and the "Record Librarian" too will have become just a footnote in the history of the profession. Tapes will not, however, supersede LPs because librarians think they will solve *their* problems; the LPs are the materials we have to cope with at the moment and these notes are practical suggestions for the best way to handle them.

The Storage and Issue of LP Recordings

Since the first edition of this book was issued many changes have taken place in the public gramophone record library, but the most important in many ways has been the rapid decline of the "indicator" and the growth of the provision of "Browser" boxes. Mrs. Hitchon contributes an essay on "indicators" (for although she at Hendon and Mr. Bryant at Widnes pioneered "Browser" boxes, she is aware that indicators are still in use and in some circumstances may still be the only possible solution when space is very limited). Opinion is now divided as to whether record libraries should be completely open access, or whether the more restricted "record sleeve indicator" method of display should be used (not to be confused with the earlier indicators described by Mrs. Hitchon). The advantages of either method are not, as is so often the case, as clear cut as the advocates of each system claim. Some of the arguments for and against each method are, therefore, given below:

FOR OPEN ACCESS	AGAINST OPEN ACCESS, BUT IN FAVOUR OF THE RECORD SLEEVE INDICATOR
Closed access is outdated for books and is already outdated for records.	Records are not books, and arguments based on book techniques are irrelevant.
Open access saves space and is, therefore, an advantage when space is short.	Fewer records and sleeves can be accommodated in browser boxes than sleeves only. The actual records can often be fitted into space which would not be suitable for public access.
Problems arise in connection with the storage of records in browser boxes, as they are not as well supported as on proper record shelving; but in busy libraries they are out on loan more often than not, and in any case the advantages of complete open access outweigh the disadvantages of less satisfactory storage.	Browser boxes are not suitable for storing LPs for long periods. Busy libraries may have few records in the boxes at any time but those with less demand may have a large proportion of their records stored in this way.
Records and sleeves are all in one place. The public do not have to collect records from another part of the library.	Records stored in browser boxes must be protected from sunshine, radiators, etc. but record sleeves only can be placed in any well lit and heated part of the library and will not suffer.
Theft and damage through handling the records is low.	Cases of large-scale theft of records on open access can be quoted, and few if any major record shops allow customers to handle both records and sleeves; and there is little point in stealing sleeves only.

Arrangement of Record or Sleeves in Browser Boxes

Beautiful young ladies smile at us from some record sleeves, but in other instances we are attracted by less inviting means, such as obscure modern paintings, old masters, or typographical exercises. Few sleeves, however, tell us quite simply what the recording contains and to gain this information is often quite a problem, to be solved only by playing the disc!

Some simple means is, therefore, required which will make it easy to place records in the correct sequence after issue. One obvious way is to affix a small strip of white Scotch tape in the same place (say the top right- or left-hand corner) on each sleeve. On this tape the name of the composer or author under which the record is filed is written so that the filing information appears *on each record in the same place*. Instead of the full name of the composer or author a selected number of letters could be used, as is often the case in the 920 Dewey biography classification. Libraries owning DYNOTAPE machines could use a strip of this special tape with the appropriate wording stamped on. An obvious refinement is to use different coloured tapes for different musical and other form divisions thus bringing together for example all the piano concertos of a given composer.

I am aware that unlike books, the majority of which are by one author about one subject, many discs contain one or more types of music by different composers so that exact classification and allocating of filing symbols can be difficult. If, however, when the record is catalogued a reference is made in the entry to the filing code reference under which the sleeve, or sleeve plus record can be found in the browser boxes, it will be easy to find the record even from an analytic entry for an item on that disc which occupies only one band on it.

For example: a disc called *Romantic Piano Music*, which contains one full length Chopin sonata, has been placed under the name of this composer in the browser boxes. The code CHO on, say yellow tape, has been used on the sleeve, to denote piano music by Chopin. On all other catalogue entries refering to the other contents of this disc a note is made: Filed under CHO/Yellow. Whichever item on the record is required can thus be easily traced in the browser boxes.*

At Walthamstow we found that sorting and filing sleeves by an alphabetic code was far slower than sorting by a numerical code. This is obvious to students of classification systems, and to some extent accounts for the wide use of Dewey in spite of all its faults. We, therefore, compiled a list of the most frequently recorded composers, using the *Gramophone* quarterly Classical catalogue. We were able to arrive at a basic 150 composers, which in practice accounted for well over 70 per cent of the musical records issued. A schedule was prepared of these 150 composers in alphabetical order and a number allocated to each. Minor, or new, composers not fitting into this main sequence, were allocated places in the sequence by the use of a letter code. A "Decimal" System based on 100

*See also E. T. Bryant. *Cataloguing Procedure suitable for Public Libraries.*

major composers would have satisfied the classification theorists far more than the schedules that resulted, but was rejected for the following reasons:

(a) Limiting the basic composers to 100 would have meant that the basic listing would have covered roughly only 50 per cent of music records issued instead of the 70 per cent using the basic 150.

(b) If a Decimal scheme had been used all numbers would have had to be given a minimum three digits to prevent confusion when the decimal point was used.

(c) As the books in the library are classified by Dewey it could be possible for a borrower or visiting librarian to assume that the sleeves were in Dewey order.

The basic schedules are printed as an appendix to this article. They are published only as a basis on which it is possible to build, not as a final scheme, but it must be added that the system based on them works excellently, keeping the browser boxes in a correct sequence with the minimum of staff time. Records and specific items on them can easily be located from the catalogue.

If sleeves only are displayed in the browser boxes there is no need to worry about the siting of the boxes in the library. Questions of warping caused by sunlight or the heating system do not arise, so that when plans are being prepared attention need only be given to the ease with which those using the library can use the boxes to select the records they desire. The actual records can be stored under conditions as ideal as possible. Should open access be decided upon, then the siting of boxes *must be given far more attention* and convenience of use weighed against other factors. Records housed in browser boxes close to a large south-facing window could suffer the same fate as those stored on the back seat of cars on sunny days! A similar disaster could befall records in boxes placed next to radiators, or other means of heating.

Record Shelving

With regard to the ideal conditions for storing LP records, the laymen might well expect that the experts would have long ago made up their minds on so simple a point, but this is not the case. The most exhaustive survey to date (1) comes out firmly for *vertical* storage of LPs with slight even side pressure on the discs. Bryant in *Music Librarianship* (2) states that "There is much to commend the storage of records in flat position", but the same author in *Record Collecting* (3) comes out strongly in favour of *vertical storage*! The author of this chapter feels that after Pickett and

Lemcoe's exhaustive work on the subject, any further writing on the topic is almost impertinent and gratefully reprints the relevant page of this treatise.

The shelving should be kept away from all forms of heating and the ideal temperature would seem to be about 60°F (15·5°C).

Record shelving is available from many makers of library furniture but when expense is being kept to the minimum there is much to recommend the excellent "Lundia" shelving made by Remploy Ltd. This can be supplied with cheap strong hardboard partitions, and has the added advantage that should the library decide to change to open access at any time, it would still have an easily dismantled set of useful shelving which can be used for book shelving, and not a useless set of expensively divided cases of little use apart from the purpose for which they were designed.

Browser Boxes

Browser boxes are not so easily obtainable ready made, but this situation will be remedied as the demand for these items of furniture increases. Rough drawings for two basic designs are included in this book. The first being based on Mr. Bryant's excellent early design for Widnes and the second based on a very simple pattern used in many record shops and libraries. These are only basic designs and can be adapted as required. It must be emphasised that if it is intended to use full open access, the browser boxes must be more strongly made than if covers only are to be displayed. A wise policy would seem to be that it is best to build strong browser boxes in any case.

Records in Transit to and from the Library

Many libraries had fibre boxes made, able to take up to sixteen 78s, and these are still used when LPs are issued. Whilst there seems no reason why these should not be used if supplies are still on hand, it would seem rather wasteful to have such boxes made if a new library is being started. If boxes are used, it would appear wise to have some place to record the issues on the actual recording, otherwise an excellent record of the number of times a certain box has been used will result, not a record of the times any given recording has been borrowed!

Normal manilla record covers were in many cases fitted over the maker's covers to protect them whilst records were either being stored or in transit. This extra cover would of course take all date labels, etc., and also keep the record sealed away from dust whilst not in use.

Covers a little larger than the normal 12 in size are essential, as in some cases the maker's cover is almost impossible to withdraw once fitted into

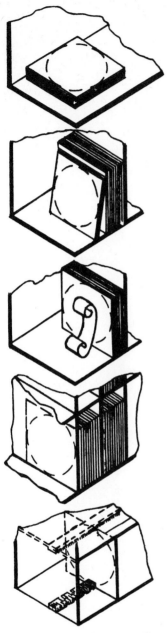

Horizontal Stacking—Poor; causes surface imprint in all discs and warp in plastic and shellac discs because of different boundary conditions of restraint and temperature on different sides.

Off Vertical Stacking—Poor; causes both surface imprint in all discs and warp of plastic and shellac discs from poor boundary conditions and gravity loads.

Spring Loaded Vertical Stacking—Poor; causes surface imprint, poor boundary conditions.

Full Compartment Vertical Stacking—Good; recommended maximum 20 disc/compartment. Compartments in use should be kept full of discs or discs and fillers.

Template Controlled Vertical Stacking—Good; slotted template can be made of metal with very thin "fins". Slots should be well aligned vertically and bottoms of slot should be at or below shelf level.

Fig. 2.   Very long time disc storage practice and shelf design.

(Reproduced by kind permission of The Librarian of Congress from "Preservation and storage of sound recordings" by A. G. Pickett and M. M. Lemcoe.)

89

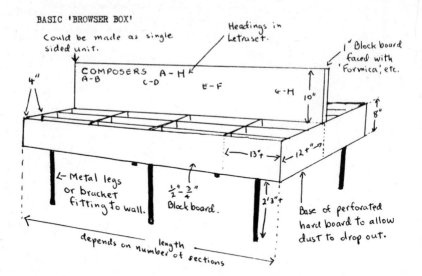

BASIC 'BROWSER BOX'

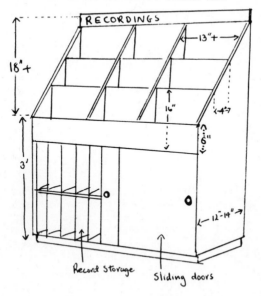

BASIC COMBINED BROWSER BOX AND STORAGE UNIT

Fig. 3.   *Storage and issue of sound recordings.*

the outer one (also the centre hole provided for 78RPM records is no longer needed). The use of some such outer cover keeps the often attractive maker's sleeve clean. At least one library now provides polythene bags to protect record cases in wet weather. Whether more elaborate bags are worth the expense involved is, however, a debatable question.

Methods of Recording Damage to LPs

GENERAL. Long-playing records are very easy to damage and one careless user of a record library could spoil the pleasure of many others, and cost the library authority a great deal for replacements before being traced; one is therefore very surprised at the lack of any definite checks made by the majority of libraries. The obvious reason is, of course, lack of staff, but this is not so in all cases. Record borrowers have more spent per head on them than most other users of public libraries and unless steps are taken to see that a *few* do not spoil the pleasure of the *many*, the case against record provision will be made far stronger. Once borrowers get used to certain standards they react rather unkindly against any tightening up of checks, so that new record libraries would be wise to adopt a firm attitude at first and then relax once the standards of the users of the library are known.

SOME METHODS USED TO RECORD DAMAGE.
(i) *Clock Face*. Damage is noted either on the date label, indicator card, or similar record as "Damage at 6 o'clock side 4".
Comments. This method has at least the virtue of simplicity, but must of course always remain rather inexact, and in fact must take more time to record (and translate back) than the now more general "diagram" method being used by a growing number of libraries.
(ii) *Diagrams*. A card or slip is kept showing both sides of a record in diagrammatic form. Faults pointed out by borrowers are noted on this and, in the case of new faults, the condition of the record on issue to a borrower may be compared with the state in which it was returned.

Comments. Woolwich had excellent printed diagrams made which have now been photographically copied for "Rotaprint" reproduction.

Diagrams suitable for 7 in, 10 in and 12 in records are now available at reasonable cost.

It may be objected that it is pointless to let borrowers take away the actual checking diagram, as they could themselves add any new scratches they make whilst the record is in their charge. This is quite true, but experience has shown, in many libraries, that a fund of goodwill is built up by trusting borrowers, and few cases of the insertion of new damage have been found. Those with less faith in their borrowers and human nature in general may, if they wish, retain the diagrams of records on loan and use them as part of the "charge". As a suggestion for research, it would appear that some modified form of "photocharging" linking a picture of the checking diagram with the borrower's ticket could provide a solution to the problem.

Smaller checking diagrams could of course be used if it was decided to use them as part of the charge, but full-sized diagram cards provide a more definite check.

Charges made for Damage

Many libraries charge from 2s. 6d. to 5s. for serious scratches on LPs. If inexact or inaccurate methods of recording damage are in use, it is difficult to ask a borrower to accept responsibility for such damage, but the goodwill created by more exact methods of recording damage must be an important factor in keeping the general condition of the records satisfactory. If borrowers understand that the library can trace those who damage records, they at once feel that they are not likely to be asked to pay for damage they themselves have never caused.

Records which had been so badly damaged that they had to be replaced were in most cases charged on a sliding scale which varied with the number of previous issues. See examples of charges below.

SCALE OF CHARGES FOR DAMAGED LPs.   These figures are based on an expected life of 100 issues per record.

(a) If the damage is such that the record has to be replaced the borrower will pay the amount as set below, but will retain the record.

(b) Marks which sound, but which do not cause the actual replacement of the record, will be charged at about 5s. per minute of audible damage.

(c) If the record is such that the undamaged side is a complete work then only half of the listed charge will be made, but the library will retain the record. The borrower can however pay the full charge and retain the record if desired. (See table, page 93.)

This acquisition price was chosen for the sake of easier calculation and is of course subject to change due to fluctuations in the Purchase Tax on records.

Issues	*Original Price Approx. £2*	*Approx. £1*
	£ s d	£ s d
1–10	2 0 0	1 0 0
11–20	1 15 0	17 6
21–30	1 10 0	15 0
31–40	1 7 6	13 0
41–50	1 5 0	12 6
51–60	1 2 6	10 0
61–70	1 0 0	9 0
71–80	17 6	8 0
81–90	15 0	7 0
91–100	12 6	6 0
Over this	10 0	5 0

Borrowers' Tickets, Issue Recording, Etc.

GENERAL. Very many libraries used a charging system that linked directly with the indicator. As an appendix is included on this aspect of record libraries by Mrs. Hitchon (p. 54) I have not gone into great detail regarding my findings.

BORROWERS' TICKETS. In nearly all cases some variation of the normal "Browne" charging method was used and in many cases actual book tickets were used as Record Library tickets with some suitable marking.

In one case all entries regarding issues, damage, etc., were made on cards kept for each borrower. These were kept in name order when not in use, and date order when being used. No charge cards were used, as a note was made on the borrower's card, of the record at present on loan. As library users often seem to mislay their tickets, there seems quite a lot to be said in favour of this method. Such a method also provides a very good record of the use individuals make of the library and also a check of the damage they cause.

CHARGE CARDS, ETC. The use of a charge card to act also as an indicator card was very popular. The method is very simple and tends to prevent records being shown as "in" when they are in fact "out".

COMMERCIAL INDICATOR AND CHARGING SYSTEMS. Under this heading I place all the visible index units made by Roneo and other such firms. All of these were so linked with the indicator used that readers seeking further information should consult Mrs. Hitchon's appendix on this topic.

Order of Filing Records on Shelves

GENERAL. The two main methods used were, Maker's prefix and number order, Library's own accession number order. Librarians using either system found it hard to understand how the other person got on with whatever was the alternative system. To be dogmatic on this point would be pointless so the main advantages and disadvantages of each have been noted below:

(i) Maker's order. *Advantages*: Direct link with Maker's catalogues, reviews, etc. *Disadvantages*: Numbers and prefixes tend to be rather long and complex since LPs were introduced. Also as many companies now re-issue records with an entirely new prefix and number, it is possible that a library could still have the record in stock under the old number. This copy could be overlooked if the record was looked for under the latest number (examples, "LXT" series issued as "ACL" Decca, "ALP" series issued as "RE" RCA)

(ii) Accession Number. *Advantages*: Number remains quite simple, i.e., G 5066 etc. Members do not ask for records not in stock. (Some Librarians using maker's numbers stated that borrowers very often never checked if a record shown in a maker's catalogue was in fact in stock). Changes caused by commercial regrouping, re-issue of records under new prefixes, etc., in no way affect the catalogue if a local accession number is used. Providing the recording is identical, it can be traced without reference to the number it may have in the commercial catalogues at the time. *Disadvantage*: Maker's catalogues etc., do not provide a direct link with the actual Library stock.

I have no doubt that numerous points in favour of either method will be raised by readers, and Miss Britten of the BBC Library has very definite views on the sanctity of prefix codes, but her library is unique and serves a very different purpose from that of a public library collection.

REFERENCES

(1) Pickett, A. G. *and* Lemcoe, M. M. *Presentation and storage of sound recordings.* Library of Congress, Washington, 1959.
(2) Bryant, E. T. *Music Librarianship.* James Clarke & Co, Ltd, London, 1959.
(3) Bryant, E. T. *Collecting gramophone records.* Focal Press, London, 1962.

COMPOSER CODE

ABRAHAM	1	GLUCK	51	PUCCINI	101
ALBENIZ	2	GOLDMARK	52	PURCELL	102
ARNOLD	3	GOUNOD	53	RACHMANINOV	103
AUBER	4	GRANADOS	54	RAVEL	104
BACH	5	GRIEG	55	REGER	105
BALAKIREV	6	GROFE	56	RESPIGHI	106
BARTOK	7	HANDEL	57	RIMSKY−KORSAKOV	107
BEETHOVEN	8	HAYDN	58	ROSSINI	108
BELLINI	9	HEROLD	59	SAINT−SAENS	109
BERG	10	HINDEMITH	60	SARASATE	110
BERLIOZ	11	HISTORY OF	61	SATIE	111
BIZET	12	MUSIC IN SOUND		SCARLATTI	112
BLISS	13	HOLST	62	SCHOENBERG	113
BLOCH	14	HUMPERDINCK	63	SCHUBERT	114
BOCCHERINI	15	INDY	64	SCHUMANN	115
BOITO	16	IPPOLITOV−IVANOV	65	SCRIABIN	116
BORODIN	17	IRELAND	66	SHOSTAKOVICH	117
BRAHMS	18	JANACEK	67	SIBELIUS	118
BRITTEN	19	JOSQUIN DES PRÈS	68	SMETANA	119
BRUCH	20	KABALEVSKY	69	SOUSA	120
BRUCKNER	21	KALMAN	70	SPOHR	121
BUSONI	22	KETELBY	71	STRAUS, O.	122
BUXTEHUDE	23	KHATCHACHURIAN	72	STRAUSS, J. sr.	123
BYRD	24	KODALY	73	STRAUSS, J. jun.	124
CHABRIER	25	LALO	74	STRAUSS, Joseph	125
CHAUSSON	26	LECOCQ	75	STRAUSS, Richard	126
CHOPIN	27	LEHAR	76	STRAVINSKY	127
COATES	28	LEONCAVALLO	77	SULLIVAN	128
COPLAND	29	LIADOV	78	SUPPE	129
COUPERIN (F)	30	LISZT	79	SZYMANOWSKI	130
DEBUSSY	31	LITOLFF	80	TALLIS	131
DELIBES	32	MAHLER	81	TCHAIKOVSKY	132
DELIUS	33	MASCAGNI	82	TELEMANN	133
DOHNANYI	34	MASSENET	83	TIPPETT	134
DONIZETTI	35	MENDELSSOHN	84	TURINI	135
DOWLAND	36	MENOTTI	85	VARESE	136
DUKAS	37	MESSAGER	86	VERDI	137
DVORAK	38	MEYERBEER	87	VILLA−LOBOS	138
ELGAR	39	MILHAUD	88	VIVALDI	139
FALLA	40	MOUSSORGSKY	89	WAGNER	140
FAURE	41	MOZART	90	WALDTEUFEL	141
FLOTOW	42	NICOLAI	91	WALTON	142
FRANCK	43	NIELSEN	92	WARLOCK	143
GABRIELI	44	OFFENBACH	93	WEBER	144
GERMAN	45	PACHELBEL	94	WEBERN	145
GERSHWIN	46	PAGANINI	95	WIDOR	146
GIBBONS	47	PALESTRINA	96	WILLIAMS	147
GIORDANO	48	PERGOLESI	97	WOLF	148
GLAZUNOV	49	PONCHIELLI	98	WOLF−FERRARI	149
GLINKA	50	POULENC	99	ZELLER	150
		PROKOFIEV	100		

Colour Code:
RED = Orchestra and Organ GREEN = Songs, Solos, Chamber YELLOW = Concertos
BLUE = Vocal, Opera etc.   BLACK = Folk music   WHITE = Spoken word
ORANGE = Recitals

Technical Data and Information for Gramophone Record Librarians

by ERIC COOPER,
Music Librarian, Enfield Public Libraries

Introduction

During the first years of the development of gramophone record provision in public libraries it was by no means uncommon to find members of the profession, who had become set in their ways, expressing the view that such activities were outside the scope of public libraries. As the provision of record libraries became widespread the need for specialised administration became more apparent to many chief librarians and their staffs. To many others, however, the lesson still had to be learned and when faced with the task of starting a gramophone lending department they proceeded (unfortunately) as though dealing with books. The results were consequently very poor and provided anti-provisionists with valuable material with which to argue their case. Many others could find no answers and proceeded on their way accepting their own standards as the best obtainable, without seeking further improvement.

On the one hand students of librarianship were given the most detailed and specialised training in all matters pertaining to books, from the history of paper-making and printing to a coverage of the vast and varied range of printed information that any librarian might conceivably require, while on the other it had not been realised that prospective music librarians needed similar training with regard to gramophone records. Anti-provisionists were against such training as a matter of principle, whilst others who were prepared to give the matter thought came to the conclusion that training would be difficult and the protection of stock impracticable. During this time a number of people in charge of gramophone record collections were quietly forming their own opinions on the subject and putting their conclusions into practice. By 1954 to 1956 the results of careful administration and staff training in these libraries began to pay dividends which were gradually revealed in larger stocks maintained in better conditions. Borrowers were requested to co-operate in maintaining the improved standards, which they did willingly, because they felt they were actively participating in the groundwork of establishing new spheres of activity in public libraries.

Many libraries embarking on the course of opening a gramophone record department sent out questionnaires to ascertain methods of procedure in general use and, because of the diversity of the answers, rightly felt that it would be of use to publish their findings. The most obvious facts to come to light were the almost complete lack of properly experienced or trained staff to administer the departments, the general absence of any standardised methods, apart from the complete mutual acceptance of closed access, and the unfortunate lack of determination to keep stock in good condition during its useful life. It is the latter problem with which this section will attempt to deal. An increasing number of gramophone record and music librarians are concentrating on this particular aspect but are again in danger of falling into the trap of producing a variety of methods of differing efficiency. As with other branches of librarianship where the widest knowledge of the materials we handle is required, so it must be with gramophone records. As training and experience enable staff to administer book stocks and archive material with maximum efficiency, the same standards must be applied to gramophone record stocks. The following pages contain the bare essential information sufficient to commence operating a common-sense method of control on excessive wear and tear of public loan collections of gramophone records. Arguments that oppose such methods will not do if the new service is to grow in usefulness and avoid falling into disrepute.

All too often arguments against so called "technical" methods of control are offered to cover up the inadequate ability of the objector.

The provision of music in public libraries has become almost general practice since the time when James Duff Brown made the first revolutionary suggestion. Gramophone record libraries are comparatively recent innovations and are still in a state of development. Music departments have been built up on sound administrative principles and the student of gramophone record libraries must follow a similar course designed exclusively for gramophone records and should not adapt existing methods devised for handling entirely different materials. Only in this way will gramophone record libraries develop along logical lines to established maturity.

Gramophone Record Manufacture

The degree of efficiency one is able to achieve in performing a particular task is governed by the amount of knowledge one has about the work in hand. It must be thoroughly understood in all its aspects if anything approaching maximum efficiency is to be obtained. Highly specialised knowledge contributes immensely to our confidence and ability to carry out library duties, and in turn creates amicable relations with borrowers, since they will appreciate sound principles working out in practice. Without good public relations created in this manner the gramophone record librarian will not achieve a great deal, for if the public sense that your knowledge is incomplete and that you lack confidence in dealing with them, then they will not feel constrained to take proper care of the records they borrow.

This may appear fairly obvious, but a few visits to gramophone record libraries will show in what varying degrees it is actually practised. Also it clearly applies to librarianship as a whole, but it becomes of paramount importance when we are called upon to handle unfamiliar materials that require specialised consideration. Too many have failed to obtain reasonable results through trying to treat records in the same manner as books. A knowledge of how gramophone records are manufactured is, therefore, essential for those librarians called upon to handle them. Without knowing something of the production processes involved it is hardly possible to realise a record library's limitations and how it must be treated in a public library service. If we realise that gramophone records are the product of precision engineering of the highest standards, and that they must be treated as such, then we have made the first step to achieving that most desirable state of efficiency and confidence referred to above. For this reason, it is essential that the following outline of manufacture, from recording to the finished article, should be carefully studied.

In the past fifty years sound recording has developed into a science and an art. The simple crude methods of the nineteenth century have given way to technical processes of the highest possible standard. Improvements in recording and sound reproduction have been constantly taking place since the Second World War and in the interests of keeping this section to reasonable proportions only microgroove records will be considered fully.

Recording

Until about 1947 records were cut direct on to soft wax discs revolving at 78 RMP that gave recording times seldom exceeding 4½ minutes. Under these conditions it was difficult to obtain continuous recordings without first overcoming serious technical problems. Even so, in the recording studio the performance could be split up into convenient sections, but recordings of public performances provided the engineers with only one chance and no room for errors. The magnificent recordings that were made under these conditions seem even more remarkable now than they did when they were issued.

Today recordings are made direct to magnetic tape and from the point of continuity the performers and engineers undergo a little less strain than formerly. But problems remain and hi-fidelity recording has added many more. The procedure using magnetic tape is very similar to the way in which a film is made, in "rushes" which are edited and joined together. To give an idea of the course a recording session follows, a large-scale operatic work will best serve to cover the various points of interest. During preliminary rehearsals the engineers place several microphones in various parts of the studio or hall, an operation which calls for considerable skill and which influences the exact balance that will be obtained during performance. Although the tape-recording method provides flexible recording time, it should not be thought that the work is recorded from beginning to end in the way one would listen to it in the opera house. For the sake of economy the largest participating forces are often rehearsed and recorded in all the concerted numbers with the leading artists, at the beginning. After several sessions the best of these "takes" is selected. Then the next part is recorded, and so on until the last sections, which may only require the orchestra, are completed. Such a project may take anything from a few days to several weeks and must be made to fit in with the leading artists' other commitments. Due to this factor (and to the high standards for which the participants aimed) one particular operatic recording took eighteen months to complete. There was an interval of many months before the artists could be reassembled from various points of the globe to complete the work started some twelve months before.

So the recording progresses stage by stage to its completion with each phase being listened to by the artists and the artist's manager to select the best of the "takes" involved. The tape is then cut, edited, and joined together into its proper sequence by staff who are both musicians and engineers. Then it is subjected to final checking and correction where necessary. Sometimes records have been issued for sale with poor tape joins that are distinctly audible and, on rarer occasions, small sections of the music have been completely lost due to poor editing. These unusual events provide a useful reminder that nearly all recordings are of the highest standards when one considers the minimal margins of error that listeners will now tolerate.

On reading the foregoing paragraph, one cannot avoid the feeling that the spontaneity of a live performance must be missing, but despite this, it cannot be denied that the great majority of recordings set a very high standard of accomplishment. However, the gramophone should be a good servant and not a demanding master that finally prevents us from continuing to enjoy live concerts. The unwary music lover who listens too much to many records of carefully tailored performances may well lose his taste for the artistic merits and qualities of live music-making. Such a listener would lose much of the joy of listening without realising the misfortune that had befallen him.

Transfer of Tape to Disc

The next stage is to transfer the information on the tape to a disc from which gramophone records can eventually be made. The point has already been made that, if, as in bygone days, the recording was cut as a groove on a soft disc, the engineers could only exercise control at the time of cutting. Mistakes or poor quality made it necessary to record the whole side again, and often such mistakes could not be detected until a special disc could be prepared for playback. In addition to instantaneous replay, tape provides audible monitoring at the time of recording, apart from visual control read from recording level indicators. Mistakes can be cut out and replaced with corrections during tape editing. The recording can be heard at any stage, and provides an accurate indication of how the finished disc will sound even before it has been made. Under these circumstances the transfer from tape to disc can proceed with reasonable confidence.

The machine used to carry out the transfer to disc is a very complicated piece of apparatus which resembles a lathe connected to a tape-replay machine. In the centre of the bed of the lathe is a large heavy turntable

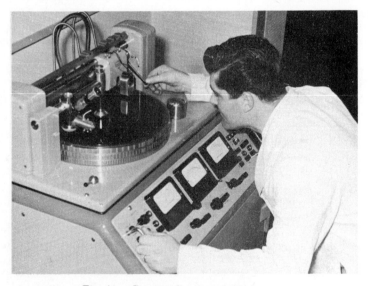

Fig. 4.   *Cutting the acetate disc.*

that is driven either by a very smoothly operating motor or by weights and pulleys suspended in a shaft below the floor. This latter system is not now in common use although it has many good points in its favour. The turntable must turn at a constant speed, unaffected by any fluctuation of power supply. Above the turntable is a parallel tracking carriage that takes the cutter head from right to left across its surface. The cutter head, for the sake of simplicity, might be compared to a gramophone pick-up head working in reverse and performing an exactly opposite function. While the pick-up takes the music from the record, the cutter etches it on to the record. The comparison is meant for the reader who has no idea of what a cutter head is, and should not be taken too literally. The cutter, which is the equivalent of the stylus in a pick-up, is made out of diamond and shaped to a triangular point. The tape-replay machine, attached to the cutter, sends the recorded information to the cutter head causing the cutter to vibrate. If this is lowered on to a smooth, soft revolving disc, the vibrations will be etched into the surface in the form of a groove which contains minute vibrations representing the original sound. A gramophone pick-up with a round stylus lowered into the same groove will reverse the process and transmit the vibrations, in the form of a low voltage signal, back to an amplifier system and loudspeaker. Again the reader must understand that this is an over-simplified explanation of a very complicated process, although in fact this is basically what happens.

The operator in charge of the cutter places a metal disc, covered with a thin even coating of lacquer or acetate, on to the turntable, which he sets in motion. He then switches on the tape-replay machine and immediately lowers the cutter head on to the disc. From this point on a great deal of the operation is controlled by the machine itself once the operator has set the level, volume as we call it, of the recording. As the tape begins to play, the signal that is transmitted to the cutter can be heard through a monitoring loudspeaker, so that the actual sound can be checked simultaneously with the recording level indicators. All the sounds captured in the magnetic coating on the tape are now transmitted to a small, vibrating cutting edge which etches the complex sound frequencies into the soft lacquer of the disc. The waste, or swarf as it is called, is sucked away by a vacuum. The line traced on the surface is not much thicker than a human hair, yet the vibration of the point that traced it cuts into the sides all the combined sound frequencies of a full orchestra, chorus, and soloists. The movement of the cutter is not just a simple side to side vibration, but is many vibrations of different intensities all brought together. The lowest sounds cause the maximum movement, but while moving from side to side the cutter also moves or vibrates within that movement thus registering the next lowest sound. This additional movement operates for each simultaneous but separate sound-frequency plus all the resultant harmonics in a range covering 20 to 20,000 cycles per second. All this is marked clearly into a V-shaped groove that measures less than ·003 in across the top. At points in the music where the sound is loud or the frequencies low the distance between the grooves is automatically widened to avoid the possibility of the grooves running one into the other.

In the quieter passages the grooves are cut closer. The rate of cut, as it is called, is governed by the speed at which the head travels across the lateral carrier and ensures the maximum playing time to the side of a record without any sacrifice of sound quality.

During recording the amount of lateral movement of the cutting tool is carefully controlled. Special attention is given to the lower and extreme upper sound-frequencies. Without this control on the cutter's movement in the lower register, the vibration would be so great that the band between the grooves would be insufficient. The grooves would run into each other or be so close that the thin walls between would break down during playback. No pick-up could follow the violent movement of the grooves and a disc would have to be the size of a cartwheel to contain any reasonable amount of playing time. To overcome this, the engineers reduce the volume in a falling curve with the deeper sounds. The lower the note, the less volume used in recording.

The opposite procedure is applied to the treble or upper frequency range. High sounds recorded at the same level as the middle frequencies would not cause the cutter to move sufficiently and the sound would be inaudible in playback. To counteract this effect all sounds above a selected level are increasingly amplified in an upward curve. This then, without discussing the velocity and amplitude, is what is called the recording characteristic. Immediately the side has been cut it is packed into a dustproof container to await the next disc that will constitute the other side of the final record.

At this point the reader is bound to think that there is some need to refer to stereo. All that needs to be said at this stage is that the sound to be recorded is divided between two or more microphones and is recorded on to separate tracks on the magnetic tape. The cutter head used for making the disc is a more complex piece of equipment than the mono one. It contains two separate heads each joined to the one cutter which, as Stanley Kelly (one of this country's leading audio engineers) once said, has "to waggle its hips in all directions simultaneously". The result is that the signal is divided with sounds from the left of the orchestra on one side of the groove and those from the right on the other. This is stereo reduced to maximum simplicity. Those who wish to know more of the technique would do well to refer to such a book as *Tinfoil to Stereo* by Oliver Read and Walter L. Welch. Such advanced detail is not needed here.

Making the Metal Master

Obviously the acetate discs themselves are too fragile and susceptible to damage to be of any use as gramophone records and it is necessary to convert them into a tougher and more durable medium. For this purpose a metal copy is made from the acetate. The process is not so incredible as it sounds, although it inevitably calls for skill and precision. To make the acetate conductive it is sprayed with a coating of silver before being immersed in an electroplating tank and coated with nickel. The plating is again repeated, but this time with copper. The coating is about the thickness of foil and this is then separated from the acetate disc by

Fig. 5. *Spraying with a coating of silver.*

suction. The metal is a reversal of the disc on which it was grown and has ridges that correspond exactly to the grooves on the acetate. Since it has little more substance than thick tinfoil it has to be mounted on to a thick metal plate. In this form it becomes known as the master and, if pressed into a soft material, it will produce the impression of a gramophone record. However, the master is too precious to be put to such a use, for if it were damaged the whole process would have to be repeated from cutting onwards. The master is carefully preserved and used only for producing metal impressions using the same method by which it was itself made. If, to correspond with prints and negatives in photography, we term the master negative, since it cannot be played like a record, then the metal disc

Fig. 6.   *Copper-plating baths.*

Fig. 7. *Separating the metal master from the acetate disc.*

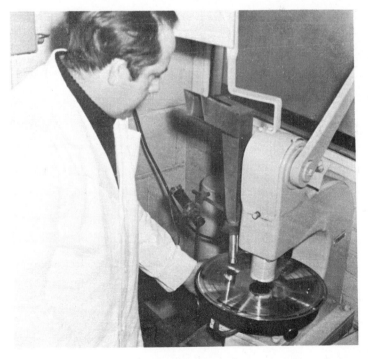

Fig. 8. *Punching centre-hole on stamper.*

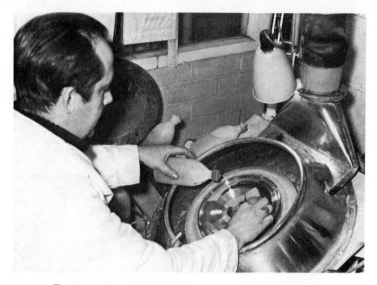

Fig. 9.   *Cleaning 'stamper' and polishing with rouge.*

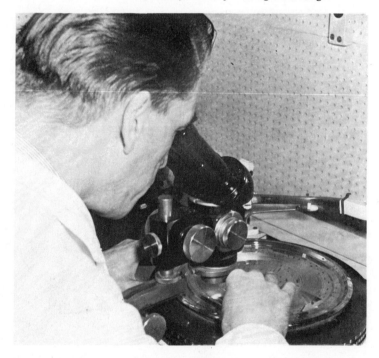

Fig. 10.   *Checking for faults and engraving them out with engraver's tool.*

produced from it will be positive, that is to say that it has grooves and can be played on a gramophone. This disc is called the "mother" and as many as required can be made from the master. With the mother the plating process is again repeated and more ridged discs are made and take the appropriate name "copymasters". These can be used as stampers, but if even more are required the plating operations may again be repeated to produce a further range by doubling or trebling the number at each stage. The final negative taken is called the stamper and the range of masters, mothers, and copymasters, etc., are preserved for further use when replacements are needed due to wear. The stamper has then to be polished with rouge, the centre hole punched out and secured to the metal plate by which it is attached to the press.

The production of these metal discs is precision work demanding immense care in handling at all stages. Faults do occur, despite high standards and rigorous checking, and although the mother is seldom played, the copymasters are checked when necessary. Irregularities, scratches, pits, or bumps are removed with engraving tools to ensure a clean silent surface. The groove has come through many separate operations since cutting and yet it is an exact copy of the original without alteration or abasement. It is difficult to realise that nothing has been lost on the way, but the sound is not distinguishable from the original tape.

Pressing

The basic ingredient from which long-playing records are made is polyvinyl chloride/acetate copolymer to which is added lubricants, extenders, stabilisers, and colouring as required. Various manufacturers have differing recipes which vary in hardness or some other small aspect, but in the main the basic ingredients vary little. The powdered ingredients are finely sifted, the remaining contents added, and the whole heated and thoroughly mixed before finally being made into pellets. The pellets are delivered via stores to the pressing shop and measured out for 12 in, 10 in, or 7 in record quantities into the shallow saucers which are then placed into an oven beside the press in which they will be used. The heater or oven is divided into compartments, with one measure of pellets for each, kept in a soft, warm state ready for instant use.

The press itself into which the stampers have been fixed is largely automatic. The operator in charge takes the record labels which are kept on a hot plate close by and places one in the top and the other in the bottom, after which he deposits a measure of pellets onto the lower stamper. In closing the press the operator sets off the automatic cycle which begins by releasing steam heat through the pipes located behind the stampers. The stampers heat instantly and press out the already hot and

Fig. 11.   *P.V.C. being poured into vat for heating.*

Fig. 12.   *Heating cabinet for storage of P.V.C. pellets.*

Fig. 13. *Record being removed from press.*

soft PVC at 11 tons to the square in, forcing the unwanted material through the sides. After a pre-set time of about 10 seconds the heated steam is automatically switched off and cold water is pumped into the pipes, rapidly cooling the record. At this point the press automatically unlocks and the operator can open it and remove the record while it is still slightly warm and thus quickly and easily cut off the waste around the edge. Although the pressing cycle is automatic the number of records pressed per hour depends on the speed at which the operator can reload the press. In between loading he cleans the edge of the last record, checks it for pressing faults, and prepares for reloading. The making of the record from studio to the production of the commercial disc is now complete and for the first time one can now hear the record in its final form.

The record now passes through the quality control department for inspection. This will be dealt with more fully in due course as it is a matter which requires close attention in its own right. At the conclusion the records are finally placed in polythene bags and outer sleeves before being sent to the stores where they are stood on edge in racks. In due course they leave here and travel to the wholesaler, then to the retailer and customer.

The foregoing paragraphs are only an outline of the business of producing a gramophone record and are set out here for the purpose of creating some understanding of the nature of the product, and to make it clear to the reader that it is a product of precision engineering which by its very nature requires special consideration quite different from other library materials. The minute groove on each disc, its bottom radius little more than ·0007 in, contains the whole spectrum of the recorded sound, is pressed into soft plastic that despite its strength is easily damaged when subjected to physical stresses even slightly beyond the limits its makers intended. If we realise to some extent the true nature of the records we handle, such knowledge will go a long way in aiding us to protect our stock, to knowing the special precautions we must take to safeguard them, and exactly why we take them. The following pages are devoted to that end.

Manufacturing Faults

In discussing the faults that occur in the actual making of gramophone records we pass from purely theoretical considerations to practical ones that directly affect gramophone record librarians. The subject is, in a sense, a halfway mark in that, although these occur in the factory and might be discussed under the heading of manufacture, the repercussions are of direct consequence in the gramophone record department. By virtue of having a foot in both camps so to speak, the subject will serve as a bridge to carry the reader from the factory to the library. Each fault, its cause and effect, increases our understanding of the overall subject of the care of records in a public loan collection. Having established the reason for placing this information at this particular point, let us revert for a moment to the factory and quality control.

It is not common practice to carry out 100 per cent inspection of many manufactured and machine-made commodities in industry. During the past few years it has been found more effective to plan inspection on a percentage basis. The subject is a little involved, but it works out in practice, especially when one realises that handling, which is an additional source of damage, is cut to a minimum. However, it is plain that some faulty records must escape inspection and reach the purchaser, and when the number of records purchased runs into hundreds as in a public library, attention to this aspect becomes very important. All records received into the library must be thoroughly scrutinised for any blemish and any disc not coming up to a reasonable standard must be rejected. One thing that is certain is that the public will not be encouraged to maintain a high standard of treatment if the staff reveal the slightest laxity or indifference in this direction. Staff in charge of collections and those assisting them

Fig. 14. *Quality control – checking for visible and audible faults.*

Fig. 15. *Testing for warping and packing.*

must maintain the highest standards in checking new stock for this reason, and if the supplier does not understand the necessity for this and is reluctant to co-operate, the firm is of no use to the library and must be replaced by one that will. The manufacturers themselves are aware of the nature of this problem and realise that poor records are hardly a good advertisement, and so instant replacement of records below an acceptable standard by dealers acting as the distributors should always be possible. The librarian can be sure of support from the makers in this matter.

Many newcomers to handling records are puzzled when checking precisely what to look for, and do not understand how to identify the imperfections when found and to decide whether or not the damage is serious. Checking demands common sense, practice, and some degree of confidence in one's own decisions. Some people are not cut out for this work because they lack this confidence, and can never acquire it. Occasionally someone may be discovered who lacks all three qualities, but whether one or all three is missing he should never be left in charge of a public loan collection, for the expense will be considerable and unnecessary. The majority of people find little difficulty with checking once they have learned what to look for. The following list of the most important and (or) the most common faults serves as a basis for training. If committed to memory, blemishes on records can be tabulated and, with experience, the extent of the defect assessed without the necessity of playing the discs. But in the beginning it is wise to play all records that are rejected so that the sound can be associated with the visual aspect of the fault.

The main requirements for doing this work are strong natural and artificial light, as all records should be checked in both. It is possible sometimes to see damage in one and not the other. Two hand glasses are also required, one X10 for quick examination of marks and X20 for close high magnification of a small area of damage. Finally, a barely damp sponge should be used to wipe each record because dirt and dust can cause confusion and delay inspection. Other requisites to assist and speed the task will be discussed, with the particular type of defect with which they can be of use.

SCRATCHES.   Scratches are, without any doubt, the most common form of damage encountered. Before the days of polythene bags, or "inners" as they are sometimes termed, scratches often accounted for 60 per cent of the rejects that had to be returned to the supplier and as many as three to four records in every ten examined had to be discarded as unsuitable due mainly to careless packing. At the present time, it is considerably reduced by the protective sheaths now provided by the makers. The introduction of the raised edge on the record has also contributed a further measure of protection. But scratches are still to be found on new records, and, because of the endless variety and seriousness each one has to be dealt with individually, previous experience being used as the guide.

The only way to acquire experience in assessing any damage visually is to play every suspect record at the point of the damage in question. To do this requires time but it is the only way to relate sight and sound together so that the eye, with continued practice, will begin to recognise just how serious or not the damage will be in playback. The ability to check records rapidly, locate damage and assess how serious it is will be of endless help in making the service run quickly and smoothly when on counter duty. Checking new stock provides an excellent opportunity to build this experience, when the gramophone can be used at once to confirm or refute the diagnosis of the examiner.

In checking scratches, three types of light are very useful if available. Strong natural daylight, *white* artificial light and *yellowish* artificial light. Magnifying glasses are then used for inspecting marks that have been located with the naked eye. Elaborate checking devices containing built-in lights and low-powered magnifying glasses are of little use. The reading type of glass these contain is usually only X5 in power and of little value in this work. Apart from this the record revolves on a pivot that maintains a constant angle to the light, when in actual fact to locate surface defects the record should be continually turning and altering its angle to the light. This is best done by rotating the record in the hands and tipping it at varying angles to the light source. This method applies to all types of fault and not to scratches alone. When a mark is found, it should be examined with the hand glass to see how extensively the grooves are damaged and the affected part of the disc played. The record should then be re-examined and the relationship between what was heard and seen committed to memory.

To return to the question of scratches, if the record is inspected in pale fluorescent light it will often appear to be without blemish, but when the same record is examined in sunlight or yellowish artificial light it will be seen to be covered with myriads of small gossamer like marks. These are not serious and are sometimes due to rough edges left on the grooves of the original acetate. These are known as crowns and are usually polished off during the production of the matrix. If these are not taken off, every groove has slightly raised edges that catch every small abrasion from dirt or handling. Merely taking them in and out of the protective packing a few times leaves them covered with these marks which are, as pointed out above, invisible except under certain kinds of light. This type of marking is mentioned because it is often, quite mistakenly, thought to be serious when seen for the first time.

Obviously not all scratches are superficial but one must be certain at what point marks of this nature begin to affect the sound quality of the record. Here experience with the magnifying glass and playing back on the gramophone will be invaluable. As a rule the deeper a scratch is the more serious its effect on the sound quality. Length is of secondary importance. If the scratch marks only the surface of the land between the grooves then it is of little importance, even though it may extend across the whole of the surface. But if it seriously disfigures the surface by its appearance then it should be rejected even though it may not sound during replay. Such marks as these have a bad effect on the borrowers who see them, thus encouraging carelessness. This particularly refers to wide bruises or abrasions on the surface of a disc that look worse than they really are. The scratch that breaks the wall of the groove to any depth, whether it is long or short, will sound and be a permanent and possibly increasing source of trouble as time passes. Reject the record and take no risks. That is all that can be said of scratches, though experience in looking for them will prove the subject to be much more varied and difficult than the foregoing paragraphs indicate.

BUBBLES.   The next type of damage is an easy one to detect. During pressing, small amounts of air or gas may be trapped in the material and form bubbles. There are several possible causes for this, but these do not need to concern the examiner. Bubbles can break down under constant playing and, although it does not happen frequently, the risk is sufficient to warrant returning the record to the supplier for exchange. Bubbles are usually audible on reasonable equipment and make a thumping sound that can be most disconcerting.

PITS OR BUMPS.   Often small pits or bumps (for which no obvious reason is discoverable) may be found on the surface of a record. These may or may not affect the playing of the disc but experience will help to decide what should be done.

Small pits may be due to several causes of which two are quite common. If the pit is sharp and round with a slight depression around it, as though something hard and pointed had been pressed into the disc while it was soft, the cause is almost certain to have been a bubble that broke at the moment the record was cooling, with the resultant crater having been only partially filled. If this is located in the land between grooves then it may be ignored. When it is found to affect the wall of the groove the record is imperfect and may give serious trouble when it is used or begins to wear. Where a pit appears as a shallow depression the cause may be in the metal master. Foreign material may have been trapped under the plating during mounting on to the backing plate. Whatever the cause the immediate surface of the stamper becomes distorted outwards and every record stamped from that batch will carry the mark. This damage or fault will seldom be serious as it is usually so shallow, but it may sound on playback. Although these have been referred to in the singular it is not uncommon to find them in groups, located in a small area.

Bumps or pimples on the record surface are fairly easily distinguished from bubbles. The bubble looks to be exactly what it is in appearance, round and convex, while the bump appears as a definite lump trapped in the material, which it is. The trapped material can be a large variety of substances ranging from impurities that find their way into the record material at the mixing stage to foreign substances that are trapped at the time of pressing. The offending materials may be pieces of paper, wood, dirt, grit, burned or oxydised PVC, and even bread or biscuit crumbs. Foreign matter can get in at any point in the process from mixing to stamping. Though examples are rare, a sharp watch should be kept for them. Lumps of PVC can be due to poor mixing, or unused fragments of the material being over heated, and at other times even due to particles of the previous record that was pressed adhering to the stampers. No record that comes into this category should be added to stock. The surface nearly always breaks down under frequent playing.

PULL-OUTS.   This is an odd name for an odd type of trouble. This is not to imply that it is rare. It is in fact fairly common and, unfortunately for the librarian, not always easy to detect because of the variety of forms it may take. The manufacturers have different titles for it, but the name "pull-out" has been taken from the book *Plastics Applied*, edited by V. E. Yarsley.

It varies in appearance from a single rough crater (the largest I have seen was nearly a quarter of an inch across!) to dozens of pin points that are so small they appear like minute flecks of silver as they catch the light. The latter type is particularly elusive. It often occurs across several grooves, in one groove wall, but not the other, with the result that in either white or yellow light it will be visible when viewed in one direction only and remain invisible from all other angles. If the area affected is a large one it often extends across the grooves rather than spreading round the record. As this may seem a little confusing an examination of some of the causes and effects will explain more clearly.

One of the causes can be due to crowns that formed on the acetate during cutting and which were not polished off at a later stage. The rough edges to the groove on the metal matrix cause the PVC to adhere to the press when it is opened. Two results can occur. Firstly the record that has been pressed will have a piece, or pieces, pulled out of the top shoulders of the groove and they may vary from the microscopic to easily observable in size. Secondly, if the pieces are not removed from the press by cleaning, these fragments may be pressed into the next disc. The fragments are cold and do not thoroughly reheat, and so do not properly fuse into the material of the next record. These too may pull out, but they can remain in place and only be observed by the irregularity and porous appearance of the affected area. It is possible for them to break down in playing and give the record the appearance that the stylus was dropped on to it while it was stationary. Checking with the hand glass will reveal that a portion of the record just left the surface and was not dug out, leaving a round minute hole devoid of signs of gouging. That the trouble is due to crowns can be deduced when the tops of one or both walls have minute pieces missing.

In a previous paragraph I mentioned a single example that measured almost a quarter of an inch across. This was due to a piece of burned material in the mix. In this case the record came back after the first issue with the additional hole to the one in the middle. Before issue there was no indication of surface irregularity other than a small, almost circular line of minute holes that could hardly affect the playing. This was in the early days of LP records and was unwisely thought not serious. The area enclosed by the.porous line was in fact a piece of burned material that had not moulded into the rest of the mix.

There is a porosity of a different kind that appears as a silver streak across the grooves from centre to edge. This is the type referred to in the opening remarks of the section, and is peculiar because it so often appears on one groove wall and not the other. In a way this should be classed as a bubble and not a pull-out, because it is primarily due to gas or liquid that is released during heating in the press. The pressure on the material is over 10 tons per square in at the centre and the pocket of gas or steam gets squashed and broken up into hundreds, or even thousands, of small pockets, that are all pushed in one direction towards the outer edges of the press where the pressure is less. In squashing they almost all come to the surface and break down against the metal of the matrix, leaving small pinholes of either smooth appearance or rough little pits.

In stereo records a similar trouble is occasionally seen, but instead of going from edge to edge the streak runs along the groove in loud passages. This is a true pull-out where the material is lifted from the groove as it is removed from the press. The record contracts as it cools and some of the material adheres to the ridge of the matrix. This is found only in stereo records and can be quite troublesome in playback. Grit or dirt on the press can leave small areas of damage that may resemble any of the above faults. In particular the shoulders of the grooves can be affected and in playback the same clicks and splatters may be heard that are characteristic of the other faults. The moral of all this is close inspection of all small areas of minute damage, remembering that these cannot be seen from all angles and in all kinds of light. Having found them, get to know just how these affect playback, and exactly what the appearance of them is.

WARPING.　Now here is a type of trouble that is a gramophone record librarian's constant companion. In every batch of records it is fairly safe to say that there will be one or two good examples and a number of more or less borderline cases. The causes are varied and quite perplexing when one examines them. The majority are due to stresses in heating and cooling during making and I often feel that the commencing stress takes place in the protective rim-guard, that raised thick edge produced by some firms to protect the record surface. With the advent of the rim-guard the number of warped and dished records increased to a considerable percentage and, although the surfaces of the older type of thick record soon became covered with numerous superfluous dirt marks that did not sound, they at least seemed to warp less often. The rim-guard can be a mixed blessing. There are causes other than those that occur in manufacture, bad storage being high on the list. Even record sleeves can cause it if they become damp, and then twist or buckle. Sometimes record labels may be the cause if one is thicker than the other, or one is a differently textured paper from the other. This is very rare, but it can happen.

All records should be checked on a sheet of plate glass and if the glass can be spun like a turntable any warp will be more readily detected. In the case of dishing or bowing, this will be seen when the record is turned over on the glass and the edge is found to be clear of the surface. Where twisting or warping has occurred the record must be discarded, since gramophone pick-ups are not designed to track on a switchback, but in the case of dishing there is some latitude allowable. If the thickness of a penny can be passed under the edge then the warping is too great but anything less can be accepted. With reasonable treatment and storage it is not likely to get worse.

SWINGERS. This is the name given to a record that has its hole out of centre. There are two possible causes for this. One is due to poor centring on the metal masters at the time of punching and the other to the matrix having stretched through stresses during pressing. This error may be as little as 20 thousandths of an inch, but the eye will be able to detect the swing of the pick-up as the record plays, hence the name swinger. All records should be placed on the turntable and the pick-up placed on the grooves to see that it is steady. This simultaneously checks for good surfaces, etc. Records that swing to such a degree that the pick-up is seen to move from side to side should be rejected. The movement can be so marked that the quality of reproduction is affected and sounds slurred. This fault is rarely found to a very serious degree.

PRE ECHO AND POST ECHO. This is an irritating business that occurs with present-day records. Fortunately it is not terribly serious, and no peculiarity is noticeable to the eye or otherwise many records would not reach the library shelves. The recorded sound can usually be heard in ghostly fashion before the actual moment of reproduction and the trouble can be due to the tape, acetate, or disc. The tape resembles blotting paper insofar that sounds recorded on it can soak through to the previous revolution of tape and this is referred to as print through. It can also be due to stress on the wall of the acetate disc when the next groove contains considerable modulation and pushes the preceding groove slightly out of shape. The acetate disc can give further trouble in this way if it should get warm during the plating operation. This effect is sometimes corrected in later pressings, but more often, the recording and all the pressings from it will be similarly affected.

There are a few other points worth noting although these do not merit a separate section. Records that have labels with silver or gold paint lettering sometimes have quantities of paint powder in the grooves. It should be remembered that this could be of a metallic nature and ought to be cleaned off with the parastat. If it persists then the record is a possible trouble spot for styli.

Discolouration of a record surface can be due to a number of causes and if it sounds in playing then it should be rejected. The nature of the sound is often a gritty surface noise or splattering sound. Possible causes are poor mixing of materials, carbon not dispersed in the mixing, pressing with damp or unheated labels and so damaging the nickel plating of the matrix. A worn matrix reveals itself with a "sunray-like" discolouration of the record that radiates from the centre of the edge. This last mentioned item is fairly unusual and can easily be confused with the more common "sunray" effect seen on a record after it had been played a few times. In this context the graining may be due to a very low frequency rumble in the original cutting machine, but is more often traceable to stresses set up in the record surface as PVC cools down.

One rule remains. If you see something that you do not recognise that is audible in playback and suspicious in appearance, then reject the record. It is better to play safe and aim for reasonably perfect new stock. Its beneficial effect on the borrowers is well worth the trouble.

To simplify the path of other members of the staff who may be called upon to check new records, the following method, although expensive, provides an easy, quick, and foolproof way to train them. Retain a specimen of each fault (or the most common ones) correctly tabulated for quick inspection so that trainees can see examples. Where a tape recorder is available make a tape of the audible faults so that the sound it makes can be heard as the trainee looks at the record. The changes can be rung on this theme by asking staff to identify the record that contains the fault they are hearing. This gives a quick indication of the person's perception and future usefulness.

Lending Conditions

Having spent some time finding out how records are made, we now have to consider the use of these in the public library. Having established that it is the product of precision engineering of the highest order and that each record is something of a minor miracle, it is not difficult to appreciate that as library lending material it merits different consideration from books. The first obvious point is that unlike a book, it is hardly suited to life in a public library. The microscopic grooves are easily damaged due to the softness of the material into which these are pressed. A look at the highly magnified grooves of a new disc will soon indicate what havoc can be caused by grit and dust, worn needles, and bad handling. The makers are very well aware of the possibility of ruining records by subjecting them to such treatment and warn their customers accordingly, because it is not possible at present to make records that stand up to such damaging factors. But as these are the constant hazards of a record lending library it might readily be assumed that records are not suitable for lending in the same way as books. A damaged or soiled book can be read, even with enjoyment, if no better copy is available, but a record in the same condition is an audible discomfort. There is no comparison between the two things, and yet it is not uncommon to find them being given almost identical treatment in many lending libraries. If records are treated in this way then they are definitely not suitable as public library material.

The point need hardly be argued that gramophone records in public libraries need special consideration if the service is to be a reasonably economic proposition, and that the librarian in charge of the department must be a specialist in matters relating to the gramophone, and the problems of playing records, quite apart from having knowledge of what is recorded on them. The requirements are of equal importance and any person deficient in any one of these qualities is not suitable for the task in hand. This is not intended to sound as though one should give up if self-appraisal reveals a weakness in one's professional knowledge, but rather that there should be no rest until the deficiency is remedied. This is by no means an easy task, but if one feels the work to be worthwhile, then it is surely worth making a commonsense effort to gather all the information that is necessary to remedy the lack of knowledge.

This is all quite possible once the nature of the gramophone record is understood, and the would-be librarian starts objectively to consider the operation of a gramophone record library with the aim of maintaining the stock in reasonable playing condition for the maximum possible time. This requires some preliminary knowledge of the conditions that are likely to be encountered in practice. To cover the ground thoroughly it would be necessary, as a preliminary step, to start with a technical history of the gramophone before getting to the crux of the matter. A moment's reflection is all that is needed to realise that such a course, though interesting, would prove ponderous and impractical. The result would be an outsize task and an oversize book. There is no point in using a large steam roller to crack a small though tough nut, when there are other means available. The best possibility that offers itself as a reasonable solution is to consider the problems from the aspect of long-playing records only, and forgetting all that happened, or nearly all, before 1950. This proved successful in the previous chapters and it will continue to serve here.

THE BORROWERS AND THEIR GRAMOPHONES.   Let us meet our public! The majority of the people who will be using the gramophone library will possess a gramophone that has been purchased during the past ten years. Many of the machines in use will be over five years of age and are unlikely to have been overhauled or brought up-to-date during that time. If the turntable revolves, and some sort of sound is emitted from the loudspeaker, then the owner is satisfied, no matter what happens to the records he plays. The reasons for this are often economic, though the user would generally not admit it. Because of the economic aspect the British public are very reluctant to make changes to, or spend money on their gramophones so long as they continue to operate after a fashion. It is not unusual to meet would-be borrowers who are certain they have wonderful gramophones despite the fact that these machines have been working for ten years without even an elementary check over. It is a sobering thought, when one stops to consider, that it is recommended practice to have a thorough overhaul of gramophone equipment about every two years quite apart from occasional cleaning and checking of all moving parts such as motors and pick-up arms. Often the proud owner thinks it a virtue that the gramophone has never needed repair or attention and when told that for the sake of his records he should take some precautions, the reply quite often is that "it sounds alright, so why bother?"

When the subject of styli comes up it is not unusual to be told that the needle is permanent and does not need changing. In extreme cases they are not even aware that there are two needles in a turn-over cartridge (one for 78 RPM and one for 33-45 RPM) and sometimes any needle at all. It is fascinating to ponder over what compulsion or ritualistic urge makes those in the latter group turn that little button over at the end of the pick-up for standard or microgroove records, if they bother at all. This is ignorance at its worst and it can ruin a public record collection in quite a short time unless there are trained and experienced staff in the library possessed with enough tact to prevent havoc when such people are unleashed on a carefully selected collection of records. The reader may well think that not all the public are quite as bad as this, and to set minds at rest it can be said that they are not. They have varying degrees of responsibility but to expect the worst is to be forearmed. The effort to protect the records for the enjoyment of the better informed borrowers must be geared to the lowest common denominator if it is to succeed in its purpose. The staff of any public lending library service must be ready to cope with all comers from the least to the best informed members of the public. All the strange ideas, misinformation, and ignorance encountered can be overcome by staff who know the answers to the everyday hazards and employ sensible public relations to cope with them. Encourage borrowers to have periodic overhauls of equipment. Use the analogy, that a gramophone is like a car in that it needs periodic checking and servicing. The ear is a deceptive organ that by constantly but unconsciously adjusting itself to deteriorating sound reproduction, leads the listener to think that all is as well as it ever was with the gramophone. Complete overhaul every three years is not imposing an excessive financial burden, and although it cannot be enforced, it should be incorporated into any printed matter that the library issues as a recommended safeguard. Not all the public will comply, but for each one that does the life of the stock will be prolonged. This of course relates to the apparatus itself as a whole, and is not intended to include the pick-up stylus. This is an entirely separate consideration which will be dealt with at a later stage.

Having progressed to the point where the public are being advised on how to maintain their equipment in reasonable playing condition then the next step, the lending and receiving back of gramophone records, can be examined. We have returned to the question of checking records. Only by this time the records are not new and we are not now looking for faults that occur in manufacture but damage that occurs through playing and handling. Furthermore, the conditions under which checking is carried out will have changed. Whereas this was previously done in a thorough and leisurely fashion in private, the examination has to be carried out under the eye of the borrower, often with other members of the public looking on. It is essential for counter staff to know what they are looking for and, if the damage is located, to know the cause. The examination must be thorough, missing nothing, and be carried out quickly and expertly to avoid discomfort to the borrower concerned and delay to others who may be waiting. This is part of the public relations aspect once more. If staff seem uncertain about what they are looking for, take too long in looking, and appear diffident about coming to a decision, then the public will have little confidence in that person and will eventually be deterred from borrowing at all. Any counter staff showing this kind of approach will never get very far in maintaining a good service in which the public have faith and which they enjoy using.

In checking new records it is possible to list every type of damage and what causes it but in examining used records the situation is rather different. With used discs the cause of damage can be more easily listed but the actual damage caused is varied indeed.

Since we are considering gramophones at this stage the logical step is to consider damage resulting from mechanical failure of the machine. Some practical information on the gramophone is needed and instead of listing the damage that can be caused to records by poor machines, a double purpose will be served if we list the components of the gramophone that can be troublesome and the different types of damage these produce. This will make a more useful list of information for reference and will immediately associate the damage with the cause.

Gramophone motors can cause damage or excessive wear to records, and some knowledge of various kinds of motors and how these operate can be of considerable use. An understanding of this field is just another part of the public relations side of the work and the benefits of knowledge of this kind will reflect strongly in the public's attitude to the staff and service. With motors, one of the most common complaints from the public is excessive motor noise. Hum and rumble are definite factors in wearing records and any information that we can give in helping to lessen or cure these problems will assist in preserving library records. The answer is really to buy a good quality motor and mount it properly in its cabinet. But not all people are in a position to afford the cost of expensive alterations of this type and are more often prepared to take advice on adapting the offending equipment, if it is forthcoming. Reference to magazines such as the *Gramophone* and *Hi-Fi News* are invaluable, and reading technical reviews and answers to readers problems in back issues will provide a wealth of information. To deal with excessive rumble, good results are possible if the motor plate is screwed through soft lead and sponge rubber to a thicker board, with the part of the board containing the pick-up cut away and mounted separately. Any rumble transmitted from the motor can no longer travel to the pick-up, since it will be separated by the width of the saw cut. If the turntable is only thin pressed steel, this can be made less resonant by a thicker rubber turntable mat and stretching a tight strip of rubber round the edge of the turntable. This will usually cure rumble to some extent, but it cannot be eliminated completely because the defect is in the motor design.

Hum is a completely different trouble, and is a very important cause of wearing records. At its worst, it can be so bad that the vibration will cause the pick-up to act as a cutter head, with a result that the needle chatters in the grooves of the record to such an extent that the sound of the damage caused is audible on all gramophones in future playings. Hum of this kind is due usually to motors mounted on springs that are too taut. If the hum is of a lower sound-frequency so that it approaches a rumbling, fluttering sound, then the springs are too slack. With some experiment on the tension of the springs and testing with an old record, a satisfactory result can be achieved. If the hum is electrical, then the fault is due to poor earthing and the user should connect a proper earth after removing any others. The best plan is to advise that all earths on the machine should go to one point. Too many earths can cause as much trouble as if there were none at all. If the hum persists, the pick-up leads can be reversed and finally the amplifier moved further from the motor and pick-up. The librarian offering this type of advice need not be a technical expert to s ggest these courses of action. It is sufficient to be able to help and in so d ing, cut down the wear on records that are borrowed. To the person seeking perfection, there is but one course to be taken to avoid the results of buying poorly designed cheap motors and that is to buy a transcription quality unit. But a correctly mounted cheap motor used with loudspeakers with negligible response below 55 cycles per second (that is the third A below middle C in the piano) will produce little audible rumble or hum. With all types of mass-produced equipment for playing records, a somewhat high rate of record wear has to be accepted, for although audible distortion can be damped down, it is not possible to achieve the same results that the use of high-quality equipment offers.

The drive systems in all three or four speed motors are identical, varying slightly in design only. The armature of the motor turns at somewhere around 1,700 RPM and to get the turntable to turn at $33\frac{1}{3}$, 45, or 78 RPM an intermediate gear is required. This is done by providing three or four different circumferences on the spindle that protrudes from the armature of the motor. This is mounted on the motor board near the inside rim of the turntable pointing up vertically. The lower end of the centre spindle of the turntable rests in a bearing in which it revolves freely. Between the rim of the turntable and the armature spindle is a rubber drive wheel which comes into contact with the rim and the spindle simultaneously, when the motor is set in motion. The speed at which the drive wheel will revolve will depend upon that part of the graduated spindle with which it comes in contact, and the reduction from the wheel to the turntable will further decrease the rate to the desired speed. The rubber wheel can be the cause of forms of distortion that borrowers will quite innocently report as a fault in the records they borrow. That is assuming they notice the trouble, of course. It is quite true to say the library staff will never cease to be amazed at the poor sound quality that many members of the public are able to tolerate and yet still apparently enjoy listening to records. The important point is to be able to identify any sort of complaint against library records that is really attributable to this intermediate drive in the motor mechanism. What does one do, for instance, if one is taken unawares and a borrower complains that a particular record sounds as though it is slowing down? Or sounds as if it is recorded at an unsteady pace? Borrowers have been known to ask if records slow down as they wear out. No time will be lost on checking the records if one understands the elementary principles of the drive mechanism. The particular fault mentioned here, is called "wow" and most expressively denotes the sound that results. The cause is hardly ever in the record and is nearly always due to the rubber intermediate drive wheel slipping because it has grease on it, or has worn shiny. Cleaning, very light buffing and french chalk applied to the edge will cure the situation.

Switching off the motor disengages the drive wheel and operates a brake on the turntable, but if the turntable is stopped by hand, or records are changed while the turntable is still in motion, then the rubber wheel will be wrenched against the turntable and the armature spindle. A warning about this can be usefully incorporated into printed information handed to all borrowers and thus preventing some of the wear that results from drive wheels that have suffered damage of this kind. The rubber drive wheel becomes torn or split from the metal it is moulded to. This will produce several types of unpleasant sound that can be transmitted to the pick-up and loudspeakers and sometimes permanently etched into the record itself. The most common problem is the flattened wheel which produces a low pitched flutter that makes itself particularly evident in pianoforte and wind-instrument recordings, causing the sustained notes to flutter and vibrate. The torn drive produces this effect with each revolution of the turntable, and although it remains inaudible in many records, this flutter never fails to appear in pianoforte, brass (particularly horns), or woodwind passages. Sometimes all three faults occur together, and this can usually be traced to the rubber having perished. Another possible cause is due to the drive becoming eccentric or warped, perhaps from heat rising from valves or motor located below. Whatever the cause, a new rubber wheel is the only possible cure. The point to remember is that stopping the motor by hand with the power on can indirectly damage records, and that the on-off switch must always be used with every record when the equipment is operated manually.

The reference to manual operation of motors is very important and a matter which must be insisted upon wherever complete manual operation is not possible. Auto-change mechanisms must not be used to play successive records stacked on the machine. The regulations issued by the library, relating to the handling and playing of records, must make this quite clear and set out the reasons for insisting on this. There is no doubt that the average cheap automatic record-player accounts for the largest part of excessive wear and tear to records in public loan collections and that it is not unreasonable to ask borrowers to play one record and remove it from the turntable before playing the next, in order to preserve records from some of the causes of damage. To state that this is not unreasonable is obvious, when one considers that the average playing time of a 12 in long-playing record side is between 15 and 20 minutes. It creates no hardship to the listener to interrupt their pleasure for a few seconds while changing discs. To keep the public aware of this requires periodic reminders to be issued, because the idea of a machine doing the work for the user is very attractive to him. Apart from this, the owner often believes that loading mechanism with a stack of records is less hazardous than manual playing. The fact that the makers recommend such a procedure is good enough for the average purchaser, who feels that this apparently foolproof mechanism is a far better machine than the single record-player. This takes us into the field of modern salesmanship, and the dangers of psychological sales methods. We will not venture far, except to say that it must be remembered that the gramophone record-player industry is geared to make a considerable appeal to the slaves of fashion, often female, who purchase gramophones on appearance rather than performance. Most radiogram cabinets are ornate glossy creations of the modern mass-production cabinetmaker's art. What goes inside is governed by the cost of the cabinet in order to keep the overall cost to a reasonable level. This is a keen market and the makers cannot afford to price themselves out of it.

As these comments may seem harsh to the reader, let us investigate the evidence to substantiate them. First and foremost, microgroove records should never be handled in quantity without protective covers, otherwise extensive scratches and abrasions will be inflicted on the discs. Stacking records on an auto changer creates these conditions which continue to operate as the mechanism is dropping and playing each disc. The raised edge to the records gives only a small amount of protection, and as discs are rarely perfectly flat they skid and slip when stacked one on another. When a warped record is present in the stack, the disc and those that follow will slip, and this slipping is one of the causes of "wow", which will seldom occur when records are played singly. Always inquire if the record was the only disc on the turntable when any complaint about "wow" arises. If it was not played singly the blame cannot definitely be attributed to the motor but the fault may well be due to warping or dishing of any one of the records on the turntable. This is one cause of record wear. The next point to consider is the changing height of the pick-up as it plays each record when a stack of discs are on the changer. Obviously the weight and angle must alter slightly with each increase in height and if by some chance a number of records is played singly the wear on the needle will damage records that are subsequently *stacked* on the turntable. If the stylus is damaged the wear is increased considerably and changes in character as each disc drops and the height of the stack changes.

Much of the damage caused to records by automatic players originates in the mechanism under the turntable that operates the changing process. This is usually connected to the base of the pick-up under the motor board and turntable, and consists of a type of long trigger that moves across with the arm as the record is played. As the pick-up nears the end of the record the trigger comes into contact with a switch that is not operated until the arm suddenly swings from the playing surface on to the run off groove at the end. The sudden swing of the pickup arm operates the switch that sets in motion the part of the mechanism that returns the arm to its rest. If the centre spindle still holds a record the process will start again, but if it is empty then the pick-up arm will drop on to the rest and switch off the power. It needs no further explanation of the device to realise that the mechanism results in back pressure against the arm. To overcome this the playing weight of the arm is increased to a point where it will track without jumping back from the switch underneath. The increase in side pressure and playing weight shortens both the life of the needle and the record.

Makers now provide a type of switch to eliminate this factor, but in my experience it does not provide a complete answer. The playing weight remains too high and the automatic switch still operates as a stopping device. A switch to disconnect the whole automatic playing process and simultaneously lighten the pick-up would be too expensive an item in a commodity that is produced primarily for cheapness. The trigger connected to the base of the arm comes into contact with the switch quite some time before the end of the record, especially if the side is a long one. At each revolution the arm moves closer to the switch and is either tapped or pressed by it, thus causing constantly increasing side pressure until the pick-up arm sweeps off the playing surface and finally sets the switch off. Any record that has been used regularly on automatic units is usually distinguished by an audible increase in wear towards the end of the side. These mechanisms are subject to failure at the beginnings and ends of record sides and in such cases produce distinct bands of damage of such severity that the affected area often feels rough to the touch. Failure of this nature is due to the machine never being cleaned or the moving parts and bearings oiled. Even oil-sealed bearings dry out in time when the amplifier is situated right under the motor. The heat can be quite intense with the lid closed, and records left on the turntable have been known to warp or dish, and even, in extreme cases, to melt.

The fact that, unlike a single playing gramophone, the centre spindle remains stationary has already been touched upon and it is worth notice that record centre holes become worn through dropping and playing. If records are left on the turntable whilst others are playing, the record at the bottom can be subjected to as much as four hours turning against the spindle if nine discs are played. Worn oversize, the centre hole becomes another possible source of "wow" if the record can no longer be accurately placed on the turntable. In any case the efficiency and constant speed of the motor are impaired when working under loads of eight to ten discs.

The point has been made that manual switches provided by manufacturers, though helpful, by no means eliminate trouble and the trend to fit such switches mainly shows a growing awareness of the basic unreliability of the product, besides overcoming sales resistance of the slightly more discerning buyer. Difficulty in coping with these troublesome machines can be kept to the minimum if a number of simple precautions are taken. One or two have been touched upon but to repeat them here will serve to emphasise them. The most important one of course is the frequent replacement of styli, as a worn stylus point used with an automatic record changer is the worst possible threat to records. Another factor is to see that the whole unit is standing level. Many records are severely mauled by heavy record changer pick-ups skating over the surface and, because it does not necessarily occur with every record that is played, the user will always try the record a second, third, or even fourth time to find out why it happens. The trouble is they rarely succeed in this and as it does not happen every time they usually blame the ruined record. This much can be added, that the raised edge or rim guard gives the pick-up a flying start, and these edges are a mixed blessing in this instance. Always advise frequent checks for the level of the machine, especially after shifting, as even the thickness of a carpet under one side and not the other can be sufficient to cause trouble. The final recommendations are frequent cleaning, oiling twice a year, and an occasional check by an engineer that understands record players every eighteen months to two years.

This is most important of all. The user can be convinced if, as I have previously said, it is likened to servicing a car. Although a car appears to be running satisfactorily one still has it serviced to avoid trouble developing instead of waiting for it to appear. Neglected machines become temperamental and records fail to drop, or get wedged. The pick-up may not come down on the record, or it may come down 2 ins in on a 12 in disc. The reverse may happen with the 10 in record and the pick-up will miss the turntable altogether and possibly ruin the stylus. If the machine is used as a single record-player and maintained in the manner suggested above, damage will be kept to a minimum. Records will be used only one at a time and so protected from dust and unnecessary handling that are just two more contributory causes of damage and wear.

STYLI. Having examined some problems of gramophone motors in a very general manner, the reader will begin to form the impression that there is no way to guarantee that record borrowers will carry out the precautions that the librarian suggests or tries to insist on. This is very true; but every borrower who does carry out all or some of the suggestions will be contributing towards a higher standard of stock maintenance in the library, thereby reducing the number of those who cause unnecessary wear. The motor is only a means to an end as far as the average gramophone user is concerned, and it is essential to make them aware of its importance. The next link in any record-player is the condition of the stylus that traces the sound track on the disc. If the gramophone motor is faulty or neglected the severity of any damage inflicted on the record by a worn stylus will be greater than it would be if the motor were running well. The more worn the stylus is, the greater the damage. This also applies to troublefree equipment, but the wear, although unnecessary, is straightforward and uncomplicated. Here is a factor that library staff can control. Having stated this, a survey of how styli are made, the work they perform and how efficiently they do it must logically follow.

Before the advent of the long playing record the playing weight of pick-ups and acoustic sound boxes was measured in ounces (where these are now measured in grammes), and there was endless controversy about which of the many types of needle gave the best all round result. For the library that has only microgroove records in stock there is only the choice of sapphire or diamond points, but where all types of record are available the position is not so straightforward. To protect library records and the styli fitted in modern equipment, the use of metal needles on 78 RPM records must be forbidden. These records are made of shellac, carbon black, cotton flock and abrasive fillers such as barytes or rottonstone. The latter ingredients were added to the mixture for the purpose of rapidly wearing the needle to the shape of the groove, with the result that each playing left a trail of minute metal fragments embedded in the grooves. The rapid wear on the metal tip removed the polished shellac surface and exposed more and more of the filler under the surface, so that in time the worn groove could wear a needle extremely quickly. No record that has been used with metal needles on old equipment is really fit for use with sapphire styli unless the user is prepared to renew the point every half-dozen sides. Although regrettable for the small minority, the obviously necessary course is to forbid the use of all equipment built before 1950 so that borrowers using sapphire and diamond points will be safeguarded from the possibility of having a stylus ruined by metal deposits left in the grooves by steel needles. Damage from a point ruined in this way could easily put an end to the useful life of a number of discs before being detected. Sapphire points used on 78 RPM records should be frequently checked for wear and changed after 200 sides or immediately wear is detected.

The figure mentioned might appear to be very low for this type of record, giving as it does an expected life of little more than 12 hours. But this is not really so low if one realises that the sapphire in use is not a true mineral but a man-made crystal.

The only resemblance that sapphire styli have to the natural stone is in the chemical structure. Whilst the latter is formed deep in the earth under the great weight of the earth's crust, the former is produced by sprinkling a fine stream of aluminium oxide powder into a tiny furnace heated by an oxyhydrogen flame. The crystal is gradually built up on a ceramic base. The great advantage of this is that the sapphire produced can be of any length or radius within reason and, because it was not formed under pressure, it has a structure that will allow it to be cut into two pieces. The two halves can be cut into sections only slightly bigger than the final stylus radius and the corners polished off to make them round. The final stage of grinding the ends into cones and polishing them to the correct tip radius is then carried out. Natural stones have a very different structure that has no "grain" and it is not possible to cut these stones as it is with their synthetic counterparts. It is this difference in structure that provides the reason for the short life of the synthetic product against the real gem stone.

The diamond stylus is of a very different order as will already be apparent. Although it is no harder than synthetic sapphire it lasts about forty times as long. Diamond styli can easily be distinguished from sapphires. Sapphire points are transparent throughout their length but diamonds are opaque. This is because the point is very small and is mounted on metal. Under magnification the appearance is not unlike that of a pencil, the point of which is the diamond and the remainder the metal shaft. The diamond chip is mounted on the metal shank and the stone and metal are ground to a cone. The final radius is reached by polishing.

In the late 1940s manufacturers began to make pick-ups of much lighter weights than before the war. The trend can be mainly attributed to the advances that had been made in sound recording, particularly by the Decca company. Weights were reduced to less than an ounce. The quality of records was further improved and with less abrasive fillers, surface noise was further reduced. These discs, although less suitable for use with acoustic machines, sounded far better with modern pick-ups using sapphire points that lasted longer than had previously been possible. But in any case the points had a short life, even if they were not chipped by the terrific forces applied to them in playing. The claims made by many makers in those now far-off days were fantastic, prophesying as many as 1,000 playings for one point even when used in the heaviest arm. Even when it was obvious that such figures were vastly exaggerated, the advertising continued and the public were gullible enough to believe them. Only a few observant enthusiasts noticed that the figures were not increased as pick-up weight dropped lower and lower, were inquisitive enough to find out why this was so, and to enquire what the real life of a point was.

When pick-up design reached a playing weight of 10 grammes the way was open for a new record material that was tough enough to stand up to this pressure. Polymerised vynil chloride discs, with microscopic grooves, requiring a turntable speed of $33\frac{1}{3}$ or 45 RPM became a fact and not just a vague rumour that had permeated the audio world for some time past. Now there were only two possible types of styli, sapphire or diamond. Diamond needles in the 1950s were very expensive and the fantastic claims of 10,000 sides playing time for a sapphire still seemed to make it the best buy. The truth was that these points had only a short life even on the new discs, and the increasing number of records returned to the manufacturers as faulty when these had in fact been damaged by worn styli forced the makers to act. In 1956 the Decca company called a meeting of their accredited dealers to acquaint them with amongst other things, the real

Fig. 16.
*Perfect
sapphire stylus.*

Fig. 17.
*Stylus
sufficiently
worn to need
replacement.*

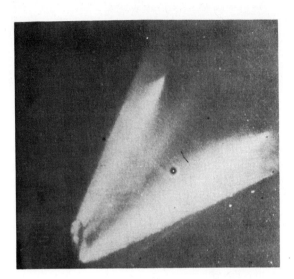

Fig. 18.
*Stylus after an
attempt to
obtain
'permanent'
use.
Permanent
stylii cause
permanent
damage.*

Fig. 19.
*Badly
manufactured
stylus. This
would cause
excessive wear
to records.*

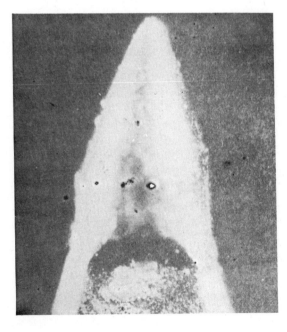

Fig. 20.
*This is the
typical condition
of a sapphire
stylus after
30 hours
use and was
obtained from
a borrower in
this library
who was
quite content
to go on
using it.*

Fig. 21.
*This is a
sapphire stylus
in perfect
condition.
The difference
to the worn
point illustrated
in Fig. 20
is obvious.*

truth about the possible life of sapphire styli. The figures announced at that time, although realistic when compared to 10,000 playings, have, even so, since proved optimistic. But now the truth was out and the makers of styli who had made these claims began to use diamond points which other makers had been offering them as an alternative to sapphire for some time past. The latter firms had always been cautious about making forecasts for sapphire points and on occasions gave a fair warning that only a limited life could be expected. Now that pick-up weights were being steadily reduced, the life of sapphire points was further reduced, possibly with an eye to a growing public that had learned the hard way with ruined records. It was not sufficient to warn the user to get a new needle when wear became audible. All the damage had been done when this stage was reached, and the only way to avoid the risk of damage was to replace the stylus frequently unless the point could be visually inspected. One firm of makers and distributors in 1951 claimed 10,000 playings for a sapphire needle. In 1955 the same point quite suddenly could only be expected to play 5,000 sides. 1958 was ushered in with 2,000 which dropped to 1,000 and then 500 before making way for their diamond that in 1960 would play 10,000 sides. This looked dangerously like another 10 year cycle developing but the better informed members of the consumer public showed their mistrust of such rash figures and so the campaign lapsed.

During recent years many libraries, although conscious of the growing demand for stereophonic records, have, until the recent announcement by EMI that all new recordings would be stereophonic only, been able to avoid the necessity of having to provide them. The new policy of this major British company was not unexpected, since this course had already been followed in America and in some European countries, notably Germany. Since the news in July 1967 several other companies have set similar policies in motion and it is quite safe to assume that within two years all *new* recordings issued will be stereophonic, and that the only monophonic discs will be those still remaining in the makers' catalogues, and some re-issues. Those libraries with stereo records are only a short step ahead of those that have yet to start a collection, since all are faced with the necessity of purchasing records on a larger scale for two distinct kinds of borrower with little chance of extra finance to provide adequately for both. Eventually mono stocks will have to be diminished. This will not be an easy task and borrowers will have to be led to expect mainly "stereo-only" libraries in the future. It should not be thought, however, that mono will disappear completely. There will be mono records available for a long time to come, but within a few years there will not be enough available to stock a library.

The position now is not dissimilar to that which existed in the 1950s when libraries were simultaneously stocking both 78 RPM and $33\frac{1}{3}$ RPM discs. But the problems were different, as will be evident from a perusal of the equivalent section in the first edition of the Handbook. In those days it was agreed by manufacturers, libraries and the public that microgroove records could not be played on 78 RPM equipment. Clear indication was made on record covers and in advertising matter that LPs could only be played on gramophones having turntables geared to revolve at $33\frac{1}{3}$ RPM, and fitted with light-weight pick-ups designed for playing microgroove discs with a stylus not exceeding a radius of ·001 in. Then we were able to observe an industry embarking on a sales campaign to a public that had only just started buying gramophones again after the war. The economic crises of the late 1940s were past and money was freely available and so honesty was not counted other than advantageous. People were in a mood to buy new equipment and the new long-playing equipment gave them every encouragement to do so.

Today times are less booming, and as a consequence the industry is less prone to frankness. Because of the possibility of sales resistance we are now informed that stereo records can safely be played by standard light-weight long-playing mono pick-ups. This comes after mountains of paper and oceans of ink have been consumed to inform us all in technical reviews and advertisements that one could only play stereo discs with equipment specifically designed for the purpose. Pick-ups, we were told, must have vertical compliance to track the hill and dale effect in stereo records that was entirely absent in mono discs. For years librarians heeded the experts and carefully kept stereo and mono collections apart, only to be told that it had not been really necessary. Sales resistance had hardened and boom times were temporarily over. Cynicism and expediency had set in. The facts remain. As LPs could not be played on standard 78 RPM equipment so stereophonic records cannot be played with monophonic pick-ups even if stereo radius (·0005 in) points are fitted. When LPs first came out in 1951, I played some discs I had from America with a 78 RPM Wilkins-Wright pick-up on a slowed-down turntable. The discs survived a few playings but were useless for playing on my first LP machine. Experiments with similar high quality mono LP cartridges on stereo discs have shown similar results. How much damage would be done with average or cheap quality cartridges must be left to the reader's imagination.

What is quite certain is that no library can offer a service unless mono record borrowers are not allowed to take stereo records unless they have a machine of fairly recent manufacture that can successfully be fitted with a stereophonic or specially made compatible cartridge.

As stated above, pick-ups must have vertical compliance to successfully track stereo records without damaging them. Few mono cartridges have sufficient compliance in the vertical plane to enable them to qualify. Mono cartridges were designed to track a groove of uniform depth and width and older versions cannot track a stereo disc without serious deformation of the grooves. The tracking weight required for mono cartridges in many auto changers would be beyond the stress limit that discs can stand without permanent damage. Some laboratory experts deny this: but laboratory conditions are far removed from the hard everyday world encountered by librarians. It was the library profession that provided quite a lot of information for the experts on the life of sapphire styli. Once again in this present case it will be librarians who will make the industry aware of what is, or is not possible in conversion of normal domestic gramophone equipment.*

Staff must have a clear and simple indication of what equipment will take a stereo or mono compatible cartridge. To avoid quoting dates of manufacture and model numbers of machines that will safely convert, the simplest course is to limit the possibility to only those gramophones that have an adjustable playing weight regulator built into the arm and are of post-1960 design. I know of some really awful auto changers of ten to twenty years of age that incorporate a crude type of adjustor either under the arm or at the rear of the arm pivot. No one in his right mind would want to convert one of these, but one never knows.

Even if a new cartridge can be fitted to such machines, do not allow them to be used for stereo records. The structure of the stop-start mechanisms alone makes them dangerous quite apart from stiffness through dirt and wear and the crudity of the mountings compared to post-1960 machines. These factors would preclude the possibility of the tracking weight being successfully brought down to 6 grammes or less. Arm resonance (or vibration) and lateral stiffness would cause groove jumping and damage. A large number of old machines were designed to operate at 10–15 grammes and were never intended to be used at lighter playing weights. It should always be remembered that the recommended playing weight for any cartridge has no relationship to the playing weight of the pick-up arm. Because the playing weight of a particular cartridge is 3–5 grammes it does not mean that the makers intend it to be fitted into *any* arm but only those arms designed to track at such a weight. Too often confusion arises over this point. The arm governs this – *not* the cartridge. Miracles cannot be performed with pick-up arms by fitting featherweight cartridges. It is like putting a cart before a horse that was never intended to pull it in any case.

Early machines with plug-in heads, such as the Collaro "Orthophonic", EMI Power Point and some of the first Acos GP series (e.g. GP 27) and Decca XMS will not convert anyway. Although these machines are very old now one still sees them all too often. Styli are still made for them and considerable quantities are sold every year. It will be a relief to be able to limit the use of these machines to playing only mono discs with the knowledge that no compromise conversion is possible.

*This has now happened.

A stereo cartridge is quite suitable for a mono gramophone provided that the terminals for left and right channels are made common (joined to one wire) and the earth terminals treated in the same fashion where there are two. Any reasonable radio shop will be able to advise the borrower how to do this or even do it for him once the librarian has cleared the machine as suitable for conversion. If the staff maintain good public relations and an air of confidence based on reasonably sound knowledge then the advice on whether or not to convert will be accepted by the borrower. Sometimes difficulty may be encountered but should it occur too often then the manner in which the advice is given should be revised, since problems usually arise through the way in which staff approach such matters. Too much diffidence can cause as much difficulty as over confident advice.

During 1967 the Sound Recordings Group of the Library Association of Great Britain produced a most useful leaflet on this subject for issue to borrowers. It is called *This concerns you* and is available in quantities of not less than 500 from The Secretary of the Sound Recordings Group, c/o Grimsby Public Libraries. Another leaflet issued by this group is a list of available mono, stereo and compatible pick-up cartridges. It is not claimed to be comprehensive and of course lacks illustrations. However, it aroused considerable interest in the industry and at least one major gramophone record company requested permission to use it for circulation to their dealers. Mr. Williams, who is Hon. Secretary of the Sound Recordings Group, has kindly given permission for it to be reproduced here.

SOUND RECORDINGS GROUP OF THE LIBRARY ASSOCIATION

GRAMOPHONE PICK-UP CARTRIDGE IDENTIFICATION GUIDE

Compiled by *David Williams*, ALA

This list has been prepared to assist librarians and borrowers to identify the various types of monaural and stereophonic pick-ups now in current use. Stereo pick-ups will play any kind of record mono or stereo, with perfect safety but mono pick-ups should not be used to play stereo or stereo "compatible" records or serious damage will be caused to the record necessitating its early withdrawal or replacement.

MONO	STEREO
Acos GP 15	Acos GP 81
Acos GP 15/3	Acos GP 81-1
Acos GP 19	Acos GP 81-2N

MONO	STEREO
Acos GP 27	Acos GP 71-1
Acos GP 35, HGP 35-1	Acos GP 71-5
Acos GP 39-1, 39-2, 39-3	Acos GP 73-1, 73-2
"Black Shadow"	Acos GP 77 "Hi-Light" (White body)
Acos GP 25	Acos GP 83, 83-2
Acos GP 29, 29/2	Acos GP 93
Acos GP 27	Acos GP 94
Acos HGP 37	ADC Professional
Acos GP 33	ADC 3 Universal stereo
Acos GP 59-1, 59-2, 59-3	ADC 660
Acos HGP 41-1 Collaro	ADC 660/E
Acos HGP 57-1 Collaro	ADC 770
Acos HGP 55-1	ADC Point 4
Acos HGP 45	ADC Point 4/E
Acos GP 61	Allphon 66
Acos HGP 63-1	Astatic 17/9
Acos GP 65-1, 65-2, 65-3	Astatic 15-D
Acos GP 67-1, 67-2	Astatic 13TX (Power Point)
Acos GP 77 "Hi-Light"	Astatic 45-D
(Red body)	Astatic 133
Acos GP 79	Astatic N-60
Acos GP 91-1, 91-3	Astatic N-67
Bang & Olufsen Professional	Astatic N-74
BJ C/12	Astatic 445-447
BSR ST 5	Audio Empire. *See* Empire
BSR TC 4	Bang & Olufsen Stereodyne SP1. SP2
BSR 12	Bank & Olufsen SP6, SP7, SP8
BSR TC8M, TC8H.	BSR C 1 ceramic
BSR TC8M/PU30, TC8H/PU30	BSR ST 8, St 9, St 10
BSR XIM ST 5	BSR SX 1 crystal
Collaro GP 27	BSR TC 8 S
Collaro Orthodynamic	BSR TC 8S/Pu 30
Collaro PX transcription	BJ stereophonic crystal
Collaro Studio, O, P or T	BJ Elac. *See* Elac 210 and 310
Collaro 560S (Schumann Merula)	Clarke & Smith. *See* EMI
Collaro RP 594 (Plug in head only)	Clarville-Eden
Collaro OS type 5399	Collaro ceramic type C
Collaro-Ronette.	*See* Ronette
Connoisseur MK mono magnetic	
Cosmocord. *See* Acos	Collel SKI (Perpetuum PE 106 or Elac 106)
Decca H	Columbia SC 1 stereo
Decca XMS	Connoisseur stereo ceramic SCU-1
Decca E (Plug in head)	Cosmocord. *See* Acos
Decca GP 27 (Chancery)	Conver stereo
Decca FFRR mono	Decca 06960/A (RCA 104)
Decca FFRR mono eliptical	Decca Deram
Decca Deram (Stereo cartridge	Decca FFSS Mk I
but may be fitted with mono stylus)	Decca FFSS Mk II
Dual CDS 1	Decca FFSS Mk III (elliptical stylus)
Dual CDS 3-DN 2	Decca FFSS Mk IV (head or cartridge type.
Dual DN 1	Also known as C4E and SC4E – cartridge
Eden 59	type. H4E and SH4E – head type for

MONO

STEREO

Eden 62
Elac KST 2

Decca arms and SME arm with adaptor)
Decca Binofluid (Ronette BF 40)

Elac KST 5 SNM 12 (perpetuum
  PE)
Elac KST 9 SMM 9 (Perpetuum
  PE 1B, 5, 8, 10)
Elac MST 1D magnetic
Elac Miratwin
Elac SNM 14
Electro-Voice 16TT
Electro-Voice 14-34
Electro-Voice 37
EMI 1 crystal
EMI Multiplay
EMI Double C
EMI CP 10186 (incorporating
  EMI cartridge 46687A)
EMI RS 3
EMI 91110 C (EMI Double C)
EMI 48496
ER 5MB ceramic
ER 5 MX crystal
ER 701
ER 702
Expert LP moving coil
Fentone. *See* Bang & Olufsen
Garrard A (Astatic A,C,D)
Garrard G (Astatic Q)
Garrard GC 2
Garrard GC 8
Garrard GC 6 (GC2 without 78 tip)
Garrard GC 7 (GC2 without 78 tip)
Garrard GCE 3
Garrard GMC5 moving coil
Garrard magnetic TOM 1
General Electric RPJ-RPX
General Electric RPX 040 OLD
General Electric VR 2
Goldring Magna 200
Goldring Magnetic 300
Goldring 500
Goldring 580
Goldring 600
Goldring ceramic CM 50
Goldring ceramic CM 60
Goldring MX 1
Goldring MX 2 (2L, 2M, 2H)
Leak dynamic LP head
Lesa B
Lesa E
Lowther moving Coil
Luxor 72411

Dual CDS 320-3
Dual DN 4
Dual DN 24
Dual DN 26
Dual DN 32
Dual DN 34
Dual DN 43
Dual DN 96
Eagle Gold M 1007G
Eagle Silver M1007F
Elac KST 22, KST 103, SM 103
Elac KST SNM 100, PE 180 US
Elac KST 100, SM 101
Elac KST 102, SM 102
Elac KST 104, SMN 104
Elac Stereotwin STS 200D
Elac Stereotwin STS 300D
Elac SNM 402
Elac SM 107
Elac STS 210
Elac STS 222
Elac STS 310
Elac STS 240
Elac KST 106 (Collel SKI, Perpetuum PE
  186)
Elac 322, 322/E
Electro-Voice EV 20 series
Electro-Voice 131
Electro-Voice 132
Electro-Voice 122
Electro-Voice 125
Electro-Voice 194
Electro-Voice 198
Electro-Voice 199
Electro-Voice EV 141
Electro-Voice EV 147D
Electro-Voice EV 169
EMI EPU 100
Empire 888
Empire 888/P
Empire 888/PE
Empire 108
ER 5 SBA ceramic
ER stereo 60
Euphonic E1
Euphonic U-1
Euphonic U-2
Euphonic U-4
Euphonic U-5
Euphonic U-8

MONO

Magnavox 560133
Magnavox 560170
Ortofon AG
Ortofon C
Ortofon CE
Ortofon A
Pathé Marconi 51
Pathé RC 5-8
Perpetuum PE 5 (Elac KST 9)
Perpetuum 1B, 5, 8, 10 (Elac
  KST 9)
Perpetuum PE 12
Perpetuum PE 7000
Perpetuum PE T048-51
Philco-Magnavox 35-2704
Philco-Magnavox 45-9678
Philips AG 3001
Philips AG 3010
Philips AG 3013
Philips AG 3016
Philips AG 3019
Philips AG 3021 magnetodynamic
Philips AG 3025 (3013 fitted
  by Philips with diamond)
Philips AG 3052
Philips AG 3113
Philips AG 3114
Philips AG 3229
Philips AG 5001
Philips AG 5012
Philips AG 5013
Pickering-Seeburg S 120
Pickering-Seeburg S 140
Pickering-Seeburg R 150
Piezo M5-8
Plessey Double Tip
Plessey-Sonotone. *See* Sonotone
Power Point 51 (red)
Power Point 56 (blue)
RCA 72345
RCA 74068
RCA 85640 orthophonic
RCA 5497
RE-SON
Reutter. *See* Trianette
ROC-OLA
Ronette PX transcription
Ronette DC-284 O
Ronette DC-284 P
Ronette DC-284 T
Ronette Studio O
Ronette Studio P

STEREO

Euphonic U-9
Euphonic U-10
Euphonic U-12
Euphonic miniconic
Garrard EV 26 (Electro-Voice)
Garrard EV 26A (Electro-Voice)
Garrard-Ronette 105
Garrard GCS 10
Garrard GCE 12
General Electric C-50
General Electric C-100
General Electric C-650
General Electric GC 7
General Electric GC 200
General Electric VR 22
Goldring CS 80
Goldring CS 90
Goldring CS 91 E
Goldring SX 10
Goldring SX 10L
Goldring SX 10M
Goldring 700 Mk.I and Mk.II
Goldring-Pickering. *See* Pickering
HMV Schumann – Short arm and Long arm
Leak Mk.4 stereo
Lesa F 5
Lesa U
Lesa U 2
Lesa W
Luxor 74916
Luxor 72786
Magnavox Euphonic BK
Magnavox Euphonic GR
Magnavox EV 26 (Electro-Voice)
Magnovox 560334-5
Mastercraft SJN-1
Merula. *See* Schumann-Merula
Micro Seiki LSM (Complete cartridge & arm)
Ortofon SPU
Ortofon SPU-G
Ortofon SPU-GT
Ortofon SPU-T
Ortofon SPU-E
Ortofon SPU-T/E
Ortofon S 15
Ortofon S 15/E
Ortofon S 15/T
Ortofon S 15/TE
Pathé STC 7
Perpetuum Ebner PE 20
Perpetuum Ebner PE 30
Perpetuum Ebner PE 45

MONO

Ronette Studio T
Ronette DC 395
Ronette DC 395-S
Ronette TX 88
Ronette Phonofluid TO-400-OV
Rothermel Senior S 8
Schumann SK 456
Schumann Fanfare
Schumann-Merula SC 474
Schumann-Merula SK 451 (Collaro
    560 S)
Schumann-Merula SK 452/3
Seeburg Juke Box
Seeburg-Pickering R 150. *See
    also* under Pickering
Shure M 5-D
Shure M 6-S
Shure P 73
Shure PC 2
Shure PC 9-WC-38
Shure WC-6
Shure PC-6
Shure WC 32
Sonideal
Sonotone 2-T
Sonotone 3-T
Sonotone N3P
Stare 57
Stella. *See* Philips
Sugden. *See* Connoisseur
Tannoy variable reluctance Mk.II
Telefunken TTS A
Teppaz ECO 60
Thorens Double Tip (*See also* Ortofon)
Trianette 100
Vaco T-45
Vaiani VA 62
Webster Electric SCI
Webster Electric WE 14-15
Zenith Corbra S 15222

STEREO

Perpetuum Ebner PE 90
Perpetuum Ebner PE 92
Perpetuum Ebner PE 188
Perpetuum Ebner PE 186 (Collel SKI,
    Elac 106)
Philips AG 3060
Philips AG 3063
Philips AG 3201
Philips AG 331
Philips AG 3304
Philips AG 3302
Philips AG 3305
Philips AG 3306
Philips AG 3310
Philips AG 3400
Philips AG 3401, 3402 magneto stereo
Philips AG 3404
Philips AG 3407 stereo magnetic dynamic
Pickering 380A
Pickering 381A
Pickering V 15 AMI
Pickering V 15 AMIE
Pickering V 15 AT 2
Pickering V 15 AC 2
Pickering Red stereo
Pickering-Seeburg stereo
Piezo SMT 29
Piezo SMT 19X
Piezo Y 152-8
Plessey Sonotone. *See* Sonotone
Pye SMT 29
Radford PC stereo cartridge
RADIOHM stereo
RCA 110-020A
RCA 110-021
RCA 110-023
RCA 115058
RCA 115059
RCA 115277
RCA 115329

STEREO

RCA 117330
RCA 118
RCA 119
RCA 200
RCA 106770
Reutter. *See* Trianette-Reutter
Ronette stereo Binofluid BF 40
Ronette 105
Ronette 106
Ronette 208

STEREO

Schumann-Merula STK 490
Schumann-Merula STK 495-1 (*See also* HMV)
Seeberg-Pickering. *See* under Pickering
Shure M 3-D
Shure M 3/N 21 D
Shure M 7-D
Shure M 7-D/N 21 D
Shure M 8-D
Shure M 33-7
Shure M 44-C

STEREO

Shure M 44-5
Shure N 55-E
Shure M 77
Singer PU 1300
Sonotone 8-T
Sonotone 8-T4A
Sonotone 9-T
Sonotone 9-TA
Sonotone 9-THCSonotone 12-T
Sonotone 16-T
Sonotone 18-T
Sonotone 12 THR
Sonotone 12 TLA
Sonotone 20-T
Sonotone 21-T
Sonotone 25-T
Sonotone 26-T
Sonotone 27-T
Sonotone 28-T
Sonotone 100-T
Sugden. *See* Connoisseur
SW 61
Tannoy Vari-Twin stereo
Telefunken A 20/1
Telefunken A 20/2
Telefunken T 20/2
Telefunken A 23/1
Telefunken A 23/2
Telefunken A 200
Teppaz stereo 60
Tetrad 11

STEREO

Tetrad 23
Tetrad 31
Tetrad 32
Tetrad 33
Tetrad 41
Tetrad 42
Tetrad 52
Tetrad 63
Tetrad 121
Trianette-Reutter SD 1
Trianette-Reutter SD 2
Trianette-Reutter SD 3
Vaco-Luxor 65977
Vaco CN 60
Vaco CN 62
Vaco CN 65
Vaco CN 67
Vaco CN 68
Vaco CN 70
Vaco CN 72
Vaco CN 75
Vaco M-50
Vaco TN-02H ST 20
Vaco TO-45
Vaco ST 100
VEB MS 8
Webster Electric SC 3
Zenith 142
Zenith 127/128
Zenith 142-136
Zenith 142-150

MONO COMPATIBLE CARTRIDGES
(Suitable for mono and stereo)

To enable mono borrowers to play stereophonic records on mono radiograms or record players it is essential that the mono cartridge be replaced by a stereophonic or "mono compatible" cartridge. If a stereo replacement is fitted the two channels will need to be parallelled (i.e. wired together) and the alternative is to fit one of the new mono compatible cartridges which are now being produced. Unlike normal mono cartridges these pick-ups have been specifically designed to play both mono and stereo records and they possess enough vertical compliance (or up/down movement) to cope with the two recorded channels on stereo discs. They will enable many mono users to play mono and stereo discs but it should be noted that certain gramophones may not accept these new compatible cartridges (e.g. some early Philips gramophones may not be convertible as these gramophones are usually fitted with pick-up arms which will only accept the Philips cartridges). Even where this factor does not apply there are still two other remaining problems when considering the conversion of older equipment. The first concerns electrical mis-matching. The function of the pick-up is to produce an electrical signal from tracing the record groove which it then presents to the amplifier of the equipment. If a replacement cartridge does not pass this signal at the correct level to the amplifier there will be a loss of volume. The output of a pick-up is measured in milli-volts (mV = 1/1000 of a volt) and it is usual to consider up to 250 mV as medium output and over this figure as high output. Fortunately the majority of gramophones will give the same (perhaps, in some cases, improved results) with a monophonic compatible cartridge but there are a number of gramophones, especially those with 1 valve amplifiers, which may not give satisfactory results if the original cartridge is replaced. The second problem is related to playing weight. Whatever cartridge is in use the correct playing weight stipulated by the manufacturer should always be adhered to. It is generally appreciated that if the playing weight is too heavy that increased wear will be caused to both stylus and record and in an effort to combat this many borrowers endeavour to reduce playing weights below those specified by the maker. *This is equally wrong.* If the playing weight is too light wear will still be caused to both record and stylus and mis-tracking will occur resulting in some cases, in groove jumping. The majority of complaints from borrowers regarding groove jumping on library records may be attributed to this fact.

It is obvious that if the correct downward pressure is not maintained the stylus will loose its freedom of movement (i.e. compliance is reduced) and so the record will tend to "see" the stylus as a nearly immovable object.

The majority of modern auto-changer arms and pick-up arms can be adjusted to suit the type of cartridge in use but there are some arms (e.g. early Collaro and BSR for example) where no adjustment facilities are provided. It would be difficult to fit a monophonic compatible cartridge to equipment of this nature and it is unlikely that the average dealer would be prepared to undertake the work involved which would demand a great deal of modification.

Many libraries already draw the attention of borrowers to the necessity of ensuring their equipment is maintained in good condition by ensuring that the pick-up arm is free and that the correct playing weight is used. These points cannot be overstressed as experience shows that the majority of borrowers do, in fact, neglect these points. Most arms are tensioned by springs which will inevitably weaken after some time, thus increasing pressure on the stylus. A new gramophone soon collects dust, grit and dirt in the various auto-changer mechanism bearings and few units are ever sent in for regular servicing by their owners.

The monophonic cartridges listed below are, at present, the only examples of this kind of pick-up known to the Sound Recordings Group although it is to be expected that others will follow in due course. In case of doubt as to the suitability of fitting a monophonic cartridge the borrower should contact either the manufacturer of the cartridge or seek information from a reputable dealer who is prepared to offer factual information and fit a replacement cartridge wherever this is possible.

MONOPHONIC COMPATIBLE CARTRIDGES
Walton-Rainer M-1
*Acos GP 91-1 S/C
Acos GP 91-3 S/C

Every endeavour has been made to ensure this list is correct but the Sound Recordings Group cannot accept responsibility for any errors or mistakes which the list may contain.

(June, 1967)

A valuable addition to the scant literature on this subject was made by Messrs Farnell of Leeds in 1968 with the publication of an up-to-date edition of their directory *Points on Pick-ups*. This is an essential aid to every librarian and record dealer.

Obviously, with so many difficulties, some method of control is required to minimise wear to records issued from public libraries. The fate of valuable discs cannot be left in the hands of the majority of borrowers who are ill-informed about stylus wear, mono-stereo conversion and the general care of records and gramophones, and who believe only the information that will not cause them financial inconvenience. Firm control is required to get the maximum number of issues from costly records. In the libraries in the London Borough of Enfield the procedure set out below is carried out without difficulty, and despite the administrative problems in what is probably one of the largest gramophone record lending networks in existence a record life of 150 issues is quite common.

When issuing enrolment forms to would-be borrowers they should be asked what type of gramophone they possess and whether it is mono or stereo and the form marked accordingly. The rules and regulations regarding the use of the library (including information on the expected life of styli) are then handed to the borrower along with the membership form. When this is returned duly filled in, the mark on the form will give the assistant on duty the information he requires to proceed without questioning the borrower further.

*NOTE: users of existing mono Acos GP 91 series cartridges may convert them to mono compatible cartridges by fitting type S/C stylus.

The printed information issued with the form tells the user of both mono and stereo equipment fitted with sapphire styli that the styli have a very short life and that they should be produced for checking under a microscope at the commencement of borrowing and every six to eight weeks afterwards. Each time a stylus is checked the borrowers ticket is stamped so that both staff and public know when the last check was made. This avoids the danger of inadequate or infrequent checking. If a borrower delays too long in availing himself of this service, then borrowing facilities can reasonably be withheld. One badly worn or chipped stylus can ruin many library records in quite a short time and make them quite unplayable for other users. The printed leaflet handed to new borrowers should give the following information quoting authoritative sources:

1 Mono sapphire styli will play approximately thirty assorted $33\frac{1}{3}$ and 45 RPM records. Stereo points will play slightly less. Worn records do not affect the life of a stylus very much, but some auto changers, especially pre-1960 models, may shorten it by as much as 10 per cent. Checking will prove this.

2 Diamond needles costing approximately £2 or more are capable of playing over 2,000 records under ideal conditions. But styli costing as little as 12/- are very good value at the price and under reasonably good conditions will play thirty times as many records as a 6/- sapphire point. Diamonds only need checking every six months.

Borrower and staff must understand that a stylus undergoes tremendous stresses and changes of temperature for microseconds of time during playing. A needle with a tip radius of ·001 in and a downward pressure of 10 grammes is exerting a tremendous weight on its point if one calculates this pressure in terms of pounds to the square inch. The groove of the record causes the needle to zigzag as it follows the sound frequencies, and tremendous forces are exerted as it thrashes from side to side. Manufacturers of needles and discs advise replacement immediately loss of "tonal quality" is apparent. But by the time this is noticed, especially on a portable machine, severe damage has already been inflicted on quite a few records. Frequent inspection under a microscope is the only safeguard against this danger. A 12 in long-playing record has up to a mile of groove. Microphotographs show grooves to be full of delicate graining, but for a stylus this is a very rough path to travel along and sixty such journeys will leave its point very worn.

The manner in which artificial sapphires are made has already been explained and the differences in structure from that of natural stones pointed out. Man-made sapphire fractures easily and in wearing does not polish like diamond but tends to wear rapidly. A microscope with a magnification of 100X—300X must be installed in the library to enable accurate checking. An adjacent table lamp of the anglepoise type to provide additional light is essential. An ideal cheap microscope is the "Naturalist"*. It is not always possible to insist that styli are replaced the moment facets appear. This is setting too high a standard and will cause discontent among the borrowers faced with frequent replacement. However the best time for replacement is the point when the facets extend far enough down the tip of the stylus to affect the radius even though this may be very slight. The Philips Company once published a valuable little booklet containing the information that when a stylus is worn sufficiently for the point to reach the bottom of the groove the rate of wear on the record increases 600 per cent.

As all points are mass produced new needles should be checked before use. It is not unusual to find faulty or poorly finished styli, or even 78 RPM needles in LP packets. Although the quality of raw diamonds is much more dependable, it is sound practice to check them also. Colour coding paint or the fixative used in mounting may sometimes adhere to the playing tip of a needle and make it unsafe to use. In view of the overall advantages of using diamond styli (saving in money for the borrower and in checking time for library staff) borrowers should be encouraged to change over to them. The library authority that allowed only diamond needles to be used would be adopting the most sensible course of action.

There need be no difficulty in identifying the various types of styli, even though these often appear identical at first sight. Although there is no agreed coding system used by various companies making needles the following information will provide a useful starting point to help identify mono and stereo points whether sapphire or diamond. In the previous paragraph there was a reference to colour coding with paint. This is a method that many makers use to indicate the type of stylus being handled. The makers of Acos styli use the following system of marking needle blades.

78 RMP	Radius: ·002 in to ·003 in	
	SAPPHIRE	One green dot
	DIAMOND	Two green dots
LP Mono	Radius: ·0007 in to ·001 in plus	
	SAPPHIRE	One red dot
	DIAMOND	Two red dots
Stereo/Mono	Radius: ·0006 in to ·00075 in	
	SAPPHIRE	One blue dot
	DIAMOND	Two blue dots
Stereo	Radius: ·00045 in to ·0006 in	
	SAPPHIRE	One white dot
	DIAMOND	Two white dots

*This microscope is no longer available, but styli may be examined in the Philips Projection Stylus Tester, specially designed for this purpose. See also p.152. Editor, April 1970.

STYLUS WEAR

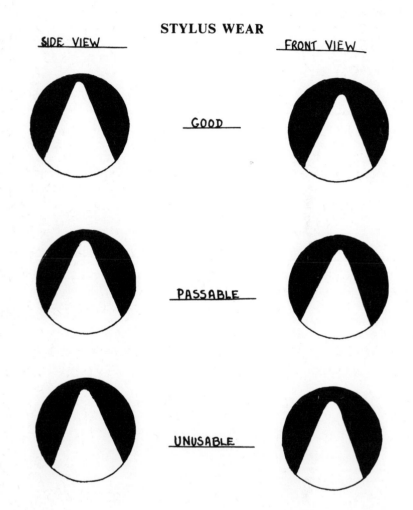

Fig. 22. *Sketch from photo-micrographs showing various stages of needle wear as viewed from front of the pick-up. Side view gives a clearer picture with light reflecting from worn facets and is recommended as the best method of examination.*

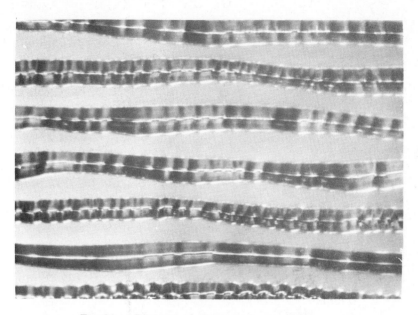

Fig. 23.   *Perfect long-playing microgroves.*

Fig. 24.   *Record played with worn stylus. Modulations have been swept out and grooves widened.*

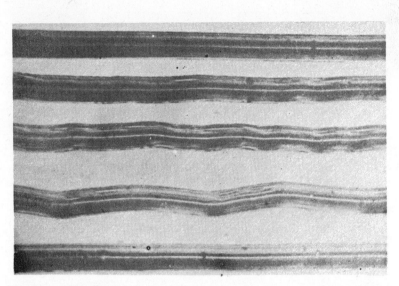

Fig. 25. *This disc has been played many times on a machine similar to that used in Fig. 24. The stylus was in perfect condition and the record shows remarkably little wear by comparison.*

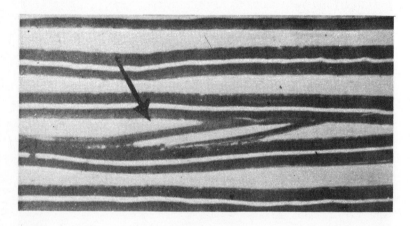

Fig. 26.

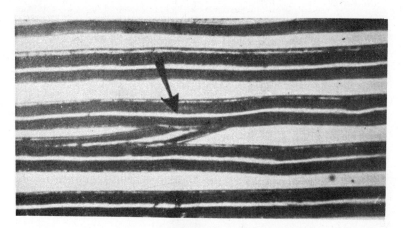

Fig. 27.

Fig. 28.

Figs. 26, 27 and 28 above, and 29 all show the effect of bad stylii and pickups. Arrows indicate the points where the pickups have been unable to trace the recorded wave-form and have cut their own tracks, ploughing from one point to another.

In the case of Figs. 26 and 27, a complete revolution of recorded sound has been skipped; the same fault in reverse causes repeating. In Figs. 28 and 29 a modulation has been ploughed through, resulting in a 'burping' sound occurring at these points.

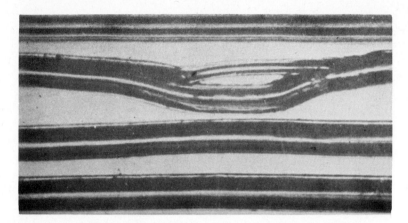

Fig. 29.

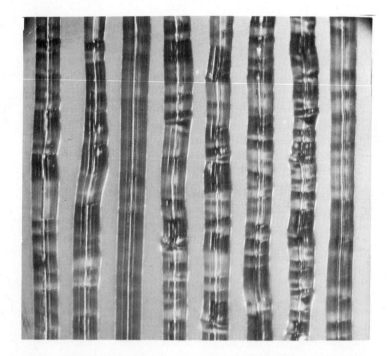

Fig. 30. *These are the grooves of a long playing record played with a worn stylus. It can be seen that the grooves are virtually stripped clean.*

150

Various manufacturers have different markings, but in the course of handling different makes one will learn what these are. Unfortunately some makers have become less discriminating with regard to tip-radius variation and one or two have given up coding. It is possible for styli suitable in size for the wider grooves of early long-playing records to find their way into stereo pick-ups. It is regrettable that the false claim that stereo discs can be played with any lightweight pick-up has added to confusion that already existed and needles of almost any size can be found in packets these days. The modification of groove widths over the past fifteen years made the variation of needle tip radii an acceptable and often welcome aid to the user. It is to be hoped that manufacturers will not use the latest development in the history of the gramophone to give up stating the radius of the point on the packet and trying to ensure that the contents are clearly labelled.

If an experienced member of staff finds that on checking a new needle for a pre-1960 mono pick-up, the radius is small enough to raise doubts about its durability in the cartridge in question, the borrower should be advised to get it changed. Should a point appear to be in the region of ·001 in and destined for the latest stereo cartridge then the owner should be given similar advice. Both cases will give a poorer standard of sound reproduction and a higher rate of wear than a point nearer to the correct size. How to distinguish sapphire points from diamond was covered earlier on and need not be repeated here.

The degree of success achieved with any checking system will depend upon the amount of knowledge that the librarian has regarding the many different makes and types of pick-up cartridges and the way in which the styli can be removed and replaced. Examination can often be carried out while the needle is still in the head, but sometimes the microscope cannot be brought into focus because the shell (or head casing) gets in the way. In these cases the needle must be removed from the pick-up head. Once the staff have acquired the necessary experience in this sphere they will be in a position to persuade the more timid members of the public that their gramophones will not disintegrate if the stylus has to be removed. This group of people, though usually well meaning, and careful, can cause a great deal of damage to the library's stock of records because they are too nervous to change a stylus. They prefer to wait until they can hear the worn needle before doing anything about it and I have previously mentioned how dangerous this is. Then they call a service-engineer to make the replacement they could have done for themselves. This represents a very easily earned fee for the engineer.

It is worth noting that dealers are not averse to deliberately omitting to supply the service manual with equipment so that the customer will be dependent on him for trivial maintenance. In nearly all cases the pick-up manufacturers intend that the user should carry out his own stylus replacement and that the cartridge is designed to this end. Time and again librarians will come across people, particularly old-age pensioners and older folk living alone, who have been told that any attempt to remove the stylus will cause dire trouble. This is untrue and such advice can only be given through ulterior motives, or ignorance, if one is to take a charitable view. The library staff can easily cope with such difficulties if they set up an advisory service, the main purpose of which is to protect library records. The first step is to compile a stylus replacement directory, listing all known pick-ups that are available with quick simple instructions on the removal and replacement of styli. This is not difficult to do. All styli sold by the Goldring Manufacturing Company have simple fitting instructions included in the box or packet for the particular needle. The Company is quite willing to supply a complete set of these on request. The slips are filed in the maker's number order and are used in conjunction with their price list, which serves as an identification guide. With this directory, library staff will have no difficulty in familiarising themselves with the appearance and method of replacement of most styli.

The few pick-ups not listed in the directory will be expensive high-quality types that will almost invariably be fitted with diamond styli. The owners of this type of equipment will usually be aware of the need for occasional checks, and, in most cases, will know how to remove the heads. Their willingness to let you handle the head will be a good indication of your success in creating an atmosphere of confidence.

To check the stylus it will be necessary to place the whole head under the microscope and with a little patience and ingenuity it will be possible to see the point from all angles. If the stylus is worn then the head has to be returned to the manufacturer for replacement. Gaps in the directory can be filled by making card entries with details of these and any new cartridges that come on the market to keep the file up to date.

Most members of the staff will have had encounters with school microscopes and know a little about using them. Separate styli can be mounted on slides in the required position by fixing them to a spot of plasticine. Contrary to the general opinion, points are best viewed from the side and not from the front. The latter method will often allow extensive wear to be missed with the type of low-powered magnification that has to be used for quick checking. The truth of this contention can be tested by viewing styli from both angles whenever time permits. The main points to remember about microscopes are as follows:

(a) Choose an instrument that is simple and uncomplicated. Avoid elaborate models and turret lenses.

(b) It should have a lens tube that can be raised sufficiently to pass a pick-up head between the lens and slide holder.

(c) Where possible have alternative lenses to increase the depth of the field of focus and eyepieces to increase the magnification.

(d) The best range of magnification is from 100X to 300X. Anything less will be useless, particularly when looking at stereo points. Magnification of much more than 200X reduces the depth of focus and the amount of light available.

(e) Always direct a beam of light from an anglepoise lamp close on to the reflector and the object to be viewed. Given such an instrument and a little practice, no stylus check need take more than 15—20 seconds.

For those readers who wish to venture into more advanced areas of knowledge on styli, cartridges, and record-playing problems than space allows me here, may I recommend *Pick-ups – The key to Hi-Fi* by John Walton? It is an admirable book and deals with a difficult subject in a most lucid fashion.

It follows, quite naturally, that some knowledge about the various types of pick-ups in current use would be helpful, as borrowers often ask about the merits and performance of one model compared with another. Full-time staff in the department should know a little about the magnetic, variable reluctance, crystal and ceramic cartridges: which current types are high or low impedance and the relative merits and uses to which they can be put, such as amplifier matching, what arms they can be put in, etc. For instance, crystal and ceramic can be matched to most types of equipment, but a borrower will be a little put out if he is advised to buy a magnetic cartridge only to discover he does not have a high gain amplifier. The borrowing public expect the librarian to know a little about such details and current developments. Apart from making for good public relations it creates a healthy respect for the lending service. It is bad for the public to feel that the staff are uninterested in sound reproduction. We obviously cannot set hi-fi standards but neither should we allow an atmosphere to develop that leads less fussy borrowers to feel that they can get away with carelessness. This will quickly lead to a decline in the service from which it would be hard to recover.

Methods similar to those used at Enfield are also in use at Walthamstow and Grimsby Public Libraries. In all three libraries high standards of quality have been maintained over periods of time that are evidence enough of the need for control on wear. It requires little thought to realise that the condition of styli is the only factor that can be controlled when the records are played on a wide variety of instruments that differ considerably in efficiency. Poorly maintained equipment and cheap auto-change mechanisms cannot be banned by the library, although some have imposed a ban on equipment costing less than £70. Unfortunate for the music lover who does not have £70 or more to spend on a gramophone!

The library should be open to use by everyone who has a machine and, provided the stylus is maintained in good condition, damage caused by mechanical failure will be kept to a minimum. This control can be exercised effectively in any reasonably organised system. Although it is not completely foolproof, it will keep the borrowers constantly aware of the need for care and will avoid the high rate of wear and damage found in those systems that take little or no direct action. When it is realised that the pressure of the stylus tip on the record can be in the order of several thousand pounds per square inch, then it is obvious that the stress on the record, even with a lightweight pick-up, is considerable. Add to this the fact that the irregularity of the groove makes the needle accelerate at speeds that cause it to become almost airborne for a considerable portion of the playing time on any record. Further, that the friction caused by forces, several times the force of gravity, causes the tip to reach temperatures near melting point for microsecond periods of time. All these factors confirm the need for a direct form of inspection.

All consideration of equipment beyond this point will, because of the difficulty of control, have less bearing on the question of wear in the library and is only necessary to form a reasonable background of knowledge in the running of the department.

Pick-up Arms

It is not uncommon for pick-up arms to be out of alignment, but trouble resulting from this margin of error will not be serious provided the needle does not become excessively worn. One will have to rely on the manufacturer, who will seldom be greatly at fault. This is a problem that can be greatly overestimated. However, one or two alignment protractors can be kept for loan to the public on request. These are available from various sources. It is far more essential to have one or two pick-up weighing devices available for loan, so that weight adjustments can be made when over weight is suspected. Frequent need for stylus replacement, every twenty sides or less, often indicates the need for adjustment. No auto-changer should track at more than 10 grammes for older machines, or less than 6 grammes for modern ones. With manual players the weight should be kept to that recommended by the maker of the cartridge for the arm in question. Attempts to track a lighter weight are to be discouraged as this can cause as much damage as over weight. Stroboscopes for testing motor speeds are also a legitimate library tool for loan.

Borrowers should be advised of the necessity of keeping the bearings of the pick-up arm clean and lightly oiled to avoid any lateral or vertical stiffness. Stiffness in the arm can cause severe damage to records. The public should be made aware that it is essential to keep the player perfectly level as this can be one of the causes of jumping and repeating when records are played. This is only occasionally heard, but is evidence of a constant unnecessary stress on the records being played. Some idea of the different types of arm and the efficiency of the performance of each can be useful on occasion. Information of this kind can be gained by reading the reviews of new equipment published in the *Gramophone*.

Amplification

Earlier in this section the hint was given that more details would be forthcoming on recording and recording characteristics and this seems to be the appropriate point to tackle the problem.

Early acoustic records were made on the constant velocity system which was quite satisfactory for records with a restricted frequency range. But when electrical recording came into being in 1925 new problems faced the recording engineer. If the cutter was allowed to etch the groove on the wax master without any control, the recorded sound would have been very uneven, and to contain the movement of the cutter the record, as previously stated, would have had to be as big as a cartwheel. The treble would have been smothered by the over-recorded bass and the upper frequencies would have been so weak that they would have been lost in the surface and background noise. New methods of recording were devised to overcome this problem and these methods have become known as recording characteristics. Briefly the engineer will, in the recording process, attenuate the bass from a certain frequency, downwards, so that the groove cut upon the disc will be contained within certain limits. At the same time, so that the treble will be properly balanced in playback, the engineer increases the strength of the treble frequency from a selected frequency upwards. This produces a correctly balanced treble in relation to the remainder of the recorded sound. It is obvious to the reader, that if the record were played back so that this corrected sound was reproduced, the result would be accentuated treble and hardly any bass.

This recording characteristic must be corrected in the first stage of amplification on any gramophone. So long as the idea is understood, it will not be necessary to go into detail. Sufficient to state that this work is carried out by the pre-amplifier. This description makes the whole process of recording characteristic appear deceptively simple, but there were snags involved, the chief one being that until 1956 no two companies making records throughout the world could agree upon a standard characteristic. Each group of companies selected different frequencies from which to attenuate their bass and different frequencies to boost the treble. Bass would be cut from anywhere between 700 down to 250 cycles per second, while treble would begin to be boosted anywhere from 1,500 cycles per second upwards. Gramophone designers compromised by making their instruments in such a way that all types of record sounded acceptable in playback. Designers of high-fidelity equipment increased the perfection of their equipment by providing channels that could be selected by press buttons to provide the exact playback compensation for the particular make of the record. For those who are still wondering, that is the purpose of those controls you have never used that are marked with such strange devices as NARTB, CCIR, AES, and RCA ortho, to name but a few!

The average borrower rarely knows the meaning of these terms and the unprepared librarian could easily be trapped by such questions as "Why are A Company's records not as good as B's?" It is essential to be able to answer the question intelligently. The quality of gramophone records varies very little in actual fact. It is usually the gramophone that is the variable and often inadequate factor. The complaints against certain makes of record are usually due to the borrower's machine being unable to cope with that recording characteristic. Librarians should be able to explain to borrowers that the records are not always at fault.

For the more ambitious reader a few more details may be welcome. The two basic systems of electrical recording are (a) constant amplitude, and (b) constant velocity of the stylus cutter. In the constant amplitude system the cutter displacement is in proportion to the amplitude of the driving voltage, and in the constant velocity system, the velocity is in proportion to the amplitude of the driving voltage. Neither system is ideal for the whole frequency range in disc-cutting.

Since the stereo recording process presented new difficulties in recording and reproduction, and to prevent the position becoming even more complex, in 1956 the major recording companies and recording engineers met together in Switzerland to standardise recording techniques for stereo and mono. Apart from adopting the present system for stereo, they agreed that in future only two recording characteristics should be used, that of CCIR and NARTB. All present-day recordings, both mono and stereo, are made under the particular combinations of constant amplitude and constant velocity that bear these initials. Only recordings made before this date will be subject to the considerable variants mentioned above.

Most early records were cut on the constant velocity system, but this system produces the fault already mentioned, of making the cutter travel too far in bass passages. Nowadays, indeed since the early days of electrical recording, it is the practice on reaching a certain point in the lower frequency range to switch over to constant amplitude. This is known as the turnover frequency. At the upper end of the range the engineers revert again to constant amplitude. This point may be anywhere between 2,000 and 5,000 CPS. Since the advent of long playing some companies — American Columbia and RCA, whose products are often marketed by Philips and Decca respectively in this country — have employed an additional twist at the lower tail end of the range by making a further change to constant velocity to increase the signal to noise ratio in the region of 50 to 100 CPS. Not all records have this, however.

To obtain good results from all records, the gramophone used should be capable of dealing with these corrections in recording, and reproducing a flat response. A pre-amplifier stage should be able to deal with the low frequency turnover and the treble roll-off. Only the most expensive gramophone amplifiers marketed as separate hi-fi units provide the number of channels required. Hence the reasons for the complaints from borrowers that certain records are not good or not as good as other makes. It just is not true. All records are of a reasonable standard, provided they are played on a gramophone that can do the job. Complaints arise from owners of equipment of a general nature sold at a low price as a commercial proposition. It is not reasonable to expect these commercial machines to be other than a compromise. I include a list of the various characteristics of gramophone records with the low frequency turnover and roll-off characteristics, as it can conceivably be of use in a library when queries arise on some pre-1956 records, historical re-issues, and "club" records.

TECHNICAL DATA

PRE-1956
LIST OF RECORDING CHARACTERISTICS

These still apply to many discs still in current catalogues and to many re-issues and "club" records, issued under labels different from the original company and where a new master has not been cut.

MAKER	TYPE OF RECORD	TURNOVER	ROLL OFF
Angel	33	NARTB	AES
Allegro	33	LP	NARTB
AnRTB	AES		
Atlantic	33	NARTB	NARTB
Caedmon	33	NARTB	NARTB
Capitol	33	AES	AES
	45	NARTB	AES
	78	AES	AES
Capitol-Soria	33	AES	AES
Cetra-Soria	33	LP	NARTB
Columbia	33	LP	NARTB
	45	NARTB	NARTB
	78	AES	NARTB
Concert Hall	33	LP	NARTB
Cook	33	NARTB	AES
Decca	33	AES	AES
	45	AES	AES
	78	AES	AES

MAKER	TYPE OF RECORD	TURNOVER	ROLL OFF
Elektra	33	NARTB	NARTB
EMI	33	AES	AES
Handel Society	33	LP	NARTB
Haydn Society	33	LP	NARTB
London	33	LP	AES
Mercury	33	AES	AES
	45	AES	AES
	78	AES	AES
MGM	33	NARTB	NARTB
	45	NARTB	NARTB
	78	NARTB	NARTB
RCA Victor	33	ORTHO (NARTB)	ORTHO (AES)
	45	ORTHO (NARTB)	ORTHO (AES)
	78	ORTHO (NARTB)	ORTHO (AES)
Remington	33	NARTB	NARTB
Stradivari	33	LP	NARTB

General Care of Records

Any library lending stereo records will have to operate a checking system for styli to make sure that borrowers have the correct playing equipment. Without some precaution records would rapidly be torn to pieces. When the stylus has been checked the borrower should be issued with a ticket that instantly indicates that he is able to borrow all types of records, including stereo. This will avoid stereo records being issued to "mono-only" borrowers during busy periods. Frequent checks of stereo sapphire points are necessary as the average life of a stylus, used on other than transcription equipment, is little more than ten to twenty records. To safeguard records, borrowers should be advised to use a diamond stylus with a tip radius of ·0007 in. Under reasonable conditions stereo discs have a useful life that is only about 25 per cent shorter than mono.

Dirt and dust are the greatest enemies of records and styli. PVC is very subject to static charges which attract dust to the surface of the disc. This factor increases wear to record and stylus to a very considerable degree. The tendency to static charges can be eliminated by using a device called the Manual Parastat, which is made by Cecil Watts of Darby House, Sunbury on Thames, Middlesex. No library should issue records without treating them with this device when they are purchased. The cleaning treatment should be repeated as often as possible *without* fluid, with the large Parastat machine where a library has one. Periodic treatments with the machine will prolong the life of the records.

Provided the surfaces of the records are not handled or fingermarked in any way by staff or public, it will only be necessary to dust the records on return with a silk cloth. Constant use of anti-static fluids, detergents, and water is harmful and should be avoided.

Records issued to the public under the conditions suggested in the foregoing pages will have a substantially increased life. The library stock will be able to increase to reasonable proportions even on a modest budget. In time records of historical importance can be withdrawn, while still in reasonable condition, to help form the basis of an interesting reference collection, without robbing the main stock. There will be no need to continue to issue records that are damaged or misused once this stage is reached. The stock can, and should be maintained in perfect condition. Once borrowers begin to experience the benefits of a well-run library the staff will begin to receive an ever increasing measure of co-operation from the public.

Tapes

During the past few years we have been able to observe a dramatic increase in the use of magnetic tape. Domestic recorders have improved to a level of efficiency beyond comparison with machines of ten years ago. It is a matter for regret that no sustained attempt has been made by any library to devise a public-lending scheme for tapes. Some schools of librarianship give token instruction in the administration and care of gramophone records but I know of none that give any guidance on tapes. This is a sad state of affairs when one considers that many young people entering the profession now, will, in ten years or so, be handling collections of material in this form. They will have to learn by trial and error. It seems wrong, when there is enough information available to give some helpful instruction on the subject. Tape is being used in increasing quantities in industry and education and librarians in these fields will be the first to have extensive collections of taped material in their care.

In the public library sector there has been an attitude of "wait and see" and "is anyone else doing anything?" for too long now. It is time to take a look at available materials and start pilot lending schemes. There will be problems, just as there are with lending discs, but I do not feel that these will be as difficult to cope with as many librarians seem to think. The problems of visual checking and accidental erasure are the two most common arguments offered against provision. I do not think these points are as vital as some people would have us believe. Most modern tape machines have excellent safeguards against spilling or breaking tape and all are fitted with press-button locking devices that prevent accidental erasure. The public does not consist of vandals but, in my experience anyway, of careful and responsible people. Nearly twenty years of lending records has not diminished my belief that this is so.

The problems that need some attention are those of storage and ageing of tapes in the library. Outside the library two other points arise. First, and most important, is the matter of damage to the recorded sound caused by replay heads that need cleaning and defluxing. Secondly, of poorly rewound tapes. The former problem can cause the build-up of background noise on the tape similar to needle wear on discs. The cure is simply to clean and deflux the heads. Cleaning is easy enough. One can buy a device to deflux heads from any tape-recorder dealer, but this can be done without going to this expense if one possesses a hairdryer, electric razor, or similar gadget. Switch the dryer or razor on and approach the tape heads; pass it over the heads and then retreat from the recorder before switching off. Anyone catching you in the act will probably be amused, but the reduction of background noise will be worth any derision! To ask borrowers to do this will be easier and more entertaining than checking styli. On the matter of poorly rewound tapes, I have little helpful to suggest except to point out that it is not an awfully serious problem and new tape machines on the market show a continued improvement on this point of performance.

To return to the question of storage and preservation of cellulose-acetate and Mylar base tapes, it is necessary to remember that collections of material for loan and sound archives will have a much longer expectation of useful life than constantly used disc collections. The need to safeguard tapes will be as essential in the future as the preservation of written and printed archives. The information covering this subject is rather too detailed to elaborate on here at the present time of scant provision. This will not be the case for many more years, however, and students and librarians could not do better than consult the section on Magnet Tape in *The Preservation and Storage of Sound Recordings* by A. G. Pickett and M. M. Lemcoe, before taking charge of any collection of tapes.

The increase in availability of instructional courses and music in tape cassettes for use on special replay machines without erasure facilities is a significant trend. Many of these do not have to be rewound after use. Schools, colleges, and universities are employing tape now not only for languages but for all forms of instruction. Librarians will need to be trained to take a proper role in these developments.

As far as training for librarianship is concerned I feel that there is too little attention given to the increasing role that audio-visual aids will play in the coming years. A few lectures on computer-programming and photo-charging represent the extent to which librarianship has moved into the twentieth century. The book was man's only means of storing and communicating information for centuries, but in the last twenty years events have moved so fast that within two or three decades domestic video-tape machines will be as common as the piano in the Victorian drawing-room. Methods of education and the use of leisure time will be completely transformed. Librarianship has the choice either to ignore the portents or to go forward to meet the challenge of the inevitable. All developments should be examined, and all efforts made to train new librarians to take their place in a changing world. Even now, should music librarians be entirely responsible for instructional records on painless childbirth and recorded Latin readers? Surely all librarians should be trained in the methods set out in the foregoing pages, so that recordings of plays, poetry, history, etc., could be shelved in the appropriate places in the library and the music librarian be allowed to be just that, and not jack of all trades? The information I have set out here makes it possible. I feel that we should all try.

A Basic Stock List

by JOAN PEMBERTON SMITH, MA, ALA
formerly Librarian, British Institute of Recorded Sound

The following is a list of 400 recommended works which should be represented in any average record library, and is intended as a guide for librarians with little knowledge of music who may be deputed to start a library from scratch.

The first important point to clarify is that this is a list of *works*, not recordings, and this is intentional, since it is obvious that a list of recommended recordings becomes out-of-date before it is even printed; this list of works, however, should be a permanent guide to the librarian who cannot easily decide from his own knowledge which works to prefer, when money is limited. New recordings of standard works are constantly being produced, and the librarian is directed to the many books and periodicals which give constructive advice on them. Since the works given in this list are mainly in what is termed the "standard concert repertoire", there should be little difficulty in tracing recordings.

It will not be difficult to spot gaps in this list: there are, fortunately for musicians, rather more than 400 good works in the musical repertoire, and deciding what to leave out becomes a heart-searching task. What I have tried to do is to make the list both standard and representative – that is to say, I have included as many popular works as possible, since these will always be in demand, but at the same time I have included several works which do not come into this category, but which are representative of a country or a musical style, so that the collection is fairly balanced, rather than weighted in favour merely of works which would give a boost to the library statistics. This has meant sacrificing another Sullivan operetta in favour of representing Kurt Weill, and giving a place to American composers by cutting down on Britten and Vaughan Williams.

Operas get a good representation in this list, as I think most librarians will find them in great demand. After deliberation I have had, for reasons of space, to exclude music before the time of Bach (with the one exception of Monteverdi), as it is difficult to recommend isolated works here, and much is still unrecorded. Librarians are advised to build up in

162

this field later, with reference to the Deutsche Grammophon Gesellschaft Archive Series.

Of the 400 works given here, 200 are marked with an asterisk, indicating that these are the ones to be given priority in an initial selection. Where I have used titles such as "Miscellaneous songs" I intend to suggest that a recital record of various well known songs should be bought, for example, of Dietrich Fischer-Dieskau singing a selection of Schubert's songs; such a collection, as also some short overtures, have been counted here as one item. Opus numbers and keys I have given only where essential to the identification of the work. Titles are given in the original language, where this is French, German, Italian, or Spanish, and in English for works in other languages: where there is an accepted English title I have given this in brackets. Foreign musical terms, such as "Oratorium", "Konzert", "Sinfonia", are translated into English. Finally, the works under each composer are grouped in the order in which they appear in Grove's *Dictionary*, i.e. operatic, choral, orchestral, chamber, instrumental, vocal.

BACH	Christmas Oratorio
	Mass in B minor
	*Passion according to St. Matthew
	Church cantata no. 21
	Church cantata no. 80
	Church cantata no. 140
	Motet: Jesu meine Freude
	Brandenburg concerto no. 1
	Brandenburg concerto no. 2
	*Brandenburg concerto no. 3
	Brandenburg concerto no. 4
	*Brandenburg concerto no. 5
	*Brandenburg concerto no. 6
	Suite no. 3 in D
	Concerto for piano and orchestra no. 1 in D minor
	Concerto for violin and orchestra in E major
	*Concerto for 2 violins and orchestra in D minor
	Goldberg variations
	Miscellaneous keyboard works
	*Miscellaneous organ works including Toccata and fugue in D minor
BARBER	Adagio for strings

BARTOK

*Concerto for orchestra
Concerto for violin and orchestra
*Music for strings, percussion, and celesta
Sonata for 2 pianos and percussion
Quartet for strings no. 2
Quartet for strings no. 6

BEETHOVEN

Fidelio
Mass in D
Selection of overtures (*Leonora* no. 3, *Egmont, Coriolanus*)
Symphony no. 1
Symphony no. 2
*Symphony no. 3 (*Eroica*)
*Symphony no. 4
*Symphony no. 5
*Symphony no. 6 (*Pastoral*)
*Symphony no. 7
*Symphony no. 8
*Symphony no. 9 (*Choral*)
Concerto for piano and orchestra no. 1
Concerto for piano and orchestra no. 2
*Concerto for piano and orchestra no. 3
*Concerto for piano and orchestra no. 4
*Concerto for piano and orchestra no. 5 (*Emperor*)
*Concerto for violin and orchestra
Septet
*Trio for piano and strings op. 97 (*Archduke*)
Quartet for strings op. 18 no. 4
*Quartet for strings op. 59 no. 1
Quartet for strings op. 95
Quartet for strings op. 127
Quartet for strings op. 130
Quartet for strings op. 131
*Quartet for strings op. 132
*Quartet for strings op. 135
*Sonata for violin and piano op. 47 (*Kreutzer*)
Sonata for violin and piano op. 96
Sonata for cello and piano op. 69
Sonata for cello and piano op. 102 no. 1
*Sonata for piano op. 13 (*Pathétique*)

*Sonata for piano op. 27 (*Moonlight*)
*Sonata for piano op. 53 (*Waldstein*)
*Sonata for piano op. 57 (*Appassionata*)
Sonata for piano op. 101
Sonata for piano op. 106
(*Hammerclavier*)
Sonata for piano op. 109
Sonata for piano op. 110
Sonata for piano op. 111

BELLINI   *Norma*

BERG   *Wozzeck*
                 *Concerto for violin and orchestra

BERLIOZ   *La Damnation de Faust*
                 L'Enfance du Christ (The Childhood of
                 Christ)
                 *Symphonie fantastique
                 Harold en Italie

BIZET   *Carmen*
                 *Symphony in C
                 L'Arlésienne suites

BLOCH   *Schelomo*

BORODIN   *Prince Igor*
                 *Symphony no. 2
                 Quartet for strings no. 2

BRAHMS   Symphony no. 1
                 *Symphony no. 2
                 Symphony no. 3
                 *Symphony no. 4
                 *Variations on a theme of Haydn
                 *Concerto for piano and orchestra no. 1
                 *Concerto for piano and orchestra no. 2
                 Concerto for violin and orchestra
                 *Concerto for violin, cello and orchestra
                 *Quintet for clarinet and strings
                 4 *Ernste Gesänge* (4 serious songs)
                 Miscellaneous songs

BRITTEN

*Peter Grimes
*War Requiem
Spring symphony
*Young person's guide to the orchestra
*Serenade for tenor, horn, and strings

BRUCKNER

Mass in F minor
Symphony no. 5
*Symphony no. 7
*Symphony no. 9

CARTER

Orchestral variations
*Quartet for strings no. 1

CHABRIER

*España

CHOPIN

Sonata for piano in B flat minor
*Miscellaneous piano works (waltzes, nocturnes, polonaises, studies)

COPLAND

*El salón Mexico
Rodeo

DEBUSSY

*Pelléas et Mélisande
Images for Orchestra
*La Mer
*Prélude à l'après-midi d'un faune
Preludes for piano

DELIUS

*On Hearing the First Cuckoo in Spring
Paris
Summer night on the River

DOHNANYI

Variations on a nursery tune

DONIZETTI

*L'Elisir d'amore
*Lucia di Lammermoor

DUKAS

*L'Apprenti Sorcier (The Sorcerer's Apprentice)

DVORAK

Slavonic dances
*Symphony no. 4 (8) op. 88 in G
*Symphony no. 5 (9) op. 95 in E minor

(from the *New World*)
*Concerto for cello and orchestra
Quartet for strings op. 96 (*American*)
Quintet for piano and strings op. 81

ELGAR

The Dream of Gerontius
Falstaff
Introduction and allegro for strings
*Symphony no. 1
Symphony no. 2
*Variations on an original theme (*Enigma*)
*Concerto for cello and orchestra

FALLA

El Amor Brujo
El Sombrero de Tres Picos (The Three-
cornered hat)
7 Spanish popular songs

FAURE

Requiem

FRANCK

*Symphony
*Symphonic variations
Sonata for violin and piano

GERSHWIN

Porgy and Bess

GLINKA

*Overture: *Ruslan and Ludmila*

GLUCK

Orfeo ed Euridice

GOUNOD

Faust

GRIEG

Peer Gynt suites
*Concerto for piano and orchestra

HANDEL

Messiah
Music for the Royal Fireworks
Water Music
Concerti grossi op. 6
Concerto for organ and orchestra op. 4,
no. 4
Selection of operatic arias

HARRIS

Symphony no. 3

HAYDN

Die Schöpfung (The Creation)
Mass no. 9 in D minor (*Nelson*)
Symphony no. 45 (*Farewell*)
*Symphony no. 88
Symphony no. 92 (*Oxford*)
*Symphony no. 94 (*Surprise*)
Symphony no. 96 (*Miracle*)
*Symphony no. 100 (*Military*)
*Symphony no. 101 (*Clock*)
*Symphony no. 102
*Symphony no. 103 (*Drum Roll*)
*Symphony no. 104 (*London*)
*Quartet for strings op. 64 no. 5 (*Lark*)
Quartets for strings op. 74
*Quartets for strings op. 76
Quartets for strings op. 77

HINDEMITH

*Concert music for brass and strings
Mathis der Maler: symphony
Nobilissima visione
*Symphonic metamorphoses on themes by Weber

HOLST

The Planets

HUMPERDINCK

Hänsel und Gretel

IRELAND

Concerto for piano and orchestra

IVES

Sonata for piano no. 2 (*Concord*)

JANACEK

The Diary of One who Vanished
Sinfonietta

KODALY

Hary Janos
Psalmus Hungaricus

LALO

Symphonie espagnole

LEHAR

Die Lustige Witwe

LEONCAVALLO

Pagliacci

LISZT

*Concerto for piano and orchestra no. 1

Concerto for piano and orchestra no. 2
A Symphony to Dante's *Divina Commedia*
A *Faust* symphony
Les Préludes
Miscellaneous piano pieces

MAHLER

Das Lied von der Erde (The Song of the Earth)
*Symphony no. 1
*Symphony no. 4
Kindertotenlieder (Songs on the Death of Infants)
Lieder eines Fahrenden Gesellen (Songs of a Wayfaring Lad)

MASCAGNI

Cavalleria Rusticana

MASSENET

Manon

MENDELSSOHN

*Elijah
A Midsummer Night's Dream: incidental music
Symphony no. 3 (*Scottish*)
*Symphony no. 4 (*Italian*)
*Overture: *Fingal's Cave*
*Concerto for violin and orchestra
Octet

MONTEVERDI

Vespers

MOZART

Così Fan Tutte
Die Entführung aus dem Serail (Il Seraglio)
Don Giovanni
Le Nozze di Figaro (The Marriage of Figaro)
Die Zauberflöte (The Magic flute)
Requiem
Symphony no. 31 (*Paris*)
Symphony no. 35 (*Haffner*)
Symphony no. 36 (*Linz*)
*Symphony no. 38 (*Prague*)
*Symphony no. 39

*Symphony no. 40
*Symphony no. 41 (*Jupiter*)
*Concerto for clarinet and orchestra
Concerto for horn and orchestra K.447
Concerto for horn and orchestra K.495
Concerto for piano and orchestra K.450
*Concerto for piano and orchestra K.466
*Concerto for piano and orchestra K.467
*Concerto for piano and orchestra K.482
*Concerto for piano and orchestra K.488
*Concerto for piano and orchestra K.491
*Concerto for piano and orchestra K.503
Concerto for piano and orchestra K.537
(Coronation)
*Concerto for piano and orchestra K.595
*Concerto for violin and orchestra K.219
Sinfonia concertante for violin, viola and
orchestra, K.364
*Eine Kleine Nachtmusik
*Quintet for clarinet and strings
Quintet for strings K.515
Quintet for strings K.516
Quintet for piano and wind K.452
Quartet for strings K.421
Quartet for strings K.464
Quartet for strings K.465

MUSSORGSKY

Boris Godunov
Night on a Bare Mountain
Pictures from an Exhibition

NIELSEN

Symphony no. 5

OFFENBACH

Orphée aux enfers (Orpheus in the underworld)
Les Contes d'Hoffmann (The Tales of Hoffmann)

ORFF

Carmina Burana

PROKOFIEV

*Symphony no. 1 (*Classical*)
Symphony no. 5
Peter and the Wolf
Suite: *Love of Three Oranges*

*Concerto for piano and orchestra no. 3

PUCCINI
La Bohème
Madama Butterfly
Tosca
Turandot

PURCELL
Dido and Aeneas
Ode for St. Cecilia's Day

RACHMANINOV
*Concerto for piano and orchestra no. 1
*Concerto for piano and orchestra no. 2
*Rhapsody on a theme of Paganini
Preludes for piano

RAVEL
Bolero
Daphnis et Chloé
Rapsodie Espagnole
La Valse
*Concerto for piano and orchestra
Concerto for piano (left hand) and orchestra

RIMSKY-KORSAKOV
Capriccio Espagnol
Golden Cockerel: suite
Scheherazade

ROSSINI
Il Barbiere di Siviglia (The Barber of Seville)
Selection of overtures, including *La Gazza ladra, Guillaume Tell, La Scala di Seta*
La Boutique Fantasque

ROUSSEL
Symphony no. 4

RUBBRA
Symphony no. 5

SAINT-SAENS
Carnaval des Animaux
Introduction and rondo capriccioso for violin and orchestra

SCARLATTI, D.
Sonatas for harpsichord (selection)

SCHOENBERG

Pierrot Lunaire
5 Orchestral pieces op. 16
Concerto for violin and orchestra
Verklärte Nacht
Quartet for strings no. 1
Quartet for strings no. 2

SCHUBERT

Rosamunde
Symphony no. 4 (*Tragic*)
Symphony no. 5˙
*Symphony no. 8 (*Unfinished*)
*Symphony no. 9 (also called no. 7)
Octet
*Quintet for strings op. 163
*Quintet for piano and strings (Trout)
*Quartet for strings in D minor (Death and the maiden)
Trio for piano and strings op. 99
Sonata for piano in B flat D.960
Die Schöne Müllerin
*Die Winterreise
*Miscellaneous songs

SCHUMANN

*Symphony no. 1
*Symphony no. 4
*Concerto for piano and orchestra
Quintet for piano and strings op. 44
Carnaval, for piano
Dichterliebe
*Miscellaneous songs

SESSIONS

Quartet for strings no. 2

SHOSTAKOVICH

*Symphony no. 5
*Symphony no. 10
Concerto for violin and orchestra
Concerto for cello and orchestra no. 1
Quintet for piano and strings

SIBELIUS

*Symphony no. 1
*Symphony no. 2
*Symphony no. 5
*Symphony no. 7
En Saga

Karelia suite
Tapiola
*Concerto for violin and orchestra

SMETANA

The Bartered bride
My country (*Ma Vlast*)

STRAUSS, J.

Die Fledermaus (The Bat)
Selection of waltzes

STRAUSS, R.

Elektra
Der Rosenkavalier
Salome
Don Juan
Don Quixote
Ein Heldenleben
Till Eulenspiegel
Four last songs

STRAVINSKY

The Rake's Progress
Symphony of psalms
*Symphony in C
*Symphony in three movements
Firebird
Petrushka
Pulcinella
The Rite of Spring
The Soldier's Tale
Concerto for piano and wind instruments

SULLIVAN

The Gondoliers
Iolanthe
The Mikado
Patience

TCHAIKOVSKY

Eugene Onegin
Nutcracker: suite
Sleeping Beauty
Swan Lake
*Symphony no. 4
*Symphony no. 5
*Symphony no. 6 (*Pathétique*)
*Italian capriccio
Romeo and Juliet
Serenade for strings

1812 overture
*Concerto for piano and orchestra no. 1
Concerto for piano and orchestra no. 2
*Concerto for violin and orchestra

THOMPSON   *Louisiana Story*

TIPPETT   Concerto for double string orchestra

VAUGHAN WILLIAMS   *Symphony no. 1 (*Sea symphony*)
Symphony no. 2 (*London*)
Symphony no. 4
*Symphony no. 5
*Fantasia on a theme of Tallis
*Fantasia on *Greensleeves*
The Lark Ascending*

VERDI   *Aida
Falstaff
Otello
*Rigoletto
*La Traviata
*Il Trovatore
Requiem*

VIVALDI   *4 Concerti for violin and orchestra (*The Four Seasons*)

WAGNER   *Das Rheingold*
Die Walküre
Siegfried
Götterdämmerung (The Twilight of the Gods)
Der Fliegende Holländer (The Flying Dutchman)
Lohengrin
Die Meistersinger (The Mastersingers)
Parsifal
Tristan und Isolde
Siegfried idyll

WALTON   *Belshazzar's Feast*
Façade
*Symphony no. 1

Concerto for viola and orchestra
Concerto for violin and orchestra

WEBER

*Der Freischütz
Selection of overtures including *Oberon*
and *Euryanthe*

WEBERN

5 Orchestral pieces op. 10

WEILL

Die Dreigroschenoper (The Threepenny
Opera)

WOLF

Italian serenade for string quartet
Miscellaneous songs

Gramophone Record Selection Withdrawal and Replacement—General

by JOHN MORGAN, BA, ALA

Head of Music Services, Camden Public Libraries

Basic

The cumulation into one integrated and organised whole of any large number of units is a task not lightly undertaken. The basis of any structural undertaking is proverbially that of a good foundation and this is no less true for bibliographical projects than for architectural ones; indeed, the analogy is a close one. An inexperienced librarian who allows personal bias and lack of knowledge, albeit unknowingly (especially this), to comprise the foundation stones of his stock is building a veritable house of cards; balance, perspective, relationship between parts – all these characteristics are fundamental to a live, growing collection and as they are capable of being achieved objectively are not subject to personal whim and fancy. The basis of any private collection whether it be of books, paintings, records or of anything else must be that of the personal requirements of the collector, otherwise the material can have little significance; after all, as the enthusiast is spending his own money there can be little complaint if his records are entirely of Italian opera, whilst the stock held in a retail shop must bear some relationship to potential sales and this based on past experience – no customer wants to be told *every* time that his requirements can be met within 24 hours. Similarly, the gramophone record librarian has to set his own yardstick, his own basis for initial purchases and further growth. This, of course, is not to say that personal prejudice is after all the prime factor involved as this would produce unbalanced "balloonings" of stock; it does means that the librarian will have to exercise his own initiative to acquire the kind of stock that is both attractive for his own borrowers and (perhaps far more important) not only representative of the field covered but full of "shoots" to encourage and assist exploration.

No two librarians will agree in every aspect of their approach and it would be inhibiting for us all if it were so. But although complete conformity would make any professional activity stillborn there is still

176

much common ground. Thus, if one is forming a jazz collection the omission of any available Ellington records of the 1927–30 vintage would be as cardinal an error as omitting the plays of Shakespeare from a collection of speech records; "classical" music would have to have adequate representation from the pre-classical, classical, romantic, and modern periods as well as from formal, geographical, instrumental, and artist standpoints – but the relative importance placed on each of these is very much a matter for the individual librarian. It is not too difficult to estimate the importance of Ellington and Shakespeare, but the priorities for Bud Powell, Kenny Ball, Clifford Brown, Lionel Hampton – or Betjeman, Auden, Hopkins, Amis, require rather more thought. It is, however, towards the common ground that this paper is directed: to investigate what any borrower is entitled to find in any one field of recording.

Most record librarians will be presented with a *fait accompli* in that the terms of reference for the collection and the vote allocated will already have been decided by their Committee. It would be as well at this stage, however, to mention the possibilities with which they may be confronted.

VOTE. The finances will almost certainly be considered inadequate to provide a good service but within the context of permanent pressure upon one's Chief Librarian for more money there is still no reason why a balanced stock cannot be bought. Indeed, as long as a working minimum is not transgressed the smaller the vote the easier it is often enough to make decisions concerning the prime necessities of an initial stock; but when this minimum is considered by a council as nothing more than a means of obtaining a "glamour" service, difficulties of post-basic selection and maintenance are immeasurably increased. There seems little point in trying to estimate what is an "adequate" figure with which to start a service as conditions and requirements vary so considerably – a new service in a London borough, for instance, could not possibly be quoted in the same terms as an expansion of an existing service in a branch of a small town. One's whole outlook on the problem of initial selection is conditioned by what *is* provided and it is much more important to relate the available money, whatever it may be, to providing good foundations for a growing stock structure. By all means press for a larger vote when you think it necessary but don't be blind to the fact that the "bird in hand" can still be used in a professional way.

TERMS OF REFERENCE.   Or what you will be expected to buy. The possibilities presented by the gramophone record industry are legion: classical, light classical, popular orchestral and vocal, "pop", film and stage, speech in many languages, documentary, jazz, language tuition, children's, humour, educational, "imports", traditional and modern folk, sporting, demonstration, historical, "special lists", clubs and societies, national and exotic, religious, medical, mono, stereo, 45, 33, 7 in, 10 in, 12 in . . . and so on. Almost certainly classical requirements will be basic, but there is every evidence these days that expansion into other forms is taking place rapidly. The attitude that gramophone records could only be a legitimate part of the library stock as long as they were of serious classical music material is, fortunately, mainly in the past. Jazz is no longer infra dig, whilst modern folk styles, theatrical and film productions, and even the latest railway saga are all recognised as important borrowing material – they all represent somebody's interests and as such may be the means by which any one borrower is introduced to the remainder of the stock. Neither speed nor size of disc has material bearing on stock purchase (except possibly that purchases for a children's department might well be mainly 7 in discs; it might also be worth a mention at this point that about 80 per cent of the adult 45 RPM records on the market today are excerpts from parent LPs and are, in consequence, often uneconomic purchases) – the main consideration of the gramophone record librarian being content.

As the main problems of basic stock selection are associated with classical purchases, suggested techniques will refer to this group of recordings, but other groups will be mentioned in the section on "Post-basic Selection". Analysis of the stock of any gramophone record library which includes classical works reveals certain characteristics. You would always find in various proportions orchestral, vocal, choral, instrumental, chamber, and operatic works, not only in complete recordings but also in "recital" (where the artist is often of primary consideration) and "highlight" format, the latter, mercifully, relating mainly to operas; this is not to say that no records are issued nowadays of excerpts from other large-scale works, but those that are released are either aimed at the educational market or at those people newly investigating the classics. This analysis would further disclose greater proportions of titles by Bach, Beethoven, Brahms, Mozart, Schubert, Tchaikovsky, and Wagner, than by Palestrina, Berlioz, Franck, Reger, Scriabin, Weber, and Wolf – not because the latter are intrinsically less important within their own spheres of work, but because they assume less relative importance in musical development as a whole. Furthermore, the nineteenth century would absorb a fair percentage of the stock, followed by the eighteenth and twentieth centuries, whilst Germany, France, Italy, and England would be better represented than Spain, America, Finland, and Denmark. These are reasonably indisputable facts, but in themselves are evidence of the many-sided approach to balancing stock. Any attempt to reconcile all these elements in one and the same operation is not really a practical proposition and it is necessary to decide which is the most important aspect: instrumental/formal, composer, chronological, geographical, or any other; once the basic stock is formed from any one of these points of view alterations of details can be made later to reconcile the balancing of the other aspects. There is, of course, something to be said in favour of using any one of these approaches. There is much nationalism in music apart from national characteristics expressed in specific forms, i.e. Italian opera, German lieder, Spanish dances. The various historical periods, again, have particular qualities, each of which need adequate representation, and it goes without saying that a very large number of specific composers must be included.

But, for all this, I consider the instrumental/formal aspect the primary one. Of necessity, composers lived in a country at one period of time, but, whilst reflecting this to a greater or lesser extent, the nature of their output was still entirely personal; much was poured into the crucible of instrumental and vocal development within structural frameworks, moulding and improving them as they were touched by the personality of the artist. The symphonic structure served the different approaches of Boyce and Mahler; the concerto reflects large-scale contrasts and complements in Telemann and Bartok; the intimate, dramatic, and so many other aspects of human nature find expression in this approach, which has been used by composers since some form of organisation was found necessary to communicate extended musical thought. It is, for me at least, one of the broadest and least vulnerable bases not only for initial stock building but also for further development.

The Instrumental/Formal Approach to Basic Stock Selection

INITIAL STAGES.   The principal divisions are vocal and non-vocal, but these are so general that they can have little practical significance and require further breaking down. Under vocal works are included opera, choral, and songs, whilst the non-vocal group consists of orchestral, instrumental, and chamber pieces. They may be conveniently tabulated as follows, together with a further subdivision necessary for our purposes:

VOCAL		Opera
		Choral works
		Lieder & other small-scale works
NON-VOCAL	Orchestral	Symphonies
		Concertos
		Miscellaneous
	Instrumental	Piano
		Violin
		'Cello
		Guitar
		Others

NON-VOCAL   Chamber   Works with piano
                                                    Works without piano
                                                        or
                                                    Trios/quartets/quintets/
                                                    sextets/others

Each of these subdivisions is sufficiently important to be considered separately; as they will eventually comprise 100 per cent of the stock, at this stage it is necessary to estimate their relative importance. It might fairly be said that there will be more orchestral than instrumental works – but how much more? Also, that there will be fewer chamber than vocal works – but how much less? The librarian to whom opera is "the greatest" or guitar music basic diet must beware personal prejudice at this point and approach the problem as objectively as possible. The following suggestions for a skeleton stock structure, in percentages, are based on experience in a library where borrowers' interests range widely and where no one record can be expected to be static for any length of time and are subject to the variation shown in brackets:

	per cent	*variation per cent*
VOCAL	45	(4)
ORCHESTRAL	35	(3)
INSTRUMENTAL	5	(1)
CHAMBER	12	(2)
RESERVE	3	(–)

This is to say that I consider that 33–36 per cent of the stock should comprise orchestral music and that, for practical purposes, these figures should also be the basis for the financial breakdown. Thus, if the vote was £500, approx. £175 (i.e. £168–£182) should be devoted to orchestral music – the remainder *pro rata*. The "reserve" section needs little explanation; it is merely the means by which difficult decisions of inclusion and exclusion are more easily circumvented. It should, however, be said here that when stereophonic records only are being considered, both vocal and instrumental proportions are likely to be drastically revised – as songs and solo instruments have less significance in stereo versions than do symphonies, string quartets, concertos, and operas. With the above suggestions in mind, however, it should not be too difficult to revise the percentages in the light of stereo requirements. If to the more experienced music librarian this application of what has been called the "statistical approach" seems like a negation of the very necessary personal touches in stock selection, I would still find it surprising if the final balance in any gramophone record library radically differed from that proposed, whichever way the problem has been initially attacked. For those with little experience, the adoption of the above basis from which to proceed further will help to ensure a more cohesive result than by working arbitrarily. With a reasonably agreed foundation, therefore, the subdivisions need further consideration:

Vocal. Opera will require a very large allocation, probably the largest of all, not only because of its potential popularity but also because of the length of the works and consequently the numbers of records in a set. Although it is perfectly acceptable to spread the provision over complete, "highlight", and to some extent "recital" recordings, a goodly proportion of the whole vote will still be needed. Choral music, too, is often of 2-record length and will require relatively more money than for smaller-scale songs.

Orchestral. Miscellaneous works can absorb, with little encouragement, a great deal of money and can well be allotted a greater sum than for concertos; symphonies, however, are a vital part of the whole and may well, by some, be considered the most important part of this section.

Instrumental. There is very little leeway for further specific allocation here within the instruments with only 5 per cent of the total vote available; when we come to consider the works necessary for inclusion they will almost select themselves automatically in any case. The guitar section, however, with its *current* vogue, should comprise at least 1·5 per cent of the whole, even if the reserve has to be used for part of it.

Chamber. The advantages of subdivision here are tenuous. Those suggested can be used if required, but I must admit a preference here to a more fluid approach to the titles themselves.

With these considerations in mind, we should now be able to provide a more definite breakdown of both our vote and future stock, working on the basis of our previous percentages:

per cent			per cent
45	VOCAL	Opera	35
		Choral	7
		Song	3
35	ORCHESTRAL	Symphonies	12
		Concertos	9
		Miscellaneous	14
5	INSTRUMENTAL	Piano/violin/'cello/etc.	3·5
		Guitar	1·5
12	CHAMBER	With piano	4·5
		Without piano	7·5
		or	
		Trios	3
		Quartets	6
		Quintets	2
		Others	1
3	RESERVE	If division required	

At this stage we have created for ourselves a skeleton – no flesh, no personality, no growth, nothing but a substance into which life has to be breathed. Let us, therefore, finalise this skeleton; let us be quite sure we know what it is and what we are going to do with it. It is an attempt to lay down the requirements for a balanced appraisal of our basic necessities; it puts down the cornerstones of our stock and provides the primary justification for the eventual inclusion or exclusion of titles; it is the foundation upon which we add, firstly, titles of works and, secondly, recordings of those works. Thus, when £1,000 is available, the following initial breakdown will help to bring the whole into a balanced perspective:

VOCAL (£430–£470)	Opera	approx.	£350
	Choral	"	£ 70
	Song	"	£ 30
ORCHESTRAL (£335–£365)	Symphonies	"	£120
	Concertos	"	£ 90
	Miscellaneous	"	£140
INSTRUMENTAL (£45–£55)	Piano/violin/'cello/etc	"	£ 35
	Guitar	"	£ 15
CHAMBER (110–£130)	With piano	"	£ 45
	Without piano	"	£ 75
	or		
	Trios	"	£ 30
	Quartets	"	£ 60
	Quintets	"	£ 20
	Others	"	£ 10
RESERVE (£30)			

Undoubtedly many would suggest changes in detail (i.e. that the expenditure for song and individual instruments be raised, that the formal chamber proporations be revised, or that opera be lowered); this is all to the good as it indicates a positive approach to the problems. Having agreed, therefore, one's own personal basis, the next step is to add the fibre of titles to the formal skeleton.

TITLES OF WORKS.   The preceding stage is one which can be carried out in a comparatively short time, but the accumulation of titles within their formal headings is a more lengthy process and should not be undertaken hurriedly. The object at this stage is to provide oneself with as complete a list of compositions as possible which will be used not only for initial selection of stock but also for its later development. We want, therefore, lists of:

Symphonies by composer
Concertos by instruments and composer
Operas by composer
Miscellaneous orchestral works by composer

Choral works by composer
Songs by composer
Chamber music either by composer or the division suggested above
Instrumental music by instrument and composer

Most librarians will be able quite easily to fill in some part of each of these headings; there would be little difficulty, say, under "Symphonies" to begin with Beethoven 1–9, Brahms 1–4, Schubert 1–9, Schumann 1–4, Sibelius 1–7; or, when dealing with "Songs" to list works by Schubert, Brahms, Wolf, Purcell, Schumann, and Richard Strauss. But for those with the very minimum of musical background it will very likely be necessary to read one or more of the many available histories of music so that the perspectives of the art become clearer; it will be seen that the other possible approaches to stock selection mentioned previously assume no little importance in the general development of music, and in the gathering of titles every aspect should be explored. Histories will help to clarify two approaches – the chronological and the composer; when reading make your own lists of works and composers under each of the above headings and use the bibliographies and index to check and supplement them. Investigate those books which specialise in the formal aspects we have been discussing and from them continually extend your own lists – always provide your own subjective work to develop rather than rely upon other people's lists. By all means use, as a means to a personal end, compilations of suggested titles such as those included in this volume and other similar professional and bibliographical works, in publishers' lists, in record catalogues (especially the *Classical Quarterly Catalogue* published by *The Gramophone*), in periodical reviews and advertisements – in fact the more current the material that is used the more likely you will be to include works not found in the more "static" lists (i.e. those prepared at any one time in the past) – and in catalogues published by other libraries of their sheet-music holdings. These latter, and especially those from Liverpool, Dagenham, and the current series from the BBC, are invaluable for finalising your list. It may be argued that such catalogues could initially provide titles of works under their forms without resource to any other literary material and this might well be so for the librarian with a good musical background (although even here one must beware the non-inclusion of important recent works), but the acquiring of a reasonably comprehensive musical knowledge through reading and browsing (and at the same time using this knowledge in a practical way) is essential for those who have not got this background. The work should be carried out within each of the formal headings with the titles enumerated separately with sufficient space alongside for further details:

SYMPHONIES

BRAHMS No. 1
2
3
4

CONCERTOS

PIANO
  BRAHMS No. 1
2
  GRIEG
  BEETHOVEN No. 1
2
3
4
5   etc

as each work will have to be investigated separately for recommended recordings. When, eventually, you are satisfied that your catalogue of works is as complete as you either can or wish to make it, one further process is required to prepare the ground for final selection and this is to sort out the wheat from the chaff! Within such a comprehensive list there will naturally be a considerable number of works of lesser importance and it is necessary to mark in some way (asterisk, tick, etc) those which are essential to any stock, irrespective of the finances available. All the works included above would certainly fall into this category but whether or not Brahms' three string quartets would do so is a matter for personal opinion; to what extent Sibelius' symphonies or Bach's church cantatas are necessary to your stock must be your own decision, but it is better to restrict rather than to extend such essentials.

The following reading list, although by no means comprehensive, may be of some assistance:

GENERAL

DEXTER, H. & TOBIN, R., comps. *Music Lover's Pocket Book* (Evans, 1960)
EWEN, D. *The Complete Book of 20th Century Music* (Blond, 1961).
PERCIVAL, Allen. *Teach Yourself History of Music* (EUP, 1961)
SARGENT, Sir Malcolm, ed. *Outline of Music* (Newnes, 1962)
SMOLDEN, Wm. L. *History of Music* (Jenkins, 1965)
TOVEY, Sir Donald. *Essays in Musical Analyses*. 6 vols. (OUP, 1946)

SYMPHONY

SIMPSON, R. W. L., ed. *The Symphony*. 2 vols. (Penguin, 1967)
HOPKINS, Antony. *Talking about Symphonies* (Heinemann, 1961)

CONCERTO

HOPKINS, Anthony. *Talking about Concertos* (Heinemann, 1964)
VEINUS, Abraham. *The Concerto* (Cassell, 1948)

ORCHESTRA

BIANCOLLI, L. & MANN, Wm. S., eds. *Analytical Concert Guide* (Cassell, 1963)

OPERA

DAVIDSON, G. *Standard Stories of the Operas* (Werner Laurie, 1968), and others similar
JACOBS, A. & SADIE, S. *The Pan Book of Opera* (Pan, 1964)
KOBBE, G. ed. Earl of Harewood. *Complete Opera Book,* (Putnam, 1954)

CHAMBER MUSIC

ROBERTSON, Alec, ed. *Chamber Music* (Pelican, 1960)

CHORAL MUSIC

JACOBS, A., ed. *Choral Music* (Pelican, 1963)

SONGS

PRAWER, S.S., ed. *Penguin Book of Lieder* (Penguin, 1964)
STEVENS, D., ed. *A History of Song* (Hutchinson, 1960)

PIANO

HUTCHESON, E. *The Literature of the Piano* (Hutchinson, n.d.)

Not all the above titles are currently in print but none should be too difficult to obtain through normal interloan channels.

SELECTION OF RECORDINGS. We have now a reasonably concise idea of the music works we want in stock — both the essential and the less essential — and the amount of money we have available for each of the forms. This last procedure is to try and put the quart into the pint pot because whatever the finances available they will never be enough to supply the recordings required. And this introduces a prime difficulty — should one concentrate on quantity at the expense of quality? Stated baldly, however, this is perhaps not a fair way to make the point. Since approximately 1959 there has been an ever-increasing tendency by record companies to issue cheaper records (i.e. around the 20/- mark and less) but this does not mean that, per se, these discs are of a cheaper quality; on the contrary, a high proportion are of exceedingly high quality. I firmly believe, however, that to approach record selection solely from the point of view of "the most for the money" is courting disaster. A discerning borrowing public will quickly spot the great holes left in the stock and reservations for recordings not immediately available over the first year will almost certainly take much of the future development of the department out of the hands of the music librarian — and even if this is not so, the borrowing public is surely entitled to have access to the best possible stock that can be offered to them. I am not saying that cheaper records should not be bought; very many of them *must* be and will provide a very welcome increase in the number of discs which will eventually be provided, but I am saying that an approach which sets out to achieve the maximum number of records without regard to any other consideration is not only basically unsound but also unprofessional.

The quality of the stock as a whole is the quality of its constituent parts; that the performance and recording characteristics of each record bought should be examined goes without saying and at this point we become dependent upon the professional critic. Even if librarians had the time and opportunity to play every record the question of determining their comparative merits would prove almost insuperable. The *Classical Quarterly Catalogue* is very adept at quoting "x" number of recordings for "X's 5th Symphony", but which to buy? Which is the best? Which do the critics go for? Do they all agree? If not, why not? Can I get a consensus of opinions rather than just one? Of course, there are many answers to these questions, many approaches to using the facilities the critics offer, but for a basic practical approach there are few better ways than to investigate the listings of the London firm of EMG in their annual cumulation of recommended recordings *The Art of Record Buying*. This contains no reviews (these are issued separately month by month and are not, in this context, being recommended any more than the critical appreciations in other periodical publications) but a star system of recommendations, the prime value of which is its regular revision. The recommendations have a group basis which do not always agree with other critics' ideas but can be depended upon to maintain a high standard and are not to be lightly considered; remember that this is an annual publication and recordings issued after its appearance (usually in November) must not be forgotten.

It is reasonable to assume that the *Art* will suggest first-class recordings for all, or nearly all, the essential titles referred to previously – indeed, it will frequently offer a further series of alternatives; standard titles by their very nature are offered in a multitude of recordings of which there will always be a percentage of recommendations. When this happens, check to see if the reverse sides of any of the records listed include any other title required; if this is so it would become an automatic selection, especially if it were a cheaper label. These are the circumstances under which it is not only advisable to get the best value for your money but, as I see it, the prime approach to the lower-priced recordings. Artists' demands may modify this outlook in part (i.e. Klemperer's *Eroica*, Callas' *Carmen*, Richter's Tchaikovsky, or Oistrakh's Bach may be considered necessary irrespective of price) but not to any great extent. Notable amongst other publications giving guidance in selecting recommended recordings are the volumes of *The Guide to the Bargain Classics* and the *Stereo Record Guide* from the LPRL, Blackpool; the items included in the catalogues issued by this and other commercial record-lending libraries set a high standard both in performance and recording and are useful auxiliary sources.

This, then, is what might be called the "3C" approach to basic stock selection:

CREATIVE: where the proportions are balanced, both formally and financially
CLERICAL: where the formal framework is 'clothed' with titles
CONSTRUCTIVE: where the titles are related to their recordings.

Post-Basic

The implications of this heading are clear enough – when you have put together your initial stock of records, by what means and with what material is it going to be further developed? There will undoubtedly be many gaps from the classical lists prepared earlier and these can be reduced slowly; the lists themselves both of titles and recordings should be thoroughly revised in the light of the knowledge and experience acquired in their formation and used continuously for stock checking; the new monthly record issues must be closely investigated to ensure that no release sufficiently important to be included in your own library is missed (and here detailed review reading of several periodicals is very often necessary to determine a record's objective qualities); counter staff should be encouraged to note details of works and/or recordings asked for by borrowers but not reserved in order that their current omission may be assessed for possible future purchase; all discographical (dreadful word!) material (advertisements, new books, record company materials, periodical articles) should be absorbed – there really is no end to the sources by which the stock of classical recordings can be expanded. This expansion, of course, will have to be related to its own finances, which will normally be the annual running costs; as issues of records are on a monthly basis it is sound practice to divide such money as is available by twelve so that a reasonable average monthly expenditure is achieved. This average should not be too rigid – for instance summer months are often quieter months for the record companies than winter – but it gives a good guide to one's financial position at any time during the year and, perhaps most important of all, helps to prevent overspending.

At this stage, progress towards increasing the number of works in stock will be well advanced and this, of course, will never cease. No library is ever too large to consider that it has a complete coverage of music works, but now that the stock is achieving substance and direction, there arises the difficult problem of duplication of titles. I say "of titles" advisedly as there will usually be little need for second or more copies of one specific recording for some time other than to satisfy a run of reservations. Almost certainly those works that need to be available in more than one copy will be amongst those designated for necessary purchase in the basic stock selection and they will have to be considered for addition as soon as the library is fully operative; the decision which extra recording to buy will again be guided by the patterns previously outlined, except that with current issues to be weighed in addition to the largely static catalogue selections many second copies will choose themselves. Unless a firm check is kept upon duplications they can easily run out of control; it is all too easy to find oneself suddenly with unreasonable numbers of copies of popular titles bought, inevitably, at the expense of other works. A separate check list of such titles, detailing record numbers and date of purchase, goes a long way towards keeping this problem under reasonable control – the titles included can be annotated with the number of copies desirable in your own stock;

	DUKAS		
(3)	Sorcerer's Apprentice	SXLP 20030;	LXT 6065;
		9/68	3/69
	ELGAR		
(5)	Enigma Variations	ACL 55; VIC 1001; ASD 548	
		1/66 6/68 2/69	

This will not only tell you at a glance that each work is understocked according to your own requirements but also that ACL 55 is likely to be in a less satisfactory condition that the other copies – it would appear that it had to do service on its own for two and a half years. Although these examples are of two isolated works, most benefit from this kind of listing is to be derived from a related series of works. Beethoven's symphonies and piano concertos, for instance, each worked out on a separate page provide a perspective of these important parts of one's stock that is quite impossible to achieve from any other source. Once started, however, it must be maintained accurately; never forget to cross out withdrawals, and ensure that you know which titles have been included in your list so that new additions will be added automatically.

The approach to cheaper labels was generally mentioned earlier, but it is sufficiently important to repeat: if *what you want* is available in a recommended recording at a cheaper price so much the better, but don't go for the bargain at the expense of quality. At the time of writing the distinction between "full-price" and "bargain" is more tenuous than ever as the price ranges are virtually continuous between 10/- and 40/-, but it is generally considered that those records below approximately 26/- are in the bargain range. The reasons for the cheaper price vary considerably: Decca's "Ace of Clubs/Diamond" labels are re-issues of earlier recordings which have already sold well at higher prices; HMV's "Concert Classics" are a mixture of old and new recordings originally designed to compete with the Decca bargains; Supraphon records have been imported at a price that was heavily subsidised by the Czech authorities; Saga's enterprise in reducing their prices to exceptionally low levels – old and new recordings – appears to be a calculated commercial venture; the Nonesuch imports with their newer range of titles have been competitively priced; DGG's original ' Heliodor" range was a sparkling lustre of re-issue now replaced by the Stereo transcription series; Transatlantic, Polydor, Decca and many other companies are currently selling cheap transfer discs of their more successful artists, and so the labels increase month by month.

These series were no doubt sparked off by the success of the various record "clubs" which were so active in the early 1960s, a success which, maintained or not, has been of immeasurable benefit to the record-buying public at large. It is quite impossible to try and name the "best" bargain label – it does not exist. Equally, it would be as pointless merely to say that they were all "good in parts" – this would be a very considerable understatement of the potential that lies here. But within this context there is generally more need to consider recommendations; Ivan March's *Guide to the Bargain Classics* and EMG's *Art* again provide a very useful quick reference, but reviews of nearly all records, irrespective of price, are to be found in gramophone periodicals – the date alongside any listing in the *Quarterly Catalogue* although referring specifically to reviews in *The Gramophone* gives a good guide where it may appear in any other periodical.

The extension of classical stock should only be one part of post-basic selection, although progression into other fields would rarely be a decision resting primarily with the music librarian. It must not be forgotten, however, that the headings listed at the beginning of this chapter under "Terms of Reference" are all potential material. "Light classical" has very grey borders with "classical" and there will normally be nothing to prevent incursions into Sullivan, Lehar and Johann Strauss operetta, Eric Coates orchestral music and similar works. Several of the other headings (viz. documentary, demonstration, humour, film and stage) virtually select themselves from the commercial catalogues, but librarians without special knowledge of, or interest in, jazz are likely to find it something of a stumbling block and it might be profitable briefly to refer to it separately.

This is not the place to provide a potted history of jazz, but it is convenient to refer to the broad divisions evident in its development, just as it is equally convenient to develop one's stock through these same divisions. The formative years from the latter part of the nineteenth century to the period of the First World War is really "pre-vintage" with so comparatively little available in the way of recordings that it is of less practical value to us that the "classical" or "vintage" period which followed it. Although dates must necessarily be vague, this lasted until the early 1930s when the small group combinations gave way to big band "swing". The mid-1940s saw the emergence of "bop", whilst the development through the 1950s was towards the "cool", together with the popular revival of classic jazz under the "trad" label. For the expert, these headings will have no value whatsoever but the tyro may find they provide a few "hooks" to hang on to.

The styles of each period are the sum total of the art of individual artists and, with jazz more than any other musical expression, the performing artist is the predominating factor; we are really concerned with the personal interpretations in the jazz idiom of all kinds of musical raw materials. The re-issues over the past few years in the Decca "Ace of Hearts" series, the CBS "BPG" label, the Parlophone "PMC" label, and the specialist RCA recordings of vintage jazz material, have provided a veritable treasure-house of early recordings, and unless a broad general resumé of jazz history is required in one's original stock (a dangerous approach as it will satisfy nobody and almost surely produce an excessive demand for "modern" jazz), no better start can be made than by buying as many of these basic records as possible. King Oliver, Louis Armstrong, Duke Ellington, Fletcher Henderson, Bix Beiderbecke, Jelly Roll Morton, and many of the lesser known combos are available in abundance and most borrowers with an interest in any aspect of jazz would be more than satisfied to know that the stock was being built on this firm foundation. Most jazz enthusiasts have specific interests which might well clash with purchases of more contemporary material, but these recordings are fundamental.

The "swing" period of the 30s and early 40s is perhaps less well served with currently available material but there is still much to be acquired of Benny Goodman, Count Basie, Bob Crosby, Artie Shaw, Muggsy Spanier, and others — this was notably the age of the big band when the soloist was in temporary decline. Charlie "Bird" Parker was the prime exponent of the succeeding "bop" era (Saga, "Eros" and CBS "Realm" labels are well supplied with his recordings) and with Dizzy Gillespie forms an essential part of any collection. So also are Miles Davis, The MJQ, Charlie Mingus, Woody Herman's "Herds", Stan Getz, and Thelonius Monk of more recent years — to name but a few. One must not forget, however, that throughout the whole of this jazz development the blues have been one of its major aspects and much recorded material is available, both instrumental and vocal. *Jazz on Record* published in 1968 by Hanover Books is obviously designed to relieve the burden of the music librarian — and, I am sure, making most of the above redundant!

Excursions into language tuition recordings are expensive if adequate service is to be maintained — expensive in money, time, and staff. The standard approach to issuing these records has been one of splitting the set amongst a circle of borrowers, each of whom is expected to pass on his currently held disc every fourteen days or so — a system which very often breaks down. It is far more satisfactory to issue whole sets for reasonable periods of loan of, say, not less than twelve weeks, but this calls for considerable financial resources. The Linguaphone series of "full" course recordings are the standard material in this field, but mention should be made of the less expensive *Daily Express* Conversational Sets and the more elementary Harrap-Didier Audio Visual Courses; also the Assimil range of "full", "preliminary" and "advanced" sets, and the Berlitz and BBC courses.

For borrowers with hi-fi equipment some consideration should be given to the purchase of technical recordings of frequency tones, stereo set-up, etc., whilst the more common stereo demonstration records will always find a ready borrowers' market. Humorous records are ideal material for library stock; so often a second or third hearing wipes out the memory of the initial entertainment but a constant varying succession of Milligans, Shermans, Newharts, Borges, and Hancocks keeps the magic alive. Modern "folk" song of the Seeger/Baez/Dylan variety currently has an enormous vogue and there would seem as much justification to add this to stock as traditional folk. Documentary recordings cover a wide field from the Argo train series to the patchwork variety of the BBC Radio Enterprises label and the poignant and sometimes terrifyingly real Kennedy records. Imports open up a vast new world and although they are dealt with in detail elsewhere I must at least refer to the "Music Minus One" series, where one of the primary parts is missing from the recording (of concertos, songs, chamber music) and thus gives facilities for practice with the complete ensemble in the home; as with many imports they are not cheap but, as they include the music score of the missing part, do offer a very real service.

And so the possibilities increase with every published catalogue. There can really be no limitation in the final analysis, although it might take some time to persuade *your* Committee that gramophone records are not solely for the reproduction of classical music but for the dissemination of every aspect of human thought and activity.

Record Withdrawal and Replacement

Stock turnover and the mechanical processes associated with it are so much a normal part of library administration that on the face of it there may seem very little need to investigate its relevance to gramophone records; in the very broadest terms this may well be so, but there are sufficient points of detail to warrant further examination. Basically, stock of any kind is withdrawn because it has ceased to serve a useful purpose and when this criterion is applied to a long-playing record we find that its "uselessness" originates in a number of sources: groove wear, scratches, warping, breakage (rare but not non-existent), and similar practical faults, which prevent the recorded sound from being properly reproduced; in addition, of course, there are the standard library reasons of loss and general stock revision.

It is perhaps advisable at this point to mention the problem of stock maintenance as this not only concerns the day to day running of a record department but also has direct consequences upon withdrawals. It will be noted from the previous paragraph (and well known by those with experience) that specific record damage is a constant source of trouble: it either happens or considerable precautions have to be taken unceasingly to try and prevent its happening. The many and varied procedures adopted by library systems for checking closely incoming and outgoing discs are ample evidence in themselves of the necessity for their existence, but checking of itself will not remove a scratch or flatten a warp — it can only record its existence. There is of course no doubt that a close scrutiny of discs in the borrower's presence makes him more alive to the dangers of mishandling and a department which deliberately adopts a policy of either partial or no checking upon issue must associate with it a very detailed system of stock control.

Agreement that checking is necessary is widespread, but there must be an increasing number of librarians who would admit that, for various reasons, the existence of the procedure does not automatically imply achievement of its objects. Both the approach of individual and often junior members of the staff and of the borrower in any given situation can complicate the matter and at times a great deal of tact may be needed not to offend; the responsibility for keeping the stock in good condition can often be interpreted by a borrower as "being too officious", especially when he may have been "handling records for years" — no one wants to start bandying experience over the counter. Again, volume of issue at specific times or in total may warrant serious consideration of restricted inspection, i.e. of more recent additions to stock, of specified popular works, etc.; and when gramophone records become as much a part of normal loan material as are books nowadays it is to be hoped that sufficient initiative will be used by librarians to adapt standard practices to the needs of their own service. Such needs, however, will certainly include a stock in as good a condition as possible and where restricted inspection is carried out it cannot be too strongly emphasised that some kind of control is imperative and will probably be derived either from an anticipated life-span of, or from the number of issues which can be expected from, each disc. This control is one of regular and frequent checking of those records which fall into either of the above criteria; both are closely related and the adoption of one or the other is often merely a matter of convenient usage. For instance, where open access is in operation and there is a specific need to keep the sleeves or their covering free from obscuring material such as date labels it may not be possible to determine how often a record has been issued; in this case a constant probing with a list based on additions to stock over a specified period (i.e. 3 to 4 years previously, or less or more, depending upon the use made of the department) will ensure that the older material is constantly under review.

This aspect of maintenance during the record's lifetime and its withdrawal for reasons of damage or wear is not, however, the whole picture. There seem to be close connections between the gramophone record and motor car industries in that both encourage a calculated obsolescence, not only through policies of continual development (nobody grumbles at this) but also through insinuative advertisement and all the implications behind "this year's model". Not only must you have Beethoven's 5th Symphony, and "Klemperer's" 5th Symphony (exploitation of the artist/composer combinations are quite endless), but also the more recent "Klemperer's" 5th Symphony. You will never be allowed to remain satisfied with your Oistrakh Bach or your Richter Schumann – as sure as night follows day there will be another public performance or another import to convince you of *its* priority. Let it not be thought for one second that I am against this plethora of "variations on a theme"; it *is* a good thing that perhaps for the first time there is a considerable choice not only of musical works but also of their interpretation; but it is equally important to point out that a recording is not necessary merely because it is new. The decision to buy any record for stock must remain valid until the record is withdrawn – and this withdrawal should not be influenced by irrelevant reasons. But recording techniques are undoubtedly advancing rapidly and a thorough investigation of reviews should certainly be carried out to determine whether there are valid reasons other than sheer novelty for stock substitution.

The mechanics of withdrawal vary slightly; if an accessions register is maintained, deletion of the number in the register may be sufficient; but for those libraries who use trade numbers in lieu of conventional accessioning the listing of records in a withdrawals book would seem to be reasonably standard practice. In both cases the confirmatory signature of a more senior librarian (or of the internal audit authority) is often needed by District Audit. These details are, mainly, for official purposes, but they do also provide necessary statistics for stock totals; from a bibliographical point of view withdrawal entails catalogue adjustments where the record is not going to be replaced.

It is reasonably obvious that unless finances are unrestricted it is not possible to replace every withdrawn record, especially where the rate of withdrawal is high; in any case, deletions from the commercial catalogues impose an arbitrary decision often enough. When a systematic turnover is in operation some proportion of annual purchases will be of new recordings whilst others will be of replacement, the proportions being adjusted to requirements. In a library with heavy issues, as much as 40 per cent of the annual vote may be required for replacements, but for most departments a figure between 15 and 25 per cent should not prove unreasonable. E. T. Bryant in his *Music Librarianship* quotes "an average withdrawal of some 20 per cent of the stock each year" and this would seem to imply a complete stock turnover every five years or so; whether or not this is so rather depends on the criterion for withdrawal. If the librarian gets rid of stock solely on the evidence of counter checks it might well be that after ten years some of the original records are available because their surfaces are still satisfactory; but with a controlled turnover based on, say, length of time in stock all records would indeed be *considered* for withdrawal during the five-year period. As indicated, deletion from the commercial catalogue is probably the most common reason for non-replacement, but the constant whirlpool of re-issues and new versions necessitates an individual appraisal for each record withdrawn. The appraisal might follow these lines:

Do I want to keep the work in stock?

> No. Don't replace.
>
> Yes . . .

Do I hold sufficient other recordings
of the work?

> Yes. Don't replace, unless the w/d
> recording is intrinsically
> valuable.
>
> No . . .

Do I reorder the same record?

> Check bibliographical sources for
> current assessment against more recent
> recordings of the work. If . . .
>
> . . .Still good. Reorder same record,
> but also consider if more copies of
> the work are required.
>
> . . .Now bettered. Replace with
> current recommendations if not
> already in stock.
>
> . . .Deleted. Replace with current
> recommendations if not
> already in stock, remembering
> that deletions very often
> appear in cheaper format.

It may be that more than one major work has to be considered or that the artist is the *raison d'etre* of the record, but the same basic questions would apply. The more popular works will probably give most trouble in this respect as calculated decisions about standard performance (i.e. *Fidelio* under Klemperer; *Carmen* with Callas; Mahler symphonies under Walter) and total numbers of copies of the work required will have to be made on many occasions. When the disc is directly replaced there is no need to change catalogue entries, but the new purchase date together with any alteration of price paid will be required in the stock register; when another recording altogether is bought, the withdrawn and replacement items are completely independent and all cards for the original record must be taken out of the catalogue, and stock register and the accession number, where applicable, deleted. The new disc, of course, will be prepared afresh.

One final point is worth consideration. Although I favour the turnover of the complete stock during the course of a number of years, largely through my own experience — and who doesn't favour what has had to be evolved in one's own library through necessity? — I am aware that "damage withdrawal" (a term I use for want of a better) does allow one to retain in stock a proportion of progressively earlier recordings which after a while assume some measure of historic interest. If sufficient of these are available to form a small reserve, their value might well increase with the years; all withdrawals (in spite of their damage) could be considered for addition to this reserve and its growing inclusion of deleted items would put what would otherwise be discarded material to good use.

The Selection of Foreign Gramophone Records

by DAVID G. WILLIAMS, ALA
Music Librarian, Grimsby Public Libraries

The last decade has seen a mushroom growth in the British gramophone record industry so that today librarians, teachers, and private individuals are offered a multiplicity of labels and companies from which to make their choice. So vast is this choice that a very substantial library could be built up utilising purely British issues and for the smaller library which so often has totally inadequate financial resources to buy gramophone records the acquisition of foreign records is a relatively rare event. Yet the librarian who neglects the foreign repertoires entirely is doing himself and his community a disservice – his own professional knowledge and his library can be greatly enriched by studying these discographical sources.

Not all records which are available from British shops are of purely British origin. In general the major companies like Decca, EMI, Philips, and CBS record, press and distribute what might be termed a purely domestic product; but other companies, especially some of the smaller ones, either acquire rights to manufacture gramophone records from tape recordings of foreign origin or, in some cases, even import finished gramophone records and merely act as distributors or agents for Britain. Saga is an example of the first kind, and although some Saga recordings are original, some, notably those on Saga/Pan have been drawn from the Austrian Amadeo catalogue. In the second category is a company like Keith Prowse, which distributes the Czech Supraphon recordings, or Polydor, which still obtains many of its Deutsche Grammophon and Archive records direct from Germany. These distinctions are rather important, since it does not always follow that a foreign recording must necessarily be imported individually by a librarian.

Nevertheless this chapter is concerned mainly to explain in brief the structure of the gramophone record industry in countries other than Britain, and it will be helpful to start by reviewing the major companies of the UK since they dominate the markets of the world. Both EMI and Decca are virtually independent of their associate companies abroad and both companies are responsible for a great deal of recording activity which is exported. CBS came on to the British scene a few years ago and although it does undertake some recording here it is mainly dominated by its associate company, Columbia, in America. (In passing it may be noted that American Columbia is in no way related to the Columbia Gramophone Record Co., which was absorbed along with HMV in the 1930s into EMI.) Philips is a Dutch company with strong links in other Continental countries, as is Deutsche Grammophon, which is known in Britain now as Polydor Records Ltd. Pye undertakes a certain amount of original recording but controls mainly American and French labels. By the time this book appears in print two American companies formerly distributed on an agency basis, will be independent concerns – they are MCA and RCA Victor. MGM has already severed its links with EMI. MCA recordings were mainly released on Brunswick, whilst the RCA label has always and will continue to be identified as RCA Victor. With the exception of Philips all these major companies have long and in some cases very complicated histories, and those who are interested will find a mass of information in Oliver Read's *From Tin Foil to Stereo* (pub. by H. W. Sams) and Gelatt's *Fabulous Phonograph.*

Gramophone records are usually imported when it is necessary to obtain a particular piece of music, or example of the spoken word, and the British catalogues do not list any suitable recordings. Sometimes foreign records are obtained to provide a recording of a certain work by a particular artist but many librarians often overlook another aspect of buying foreign discs: the fact that they often are the means of obtaining replacements when the original British pressings have been deleted. This can be especially useful, for some British companies have summarily deleted records of great artistic and musical interest apparently without rhyme or reason. When a record is deleted in the United Kingdom it does not follow that simultaneous deletion will take place elsewhere, indeed this would be quite exceptional. Similarly, although a large number of deleted records in the UK appear again as re-pressings, usually on cheaper labels, contractual obligations, copyright restrictions, and other considerations can and do sometimes prevent records from being issued again. In such cases it is often possible to obtain another copy from abroad.

Great Britain

EMI. This large organisation has associate companies in almost every country of the world. In Europe the principal EMI labels are Electrola (Germany), Pathé-Marconi (La Voix de son Maître-France), La Voce del suo Padrone (Italy), and Compania Odeon (Spain). The Odeon trademark is found in other places in Europe such as the Scandinavian EMI companies, but in most countries the HMV, Capitol, and Columbia labels are all used, except in America where Capitol uses Angel as the main EMI label. This is because Columbia belongs to CBS and His Master's Voice to RCA and many readers will remember some of the early HMV LPs, like the Toscanini recordings, which originated from RCA in America. In some countries EMI associated companies control labels not normally seen in Britain. Regal (mainly a re-issue label) is one such example and is found in many countries, whilst an example of a label controlled for one country only is Ducretet-Thompson, formerly issued here by Decca but now controlled by Pathé-Marconi as a French label. Discophile Français is also a French EMI concern. Both the German and French EMI catalogues contain many records which are no longer available from British EMI, and although EMI now have a more responsible attitude towards posterity, when deletion lists are issued it would seem that a great deal of material will continue to be available only outside this country.

DECCA. It established itself on the British market as a pioneer of the long-playing record and was one of the first companies to exploit the stereophonic gramophone record to the full. Its dominance as a major contributor to the English market is also in evidence in many other countries, where the Decca trade mark usually identifies the company. "Decca" has the advantage of being a nearly universal word, but two important exceptions are noted in the case of Germany and America. In Germany the associate company is Telefunken and the group is Tel-Dec, whilst in America, Decca is known as London. There, Decca is the trade name owned by the American Decca Co. which produces Brunswick recordings. Tel-Dec, as was the case in England, distributes RCA records, although in many countries RCA is entirely independent of Decca. The French Decca catalogues contain some items not issued in the UK such as many French operettas and some plays, but the German catalogues in general have little original material of interest and since Decca maintain a stable catalogue in the UK it is rarely necessary to obtain other foreign Decca issues.

RCA. This major concern has been a dominating member of the American gramophone scene for many decades and has also established overseas branches and organisations in most countries of the world. It was hardly known in the UK until the EMI contract terminated in 1957, for until that time RCA recordings issued here actually appeared on the HMV label. For the last ten years Decca have been associated with RCA, and although the RCA labels have been used the actual records have been processed and pressed by English Decca. This association is rather curious, for in most countries RCA and Decca (or London in America) are in cutthroat competition with one another, a fact which will become more evident now that RCA have severed their English link with Decca and have become an independent concern.

DEUTSCHE GRAMMOPHON. This company was actually at one time the German branch of the Gramophone Co. (EMI) but as a result of protracted legal complications following the First World War it became an entirely separate organisation. Deutsche Grammophon, Archive, and Heliodor are well known in the UK, but it often happens that pressings are deleted in Britain when they still continue to be available in Germany and consequently replacements for worn-out recordings can sometimes be obtained. In Germany Deutsche Grammophon is a larger concern than in England and controls some American labels like United Artists and Verve, which in England are the domain of EMI. Very often label control works on a reciprocal basis and in America it is MGM which is responsible for Deutsche Grammophon pressing and distribution. The Heliodor label is far more independent in America as a result of this arrangement and carries a number of interesting re-issues not found anywhere else. A wide range of Archive records is available from both Germany and America, many of them now being unavailable from Polydor in the UK.

CBS. An organisation with many trading links throughout the world, but it is obviously the American catalogue which is the largest. Many Columbia issues have appeared in Britain in the past, disguised in the main as Philips or Fontana issues, but recordings still appear in the American catalogues which seem to miss the English CBS company. CBS has only recently started a re-issue label, Odyssy, and some of the issues are not in fact original CBS recordings but stem from a small American company called "Library of Recorded Masterpieces". The CBS catalogue is especially strong for jazz and many issues not available here can be found in the German CBS catalogue. The French CBS catalogue is smaller but not without interest.

PHILIPS. Well represented throughout the continent, but especially so in Holland and France. Again it is often possible to find records listed which have been deleted from the British Philips catalogue, but quite a number of records exist in France and Germany which never appeared on the British market at all. This is in part due to the control which Philips has of various labels. Mercury, for example, has only recently been revived as a source for re-issue recordings in Britain (where most issues appear on Wing), but in France the Mercury label has been a cheaper label for some years. Some Philips associates' recordings are familiar to the British public in other guises, Cycnus being a case in point, some of whose recordings are available here on Nonesuch. The spring of 1968 saw English Philips following another latent continental lead when the Vanguard label (previously here associated with Pye/Nixa) was launched. Vanguard is an American concern linked on the continent with Austrian Amadeo, and both companies have a great deal of material interesting to librarians. The

Amadeo catalogue should certainly be examined since only a relatively small percentage has appeared in Britain through Philips (mainly on the GL/SGL label) and curiously enough from Saga (on the Saga/Pan label although most of the artists' names have been changed in this case).

PYE. It has no comparable continental associates in the same way as the other companies.listed above, since in Britain much of its material is drawn from other American and foreign catalogues. Chess is an example of an American source whilst companies like Disques Vogue have also made their contributions to Pye issues. Pye, like most of the other companies, however, does not rely on "importing" recordings and indeed some "Golden Guinea" classical issues appear in America as re-pressings on Nonesuch.

Most of the other British companies are smaller concerns and in the majority of cases issue recordings which have originated from other sources. In order to point out some of the more interesting examples and to note a few of the other foreign labels generally unknown to the British market it is proposed to survey briefly the continental and American scenes.

France

LE CHANT DU MONDE.   An interesting company that re-presses many Russian MK recordings which can sometimes be difficult to obtain in the UK (e.g. Prokofiev's *Simeon Kotko* or Rimsky-Korsakov's *Tsar Saltan* and *Sadko*), but it also has some French music by Satie and Milhaud which is otherwise not available. There is a good folk music section. It is a matter for regret that no permanent distribution rights have been secured in Great Britain for ERATO since this catalogue, a kind of French equivalent to Argo, contains a large and varied number of interesting recordings. In the past a few items have appeared either through Argo or World Record Club but the majority of the issues, which include a fair representation of contemporary music, remain virtually unknown to British buyers. Perhaps the notion of Erato as a French Argo may suggest there are no other labels of great merit which is, of course, untrue.

VEGA, indeed, is another important concern, which not only has many fine recordings to its credit (including an important series of French music entitled "Présence de la Musique Contemporaine") but is also responsible for distributing labels such as Ariola-Eurodisc in France. COMPAGNIE GENERALE DU DISQUE has a number of good jazz discs, some of which have appeared on Pye, and some useful childrens' records. An example of the material foreign records can provide is shown by the bird song LPs and a disc of insect sounds. The spoken word in French is well served by DISQUE ADES and by L'ENCYCLOPEDIE SONORE and some of these records together with the poetry, prose, and plays available from French Decca and Pathé-Marconi will undoubtably be welcomed by school-teachers and GCE students. With the deletion of all Vox-boxes in the UK it may be worth while to point out that VOX are not linked with Decca in France. Vox-boxes are a mixed blessing from a library point of view but for some series like the Haydn piano sonatas or string quartets they are useful for ensuring completeness of a collection. In general other French companies (of which PELCA, MONDIOPHONIE, DISQUES SFP are examples) provide little material which cannot be obtained, in many cases more easily, from other sources.

Germany

Apart from the major companies one of the more important German labels is ARIOLA-EURODISC, some of whose recordings have appeared in the past on Oriole (before its absorption by CBS) and on World Record Club. There are a number of opera and opera "highlight" recordings together with a good number of vocal recordings, but since Germans do not generally entertain any qualms on the question of translating libretti, many operas and excerpts are sung in German. There are some speech records of interest and, again, for GCE and use by the advanced student, these should not be overlooked. (In connection with this point it may be worthwhile to remind librarians of the German literature on records available from Deutsche Grammophon in Germany.)

It has already been observed that the major companies like EMI and Polydor have many issues still available in foreign catalogues where the English pressings have long since been withdrawn. In the case of these two companies this fact is especially noticable in Germany and librarians requiring replacement records should not necessarily despair of obtainirg them without first having at least checked on availability in Germany.

METRONOME has some good jazz issues since it is responsible for Atlantic and Storyville. Atlantic, formerly under English Decca control and now with Polydor, has a number of important jazz LPs such as the "Southern Folk Heritage" 7 LP set which are now deleted in Britain. Material from some of the smaller German companies has been in evidence on the British market in the past. Saga, for example, has issued some recordings to be found in the BARENREITER-MUSICAPHON and DA CAMERA contributes to the British issues of Musica Rara. However the librarian may well find something of interest from these sources and his attention is certainly directed to CHRISTOPHUS which has a great number of interesting records. Since the same company is also responsible for CANTATE which is handled by Keith Prowse it may be possible to obtain records through this source. HARMONIA MUNDI is perhaps a German equivalent to Argo and has many fine recordings. MUSICA SACRA, as the name implies, is a useful source for filling in gaps in liturgical music.

Other Countries

In this brief chapter it is impossible to deal exhaustively even with France and Germany and consequently little space is available to write at length on remaining European countries. In general Spain and Italy repeat the pattern of the major companies and little original material is issued from either country. Nevertheless there is some local activity and it is a matter of common sense to look at certain catalogues when covering specific fields such as Italian EMI for opera and vocal recordings (many of the English Columbia "La Scala" recordings will probably not appear again after deletion because of copyright difficulties) or Spanish catalogues for zarzuelas and flamenco music. In Italy it may be pertinent to remark that some CETRA records have filled many useful gaps in the recorded operatic repertoire although many of the recordings show their age when reproduced on larger gramophones. A few local issues of Scandinavian music exist on ODEON and Swedish EMI and TEL-DEC.

The United States of America

America, as might be expected, has the most complicated record industry in the world and with the vast market available there are dozens upon dozens of smaller labels and companies. The major companies are, of course, all represented but the British librarian must appreciate the slight transatlantic changes in terminology. EMI is known as Capitol and most issues are made on ANGEL because the HMV and Columbia trademarks cannot be used. For the same reason Decca uses its LONDON label and MGM is responsible for its own labels and for pressing Deutsche Grammophon, Archive and Heliodor, the latter being a re-issue label and including several MGM original recordings which are not seen elsewhere. CBS is the Columbia Broadcasting System and is generally known as COLUMBIA and the American Decca Record Co. has, in the past, been associated with the Brunswick issues which have stemmed from Decca in England. RCA Victor is the parent company of RCA organisations throughout the world and MERCURY makes its own local pressing arrangements for Philips. It is possible to indicate only a few of the remaining American companies not all of which are necessarily small ones.

WESTMINSTER is now owned by ABC Paramount but it was originally one of the first American companies to exploit the LP disc and some items from its large and varied catalogue were seen in England during the days when Associated Recordings used the Artia/Parliament/Westminster labels, and subsequently by means of EMI re-issues made mainly on "Concert Classics" and CSD/CLP. Quite a lot of Westminster records have been re-issued in America and the catalogue is well worth studying. The connection of Mercury and Philips has already been noted but apart from a few issues most of the Mercury recordings are available either from France on "Plaisir du Classique" or in England on "Wing" or Fontana SFL. VANGUARD is an important American label and has a link with Austrian Amadeo and Philips. (Some of these records have been available in Britain on GL/SGL.) Since the Vanguard label has, at the time of writing, only just been launched in Britain it is not possible to see how exhaustively Philips in Britain will develop it, but it is to be hoped that the majority of LPs will appear.

Just as Vanguard was originally founded by a small group of keen individual people so, too, was FOLKWAYS, which now has a most important catalogue from a library point of view. Not only is there a most authentic collection of folk music, especially American folk music, but there are also documentary and instructional records of all kinds. They include a history of jazz series (11 LPs), some contemporary American and other music, music lectures on such subjects as harmony, model counterpoint, arrangement, and so on, an American historical and documentary section, a language section which includes English and the use of English in language and literature and a most interesting spoken word section which includes many recordings not otherwise available. The well known recording of James Joyce reading extracts from *Finnegans Wake* is an example. It should also be noted that these spoken word recordings include readings of literature in languages other than English. CAEDMON is not unfamiliar to British librarians since a number of issues have been made through Philips. It may not be realised, however, that only a proportion of Caedmon LPs have been issued in Britain, although recently matters have improved with the issue of some of the plays. But there is still a great deal of poetry and prose (some it originally recorded in England by Philips it may be remarked!) which has still only been issued in America. The American catalogue also contains most of the Caedmon records which Philips have withdrawn. Now that America is becoming more budget market conscious it may be that Caedmon will license the re-issue of some of these older spoken word records, since this particular genre of record has been excluded from cheaper labels until now* Even allowing for the

---

*In the UK Caedmon have licensed re-issue discs on the Philips "Four Front" label. Argo are also re-issuing material now.

more limited market in comparison with classical music there should be little economic drawback since the cost of recording the spoken word is certainly much less than when orchestras, conductors, soloists and perhaps singers are all involved.

Another American label which concentrates on speech is SPOKEN ARTS, some of whose recordings have appeared in the UK on Argo. Fortunately there is now an English distribution arrangement for Spoken Arts and most of the catalogue is available here. ELEKTRA is another company whose products are represented on the British market by Polydor Ltd but again only on a limited basis. It is to Elektra that we owe the existence of NONESUCH, which uses master recordings of several European labels such as Cycnus, Club Française du Disque and so on. The folk music and popular items on Elektra are thus happily balanced by the classical recordings on Nonesuch although in the USA this label contains a wider range of records than in the UK because it includes there some discs known to British librarians on Pye's 'Golden Guinea''. The cause of contemporary music in the USA is better served than in England and one of the major sources for translantic music of our time is COMPOSER RECORDINGS INC. This represents the work of some 150 composers on more than 200 LPs. A smaller representation of American music is also available on DESTO. The LYRICHORD label produced by EXPÉRIENCES ANONYMES has filled in some musical gaps in the gramophone record catalogue although the recordings and performance qualities have not always been perfect.

It is a great pity that MUSIC MINUS ONE has not been properly exploited in Great Britain for although there is a London agent who imports them the cost is excessively high due to the small numbers involved, import duties and purchase tax. This is a great pity for most of these records would fill a worthwhile place in many British gramophone libraries. Most instruments are covered and there are about 30 odd LPs available for the piano alone, ranging from the Schubert *Trout* quintet to Beethoven's *Emperor* concerto. Many of these recordings exist in different editions so that the *Trout* quintet previously referred to can be obtained recorded by the strings alone, or with the piano part and the first violin missing. There are, of course, limitations in practising with the aid of such recordings but their potential help should, never the less, not be underestimated. Russian recordings have had a chequered history in the past and the availability of them both in the UK and the USA has to some extent been reflected by the diplomatic temperatures between Washington, London, and Moscow. In America Russian recordings have appeared on a number of labels including MONITOR and BRUNO but recently Capitol launched a new Russian series on Angel/Melodyia*. The Angel recordings

*Some are now appearing in HMV/Melodyia.

are of high quality but other Russian series tend to be more variable. Other East European labels are in evidence to Americans, some, like the Hungarian Qualiton, appearing without disguise of any kind, whilst others are cloaked like Supraphon which appears on CROSSROADS, a cheaper label belonging to EPIC.

ESOTERIC, which issued the Hadyn Society records of the 1950s and early 1960s, is another small but interesting company and an example of a book publishing company which is taking an interest in recorded sound is DOVER, known in the publishing field through its link with Constable, but which in America issues a number of language course, some 80 odd LPs of music, and some interesting spoken work LPs. Some of the classical records have been seen in Britain on labels like Saga and Delta but quite a lot are unknown. Whilst it is hardly a major catalogue the usefulness of the smaller lists is demonstrated by Dover which issues two Rossini operas and one Donizetti opera which are not otherwise available. The spoken word section includes, curiously enough, some BBC material in a "History of English Drama" series. This would seem to be material which ought to be available to British gramophone libraries on the British market but for reasons best known to Dover and the BBC these 18 records have appeared only in America! Few gramophone libraries have such comprehensive collections of British jazz that they need to import records from abroad also, but it need hardly be said that is any case the USA provides a vast range of jazz recordings from which to select. RIVERSIDE, PRESTIGE, JAZZ CRUSADE, JAZZOLOGY and VERVE provide five examples of catalogues which by themselves would provide a very wide range of jazz recordings covering practically every period and style.

American Re-issues

With the vast number of large, intermediate, and smaller companies which exist, or have existed at one time or another on the American market, there is a substantial pattern of re-issue series now available as there is in England. Decca's "Ace of Clubs" and "Ace of Diamonds" largely has a counterpart in America in RICHMOND and STEREO TREASURY, the latter being limited to stereo only issues. This in an indication that American manufacturers are following the British lead of dropping new and many re-issue records in monaural form, although the lead towards this simplification of issues originated not in Britain but on the continent where mono discs are virtually now non-existent. Considering the wild enthusiasm with which America welcomed the LP (it was the first country to see its commercial exploitation) and later on, stereo, it seems strange that it should be America which has provided the last stronghold for the mono record. The danger is that the attitude prevailing in Britain, exemplified by EMI for example, that records will be issued in stereo where *original* stereo tapes exist but where this is not the case issues will be made in mono, may not be followed in America. The so-called "compatible" record is appearing in the USA, notably at the moment from Philips/Mercury. Much valuable material recorded in mono only may not appear again unless it is capable of being "enhanced" by electronic stereo processing. Some of the more reputable and established major companies have not so far allowed these factors to influence them and it is to be hoped that matters remain so*. Of the more important re-issue labels the librarian may be interested in EVERYMAN CLASSICS, which draws not only on older material from the Vanguard catalogue but also includes some recordings new to American buyers. MUSIC GUILD performs a similar service by reviving some of the Westminster records. A rather curious situation exists where Capitol is concerned. Some recordings have been put on SERAPHIM (a label which contains some fine recordings which librarians would like to see on EMI's comparable "Golden Voice" and "Concert Classics") but Capitol has also licensed some of its mono and stereo tapes to PICKWICK INTERNATIONAL. Pickwick is not unknown in Britain, where the labels used are known as Allegro and Hallmark. Presumably the American arrangement is to correspond with the EMI re-issue scheme in Britain of "Music for Pleasure", which works in association with Paul Hamlyn and which is primarily designed to provide retail outlets for gramophone records through bookshops, multiple stores, chemists, and so on, although Pickwick in America draws from other sources besides Capitol.

With the exception of Pickwick and one or two smaller companies whose records retail at between $1.50 to $2.00 there is more or less the same division in the record industry that there was in Britain about seven years ago before the full impact of "budget" price records had been felt. Most new records retail in America at up to $6.00 and the bulk of re-issues sell at $2.50 to $3.00. For the British librarian it is well to understand this, for devaluation and the present high rates of purchase tax coupled with import duty all combine to make American records rather costly. As a rough and ready guide it may be assumed that a top price American record will cost nearly twice as much as a comparable British issue – whilst most American re-issue discs work out at about half that amount. The American librarian is in the envious position of being able to import records into his country with the knowledge that the White House is apparently more able in managing the American economy than is the Treasury, which has always found itself unable to make the ridiculously small financial sacrifice involved in abolishing import duty and purchase tax for gramophone

*Since this was written, matters have been clarified to some extent in the UK by the Trade Description Act, 1969.

records ordered by libraries. The American librarian is also materially assisted by the different kind of retail market which exists in America since retail price maintenance does not exist there. British librarians requiring a reasonable number of American records would be advised to examine the importing and exporting arrangements made by various shops and agencies with some care – in some cases it may be advisable to order via an English agency but in others it could be worth while arranging for a shipment direct from America. Many libraries in America obtain records direct from wholesalers or manufacturers and even some retail shops match these discounts of 25 to 33 per cent by making periodic offers on complete catalogues. It must be remembered, however, that if records are shipped from America on the instructions of a library, the library will be responsible for the payment of import duty and purchase tax.

East Europe and Russia

The Czechkoslovakian range of SUPRAPHON are now distributed in Britain by Keith Prowse Ltd., who maintain reasonable stocks. Some which are not stocked, however, may still be availabe in Czechoslovakia. The "Musica Antiqua Bohemica" and "Musica Nova" series are cases in point. Keith Prowse will accept orders for Supraphon to be imported but orders may not always be fulfilled and may also take some time to come. QUALITON records originate from Hungary and distribution is effected by Robert Maxwell Ltd. and Continental Record Distributors, who carry most of the Qualiton issues likely to interest librarians. Vistula Records Ltd. of London look after both the Polish MUZA and Roumanian ELECTRECORD issues. MELODYIA (MK) from Russia still have no satisfactory importing arrangement although the situation is a little better than in the past. The London Music Shop apparently is able to obtain issues more regularly than most but the number of issues is still rather limited and does not reflect the total number of records in the Melodyia catalogue. Obtaining records to import order is also a hazardous business and no guarantee can be given that orders can be met whilst delivery dates are quoted at four to five months in some cases. This seems to be a great pity since Melodyia records have much improved in technical processing and packaging over the last year or two and the latest issues in stereo have shown that Russian recording techniques now seem to be well up to European standards.

The limitations of space imposed on the writer have made it impossible to deal adequately with the subject of foreign gramophone records but it is hoped that this brief survey may be of some interest especially to the librarian or school teacher who may have tended to assume that the British

"Gramophone LP Classical Catalogue" gives the definitive answer on the availability of recorded music or the spoken word.

Specialist Gramophone Record Suppliers

The following list is not intended to be an exhaustive directory of specialist gramophone record suppliers but merely a selection of well known and long established firms and some of the trade distribution agencies whose services are used by many libraries, schools, colleges, universities, and private collectors. Some of the companies concerned which distribute to the trade do not supply customers direct and this has been noted where applicable. The effects of devaluation and the present high rates of purchase tax at the time of writing have also created difficulties and some import agencies require a minimum number of records to be ordered at any one time. Where these details are known they are also quoted.

DISC IMPORTS AND RARE RECORDS LTD (Manchester). Rare Records Ltd is the retail half of this concern whilst Disc Imports is a wholesale distributor to the trade. Over fifty European labels are imported, including the bulk of the French ones, together with many German and some Dutch, Spanish, Swiss, and Italian records. RCA, Decca and EMI import items are obtainable but American records are not supplied. Disc Imports has recently assumed responsibility for foreign records on Philips labels. A surcharge is made to dealers for records costing £10 or less at trade value, exclusive of purchase tax. The minimum orders that can be accepted are twelve records of any make, size or country of origin but Philips records may not be included. For Philips the present ruling is that a minimum of twelve records must be ordered but again such orders may consist of a mixture of sizes, prefixes and country of origin. Disc Imports supplies EMI Import Dept. Librarians may visit the warehouse by appointment to select stock. Delivery periods for imports to special order quoted as 3–6 weeks but some items may take longer. Export service operated.

SELECTA (Decca wholesale division). All Selecta depots accept orders for continental and American Decca group and RCA records from dealers. Orders are collated at one point and this system avoids any minimum orders being stipulated. A selection of foreign records is maintained at Selecta (London) and certain foreign records can, therefore, be supplied quite quickly. It is possible to visit Selecta depots by making an appointment and for librarians this useful facility allows them to see and handle the material they may require. Delivery times for items not in stock are quoted as 3–4 weeks for European pressings and 6 weeks for American.

RCA import records will not be supplied after June 1969 by Selecta since RCA will at this time be an independant concern and will presumably make their own individual arrangements.

EMI IMPORT DEPT (Hayes, Middx). EMI import pressings and many European labels which are supplied by Disc Imports Ltd. Limited selections from foreign EMI catalogues are kept in stock and for these items dealers are surcharged if less than twelve LPs are ordered. For items not in stock at Hayes, EMI create as many difficulties as possible by insisting that orders must be made for a minimum of twelve LPs from each country of origin, unlike Disc Imports who merely stipulate a minimum of twelve LPs from any country. EMI also make the same ruling for labels supplied to them via Disc Imports, i.e. for non-EMI records a minimum of twelve discs of *each label* must be supplied. Disc Imports do not make this stipulation either. In the last resort this ensures that the onus is placed on librarians of ensuring that sufficient quantities of records are ordered of each label or from each country, a practice which is both irritating and frustrating and prevents librarians from exploiting the service as fully as the equivalent Selecta service.

POLYDOR RECORDS LTD.   Import service now discontinued but operated by Continental Record Distributors.

PHILIPS RECORDS LTD.   Import service now discontinued and taken over by Disc Imports Ltd.

CBS RECORDS LTD.   No import service but foreign CBS records obtainable from EMI Import Dept.

CONTINENTAL RECORD DISTRIBUTORS LTD.   CRD have recently assumed responsibility for operating the Polydor import service and they appear to be doing so in the same efficient manner in which Polydor used to do it. CRD also supply certain European and American labels and these tend to be labels which are not handled by many other distributors.

LONDON MUSIC SHOP.   Specialises in East European Labels such as MK Melodyia (Russia), Electrecord (Roumania) and Muza (Poland). Items not in stock can be ordered but delivery times are not guaranteed. In the case of Russian records it can take four or five months sometimes to obtain orders. It is hoped that both the delivery times and the quantities of records supplied will be improved in the near future. The London Music Shop has distribution arrangements to the trade but these are limited in nature.

THE GRAMOPHONE SHOP (Glasgow).   Continental and American labels are supplied. European records take 3–4 weeks and American ones 6 weeks or so. An excellent source for obtaining many American labels. Bulk quantities of various catalogues are offered from time to time and this means that since large quantities are involved the retail prices can be very competitive. Supplies to the trade. Export service.

RECORD SPECIALITIES LTD (London).   Most European and American labels including EMI, Decca, and RCA imports. Normally European labels are supplied in about 3 weeks and American labels in 6–8 weeks. Small stock at shop includes a selection of imported records. Bulk deletions are acquired from time to time and these sometimes include foreign records. Well run and helpful information service. Specialises in supply services to libraries (processing and cataloguing of records, etc.). Export service. Selected continental catalogues can be supplied if required.

LONG PLAYING RECORD LIBRARY LTD (Blackpool).   European import records can be obtained. Information service. Specialises in supply services to libraries (processing and cataloguing of records, etc.).

DISCURIO LTD (London).   Most labels, including examples of items not easily found elsewhere (Australian local HMV pressings for example). Maintains a large and interesting stock of imported records, classical music, spoken word, etc. Export service. Supplies some foreign periodicals and catalogues.

GRAMOPHONE EXCHANGE LTD (London).   Mostly European labels and only a small selection of American records. A large and varied stock is kept at the shop. Export service.

HENRY STAVE & CO. LTD (London). Specialist EMI and Decca dealer.

TRANSATLANTIC RECORDS LTD (London).   Wholesale supplier. Dealers may order Folkways not generally available in Britain. Orders should be for not less than twelve LPs to minimise freight charges.

KEITH PROWSE & CO. LTD (London). Supraphon records not listed in the British Supraphon lists and which are often available in Czechoslovakia may be ordered. Delivery tends to be rather erratic and items are sometimes not supplied.

Sources Abroad

Among the many specialist shops and sources in other countries the following are quoted at random. Librarians may like to note that where applicable, orders are accepted in, and will be replied to, in English.

N.V. The Electric Gramophone, Spui 6, Amsterdam, Netherlands. O. G. Preiser, Fischerstiege, 9, Vienna, Austria. Musikhaus, 3–4, Neuer Markt, Vienna, 1. Chesterfield Music Stores, 12, Warren Street, New York, N.Y. 10007. Sam Goody Inc., 250, West 49th Street, New York, N.Y. 10019. The Record Hunter, 507, Fifth Avenue, New York, N.Y. 10017.

Catalogues and Periodicals

The following catalogues are "equivalents" to the *Gramophone LP Classical Catalogues* published by the *Gramophone* in England.
Schwann LP Record Catalog. (W. Schwann Inc., 137, Newbury St., Boston, USA). Occasionally publishes an Artist Index. Monthly.
Bielefelder Katalog. Publishes catalogues for classical, for spoken word and for jazz records. (Bielefelder Verlagsanstalt KG, Bielefeld, Postfach 1140, W. Germany.) Usually twice a year.
Diapason Microsillon Catalogue Classique. (Diapason-Microsillon, 61, rue La Fontaine, Paris, 16.) About every 18 months.

Apart from individual manufacturers' catalogue services which range from small printed lists to subscription catalogues which may include regular supplements, two other sources for tracing information exist in the American *Music and Phonorecord Catalog* (published by the Library of Congress) and *Der Grosse Deutsche Schallplatten Katalog*, the latter being a combined trade catalogue published in Western Germany. Both these catalogues are, however, rather more expensive and are likely to be needed only in larger libraries.

The following periodicals and journals may also be of interest:

American Record Guide. USA. Monthly.
Billboard. Cincinnati, USA. Weekly.
Diapason. Paris, France. Ten times per annum.
Discoteca. Milan, Italy. Eight to twelve times per annum.
Fono Forum. Bielefeld, W. Germany. Monthly.
Hi-Fi Stereo Review. Chicago, USA. Monthly.
High Fidelity. Great Barrington, Mass., USA. Monthly.
New Records. Philadelphia, USA. Monthly.
Phono. Vienna, Austria. Six times per annum.
(La) Revue des Disques. Belgium. Ten times per annum.

Catalogue Enquiry Service

A collection of gramophone record catalogues, British and foreign, is being built up by the hon. secretary of the Library Association's Sound Recordings Group. All catalogues and lists received are permanently filed and kept. Librarians in the United Kingdom are welcome to send enquiries for information about records which they wish to obtain or think may exist. For librarians overseas the hon. secretary will, in cases of difficulty, answer enquiries about British issues.

Communications should be sent to Mr. D. G. Williams, ALA, Hon. Secretary, Sound Recordings Group, Grimsby Public Libraries, Central Library, Town Hall Square, Grimsby, Lincs. (Telephone: 56012/STD Code: 0472.)

Museums of Sound
History and Principles of Operation

by PATRICK SAUL
Director, British Institute of Recorded Sound

Although such inventions as Leon Scott's phonautograph, dating from 1857, did in a sense record sound by making a visual record of sound waves, the phonograph invented in 1877 by Edison in America and — independently — by Charles Cros in France, was the first machine which recorded sounds in such a manner that they could be audibly reproduced.

Unfortunately, the new invention's potentialities as a means of providing posterity with aural evidence of those aspects of civilisation which are expressed in sound were largely neglected. In its earliest days the phonograph was mainly exploited as an office-dictating machine or as an amusing novelty which enabled its owner to record and hear his own voice and those of his friends. Furthermore, when "pre-recorded" cylinder recordings began to be published they were, as a rule, of little aesthetic or historical interest, consisting for the most part of such items as humorous monologues, comic and popular songs, bell solos and marches.

However, some eminent people did make records: the first musician of standing to record was the great pianist, Josef Hofmann (1876–1956), who made his debut at the age of six, and at the advanced age of twelve made some experimental cylinders for Edison (1). Other celebrities known to have made records very early in the history of the phonograph include Bismarck (1815–98), Brahms (1833–97), Browning (1812–89), Gladstone (1809–98), Gounod (1818–93), Irving (1838–1905), Florence Nightingale (1820–1910), and Tennyson (1809–92). But it was the students of folk music and of linguistics who first made serious and extended use of the phonograph for research purposes, and it was their activities which led eventually to the establishment of the first archives of sound recordings. The reason for this was, of course, that the phonograph provided a solution of what for them had hitherto been an insoluble problem: the accurate registration — impossible by written notation, however complex — of the subtle inflections, irregular rhythms and microtone intervals of the music and language of non-literate or "primitive" peoples.

Archives of Sound Recordings

What is generally taken to be the first instance of the use of sound recordings in academic research in the humanities and of their deposit in a museum as research material occurred when, in 1889, Dr. J. Walter Fewkes recorded some prayers, tales, and songs of the Passamaquody Indians in the eastern part of the United States; from 1890 he also recorded some Zuni and Hopi songs, and some of these were transcribed by Dr. Benjamin Ives Gilman of Harvard, the recordings being deposited in the Peabody Museum (2). The use of the phonograph for similar purposes in Europe was begun in Hungary in 1898 by Béla Vikar, and continued from 1904 onwards by Béla Bartók, Zoltan Kodály, and others, thousands of their recordings finding a home in the Hungarian National Museum in Budapest (3).

It is, however, to Austria that credit must be given for establishing the first *comprehensive* archive of sound recordings. The plans for this institution, the *Phonogramm-Archiv* of the *Akademie der Wissenschaften* in Vienna, were drawn up by Professor Siegmund Exner, and are dated April 27th, 1899. They were as follows (4):

1. *Languages.* Initially, to survey the languages and dialects of Europe, as spoken at the end of the nineteenth century, and gradually to extend this survey throughout the world.
2. *Music.* To record performances of music, in particular the music of primitive races, for study on a comparative basis.
3. *Voices.* To form a collection of the records of the voices of famous people.

The catalogue, published in 1922, of the first 2,000 accessions, shows that the collection – which contained few if any commercial records – was rich in folk music and linguistic matter recorded in many parts of the world by expeditions sent out by the *Phonogramm-Archiv* itself or obtained by exchange from foreign institutions. There were also a few scientific records, and a large number of "voice-portraits", including the voices of Franz Josef I, Einstein, Puccini, and – reading extracts from their own works – Hugo von Hofmannstal, Arthur Schnitzler, and Ferdinand von Saar (5). The collection, as detailed in this catalogue, did in fact provide a conspectus in sound of Viennese civilisation as it was during the first dozen or so years of the twentieth century.

Between 1899 and the outbreak of the Great War in 1914 many record archives were established, often as departments of university institutions or of national libraries. One of the most important was the Berlin *Phono-grammarchiv*, founded in 1904, which was for many years until 1933 directed by the eminent ethno-musicologist, Erich von Hornbostel, under whom an unrivalled collection of folk music was built up (6).

Other collections of outstanding importance include the *Phonothèque*

Nationale in Paris, which developed from an archive which has existed in one form or another since 1911 (7), and the *Discoteca di Stato* in Rome, which was founded in 1928 at the instigation of the composer, Umberto Giordano (8). Both these institutions benefit from legal deposit laws under which record manufacturers are obliged to furnish on demand two copies of any record published in France or Italy respectively.

One of the largest collections in the world is that of the Library of Congress in Washington, the nucleus of which was the Archive of American Folk Song, set up within the library in 1928. There is no legal deposit law applying to records in the United States, though legislation pending may introduce this; however, the principle American manufacturers have for many years given their records to the library, which also possesses some hundreds of thousands of recordings made by government departments, and many recordings of important broadcasts (9).

Among other important American archives are the general reference collection in the New York Public Library, now known as the Rodgers and Hammerstein (10), the extremely comprehensive library of recorded literature in the Poetry Room at Harvard University, and the collection of vocal records in the Historical Sound Recordings Archive of Yale University Library. In general, the provision of facilities for the study of records – both reference and circulating libraries – in universities, public libraries, and elsewhere, is far more widespread in the United States than elsewhere.

Apart from general collections, many specialist archives containing records of great value have been established. The Department of English at Leeds University, in England, for instance, has undertaken a recorded survey of English dialect (11); a similar survey of German dialect has recently been completed by the *Deutsches Spracharchiv* at Münster, and there is an outstanding folk music archive in the Department of Musicology in the *Musée de l'Homme* in Paris, the value of which to the world at large is greatly enhanced by the publication – either by the museum itself or by commercial firms – of many records of material from its collections (12).

Several private collections are in existence which contain unique material of great value. Two of the most important are the collections of Dr. Walter Toscanini in New York and Dr. Garcia Montes in Havana. Dr. Toscanini has for many years been engaged in forming a collection of recorded performances conducted by his father, Arturo Toscanini; apart from all the published records, the collection, which is very extensive, contains unpublished tests and recordings of broadcasts (13). Dr. Garcia Montes' collection contains most of the records by opera singers of any importance published during the last fifty or so years anywhere in the world (14).

Nowadays, most broadcasting organisations maintain record libraries of one sort or another; unfortunately, many of these resemble circulating libraries rather than archives, since as their stock wears out or goes out of fashion it is replaced by newer publications and there is little effort to safeguard those recordings which are of historical interest. However, some radio collections are archival in character; one of the earliest and most impressive was that established by the German radio before World War II. It consisted not of commercial records but of recordings made by the radio itself from broadcasts considered to be worthy of preservation. There is an astonishing wealth of material in the two catalogues covering the years 1929–39, and it will be regrettable if it transpires that the bulk of the collection did not survive the war. Apart from foreign material, the collection of some 50,000 recordings included the recorded voice of almost every eminent German during the period – statesmen, leaders of industry, actors and actresses, authors reading their own works – and a remarkable repertoire of familiar and unfamiliar music of all kinds, performed by the best interpreters and often by the composers themselves (15).

In the United Kingdom the BBC maintains two very large record libraries: the BBC Gramophone Library, which contains commercial records only, and the BBC Sound Archives (formerly the Recorded Programmes Permanent Library), which consists of non-commercial records such as those which the BBC makes itself or obtains from foreign radios. The BBC Gramophone Library, which contains more than 250,000 different records, is less like an archive than the other library, since although great care is taken of unusual or out-of-print records of obvious importance, the first object of the library is to serve current programme needs, and this necessitates the handling of records by unskilled staff outside the library and their despatch to radio stations throughout the BBC network. The BBC Sound Archives – which contain over 30,000 recordings – have on the other hand, been built up as a collection of historical sounds which can be used in future programmes, and its contents illustrate every aspect of life in Britain since 1934.

Both these libraries are for the internal use of the BBC; there is, however, one other archive in Britain which aims to be universal in scope and which is also intended to serve the general public. This is the British Institute of Recorded Sound, which was established in active operation in 1955 and which during the thirteen years since then has acquired some 180,000 recordings by gift, exchange, or purchase; the current rate of intake is about 1,000 records a month, and the collection includes commercial records, British and foreign, some BBC recordings, and many obtained from overseas institutions and from private collectors; for example, of folk music recorded in the field. In addition to the records themselves the Institute has a collection of related written matter – such as record manufacturers' catalogues from all parts of the world, books and periodicals about records, and documents relating to the record industry, in original form or on microfilm.

Principles of Operation

The problems facing the archivist may be divided into the following four categories, which to some extent overlap: acquisition, preservation, service to the public, and legal questions.

It is assumed that in each country there should and indeed eventually will be something in the nature of a national deposit library or archive which will obtain records in the following categories:

1. Commercial records published in the country in which the archive is situated or manufactured in it for publication abroad.
2. Commercial records published abroad by foreign manufacturers.
3. Recordings produced by radio organisations.
4. Private recordings and those produced by institutions; and
5. Unpublished commercial records

There are some fundamental principles which each national archive ideally should follow. In the first place, in order to prevent losses caused by pressure for economy or by changes in taste, the archive should be prohibited from disposing of any record of which it has only one copy. Secondly, a national archive should not take the form of a chain of specialist libraries; what is needed in each country is a fully comprehensive collection containing sounds of all kinds. The existence of such an archive would not prevent the establishment by — for example — universities and learned societies of specialist collections, and if this led to a certain amount of duplication it would be a good thing; accidental damage to a valuable record would not then be an irreparable disaster.

The third principle is non-selection; in practice this would mean that the archive would select only if forced to do so. Any record offered to it which was in reasonable condition would be accepted for preservation if it were in a form considered to be permanent; by this is meant, in effect, processed discs, published or unpublished. There should be rigorous selection of records of doubtful permanence — such as cylinders, instantaneous discs, and tapes. (To say that the archive should reject selection as a principle does not mean, of course, that it would not make greater effort to obtain some records than others.)

If, for policy reasons, some selection of processed discs were necessary, it would probably be wise to try to restrict it to "commercial" dance music, and to certain kinds of English and American "light" music; that is to say what is sometimes called "salon" music. Some people may wonder why a serious institution should bother itself at all with popular music; but even if of little aesthetic value – and this is debatable to say the least – popular art in any medium may be of considerable sociological interest; there seems to be a good case for the preservation at least of samples of all kinds of popular music and entertainment in their various stages of development.

A fourth fundamental principle is the need for documentation; every record must have kept in association with it any relevant texts or other related matter. The desirability of this will be evident in the case of folk music, folklore, and linguistic records, but the principle applies no less to other categories. The albums and sleeve notes, libretti, and other written material which are sometimes available in connection with records should not be dissociated from them, but should be treated as part of a discographical entity (16).

With regard to acquisition, a law of legal deposit or a voluntary agreement with the record industry would cover all records under category (1) above. In most of the principal record manufacturing countries the industry has an extensive export trade in records not intended for the home market; these records are often of great importance, and steps should be taken to obtain copies for the archive of the country in question as soon as they are manufactured.

It is essential for a record archive to obtain regular information about all commercial records available abroad as well as in its own country. Many records of great importance have been published by short-lived mushroom companies, and even in the case of the larger manufacturers it is normal practice to delete records from the catalogues if, for example, their sales are considered to be insufficient. Once a record goes out of print it may be very difficult and expensive to obtain a copy, and these difficulties will be much greater in the case of foreign records.

The introduction of tape-recording has led to the recording on a large scale of performances for broadcasting and also to the recording of broadcasts; there is an international agreement between many radios under which a recording made by any one of these may be made available to its fellow organisations abroad. Many of these recordings are of great historical or artistic value, and it would be a great step forward if an international agreement could be drawn up under which it would become permissible for such radio recordings to be deposited in any of the constituent non-radio archives of an interlinked system.

Recordings of broadcasts are, as a rule, made under agreement with performers' unions, copyright organisations, and other interested bodies, and the existence of these agreements is presumably reflected in increased fees payable in respect of recordings intended to be made available for exchange with overseas broadcasting stations. There are, however, few problems facing record archives which are more urgent that the necessity for establishing machinery which would enable a reputable non-radio archive to obtain a copy of a recording made by the broadcasting organisation of another country.

The law regarding the recording of broadcasts varies from country to country; in Britain it appears to be obscure and there are many anomalies. Amateurs regularly record broadcasts and exchange them with one another, and the law thus gives sanction to the casual collector which it denies to the archivist. Legislation may not be necessary, but if it were thought desirable and practicable to change the law relating to the protection of performers' copyright, mechanical rights, and broadcasters' rights in the many countries involved it would probably be sufficient to provide that in any proceedings it would be a defence to show that the allegedly infringing copy had been made, passed on or acquired for the purpose of improving the archive concerned in the case.

The acquisition of private recordings presents few problems, since private collectors are as a rule very generous in allowing an archive to copy their recordings; the source is particularly valuable in providing folk music recorded in the field.

Perhaps the class of record which raises most difficulties for the archivist is the unpublished commercial record, of which vast quantities exist in the vaults of the record companies. It may happen, for example, that one member of the cast of an opera, dissatisfied with his own performance, will refuse to authorise publication of the record. Its acquisition by a public archive may then raise a moral problem; it can be argued that if an artist will not permit the publication of a record it should be destroyed. But sometimes refusal to authorise publication does not signify that the artist is dissatisfied with it; there have been cases, for instance, in which it has been alleged that authority to publish was refused because of disputes over fees.

In general, it would be desirable for unpublished records to be treated as manuscripts are treated and for accredited archives to be able to acquire copies which could be made accessible for study, the relative catalogue entries making clear that the performance had not been approved by the artists.

With regard to the preservation of valuable sound, cylinders and instantaneous discs (sometimes known as "acetates") cannot be regarded as satisfactory media; the former are bulky and fragile and liable to fungoid growths, and according to an invaluable pioneer work the *Library of Congress Report on Preservation and Storage of Sound Recordings* (Washington, DC, 1959), the latter, even if kept sealed under ideal conditions, are liable to sudden and complete disintegration of the emulsion on which the recording is engraved. If kept under suitable conditions of temperature and humidity and free from abrasion and pressure, processed discs – either shellac or plastic – may be regarded as satisfactory means of long-term storing of valuable sounds. The position of tape-recordings is not so clear; it is obvious that a tape is in some ways an unsafe medium. It is easily erased and, if carelessly handled, may be broken or stretched. Other less obvious possible faults, which may vary according to such factors as the nature of the base material, are demagnetisation, printing (the spreading of the recording from layer to layer), and physical deterioration.

In the actual operation of an archive there are a few simple principles, the observation of which will reduce the chances of damage to valuable records. For instance, members of the public should not be allowed to handle records (which for obvious reasons cannot be lent). They should be listened to by means of headphones or through a loudspeaker in a listening room connected by telephone with the operator. It is also important that any members of the staff who handle records should be trained in their use. In order to prevent wear, any extracts from a record which a listener wishes to have repeated over and over again should be dubbed on to a tape loop, a device which allows continuous repetition. Permission to do this would have to be obtained from the copyright owners, but they would probably be ready to grant a blanket authority covering cases of this kind to a national archive. It is also desirable, particularly for a vulnerable medium such as tape, that every recording should be kept in duplicate, the two copies being kept in different buildings.

Although the acquisition of valuable records and their safe keeping are the first tasks of an archive and an inaccessible archive is better than none at all, mere possession is not an end in itself. In the long run the *raison d'être* of the archive is the public service which it can provide. This will depend largely, though not entirely, on the existence of a satisfactory catalogue.

In addition to providing a listening service, the archive should act as an information and documentation centre and should publish a periodical and occasional monographs on various aspects of recorded sound. Recitals of recorded music, poetry, and drama would also be both valuable in themselves and an effective means of drawing the attention of the public to the educational potentialities of the archive itself, and indeed of the still comparatively youthful medium of sound recording.

© 1963 Patrick Saul (Revised 1968)

REFERENCES

(1) Roland Gellatt. *The Fabulous Phonograph*, English edition (London, 1956), p. 18.
(2) *Journal of American Folklore*, III, No. X (1890), article by J. Walter Fewkes; *Journal of American Ethnology and Archaeology*, I (1891) and V (1908), articles by B. I. Gilman.

(3) Béla Bartók. *Hungarian Folk Music*, English translation by M. D. Calvocoressi (Oxford, 1931).

(4) *Mitteilungen der Phonogrammarchivs-Kommission der Akademie der Wissenschaften in Wien*, No. 1. Bericht über die Arbeiten der von der Kais. Akademie der Wissenschaften in Wien eingesetzen Kommission zur Gründung eines Phonogrammarchiv (1900); No. 58. Das Phonogrammarchiv der Akademic der Wissenschaften in Wien von seiner Gründung bis zur Neueinrichtung im Jahre 1927, by Leo Hajek (1928).

(5) Katalog I der Platten 1-2000 des durch die Mittel der Treitl-Stifung gegründeten und erhaltenen Phonogramm-Archives der Akademie der Wissenschaften in Wien (1922).

(6) Erich von Hornbostel, *Zeitschrift für vergleichende Musikwissenschaft*, Jahrgang I, No. 2 (1933).

(7) *Revue de Phonétique*, 1911, *tome premier, premier fascicule*, p. 103; *deuxième fascicule*, p. 197. For further information see article on page 000, *"La Phonothèque Nationale"*

(8) *Italian Affairs*, IV, No. 4 (July, 1955), pp. 877–9.

(9) *Folk Music of the United States and Latin America: Combined Catalog of Phonograph Records* (Division of Music, the Library of Congress, Washington, D.C., 1948), p. iii; Library of Congress *Annual Reports*, 1940 onwards.

(10) *Bulletin of the British Institute of Recorded Sound*, No. 5 (Summer, 1957), pp. 20–22, article by Philip L. Miller.

(11) *Bulletin of the British Institute of Recorded Sound*, No. 1 (Summer, 1956), pp. 2–6, article by Stanley Ellis: "Mechanical Recordings for the Linguistic Atlas of England".

(12) Collection *Musée de l'Homme* (Paris) (Paris, UNESCO).

(13) Robert C. Marsh. *Toscanini and the Art of Orchestral Performance* (London, 1956).

(14) *The Gramophone*, XXXVI, No. 422 (July, 1958), p. 47.

(15) *Schallaufnahmen der Reichs-Rundfunk* G.m.b.II. von Ende *1929 bis Anfang 1936; von Anfang 1936 bis Anfang 1939.*

(16) A more detailed note on this subject will be found in *Fontes Artis Musicae*, 1964 2/3, Patrick Saul "A documentation policy for a national sound archive".

The British Institute of Recorded Sound

by PATRICK SAUL

Director, the British Institute of Recorded Sound

The British Institute of Recorded Sound was founded in 1948, as a national archive of sound-recordings and a documentation and information centre for all aspects of recorded sound other than the purely technical. In the early 50s the Charles Henry Foyle Trust of Birmingham granted a small capital sum for the purchase of equipment and the conversion of premises, and the Arts Council and the London County Council each promised £500 a year for three years; and support for a limited period, to help to get the Institute on its feet, was given by the Pilgrim Trust.

These developments resulted from the Institute's first public activity: the organisation, in collaboration with the University of London Department of Extra-Mural Studies, of lectures by a number of eminent authorities on a variety of subjects, each lecture being illustrated by gramophone records or tape-recordings and thus drawing the attention of the public to the potential value for serious purposes of a comprehensive national collection of sound-recordings, open to the public for reference.

In 1955 leasehold premises were obtained in Russell Square and an appeal for public support in the form of gifts of records was launched in *The Times* and elsewhere. The first large collection of records which the Institute received came from the Central Music Library, consisting mainly of collections formed by Gerald Cooper and Edwin Evans. Other large collections – each containing several thousand records – received comparatively early in the Institute's history by gift or bequest – included the large general collection of Percy Scholes, an extensive Wagner collection presented by V. V. Rosenfeld, a vocal collection – particularly rich in French music – presented by the Executors of the late Lionel Dunlop, Percy Grainger's collection of English, Danish and Polynesian folk music which he amassed early in the century (presented by the collector together with photographic reproductions of his original transcriptions of the songs into musical notation), all the British Council recordings of poets reading their own poetry, and innumerable gifts from private collectors and institutions, including many public libraries.

The Institute clearly has a special responsibility to preserve British material and it thus possesses — for instance — more than 1,000 works by British composers of the twentieth century which it has itself recorded on tape (mainly from broadcasts, under one of the agreements with the BBC mentioned below). But it is also international in scope and among important items, to mention a few taken at random, are Professor K. P. Wachsmann's collection of African music; the late Arnold Baké's Indian collection; the recordings made in Colombia by the Anglo-Colombian Recording Expedition; 4,500 political 78s; 30 LPs of Dutch poetry and 40 LPs of Mexican poetry read by the poets; several dozen plays recorded by the Moscow Arts Theatre and a similar number by the Comédie Française; 1,500 Folkways LPs; most of the records available in India in 1968 of Indian classical and folk music — about 300 LPs and EPs; 80 LPs of Australian aboriginal music; and recordings made specially for the Institute by the Parliament of Australia of its own proceedings.

The average rate of intake of discs has been about 1,000 a month since 1955 and at the time of writing the archive ranks among the world's largest — as well as the most comprehensive — public reference collections, apart from those owned by radios (which are of course essentially not accessible to the public). It includes, at the time of writing 150–160,000 discs, 1,500 cylinders and about 5,000 hours of tape. The disc collection includes some duplication since it is the practice to accept two of each disc, the right being reserved to dispose of surplus copies. It is also the policy to keep every tape in duplicate, for reasons of safety.

One of the principal obstacles which hindered progress at the start was Purchase Tax, for it was discovered that this tax would be payable on all British records, even if offered as free gifts by the manufacturers. After lengthy negotiations the Government agreed to incorporate a clause in the Finance Act 1960 which has the effect, subject to conditions, of exempting from Purchase Tax and Import Duty any new record which the Institute adds to its archive. This legislation made it feasible for the Institute to approach the record industry for support, and most of the principal British manufacturers now present their records as they are issued. The Institute also buys some foreign records and acquires many by exchange with overseas archives.

The archive now contains most of the orchestral 78s and many of the instrumental 78s issued in British, but it is relatively weak in rare vocal records and popular music and light entertainment. It is expected that many gaps in the collection can in future be filled by means of tape copies of rare originals lent by private collectors, since the principal record manufacturers have said that they are ready to give the Institute the necessary permissions, subject to safeguards against further copying for illicit use. Many private collectors have indeed already generously offered their co-operation.

Apart from published records, British and foreign, the Institute – as indicated above – possesses a large quantity of unpublished material, and one of the most important sources of this is the BBC. For several years there have been two contractual agreements between the BBC and the Institute, approved by other interested parties such as the copyright bodies and the performers' unions. Under one of these agreements the Institute acquires all recordings added to the BBC Sound Archives in disc form and also BBC transcription recordings – the latter being recordings made by the BBC for transmission by overseas radios; under the other agreement the Institute itself is permitted to record broadcasts. This it does on a fairly large scale – perhaps ten or twenty broadcasts each week – since the BBC itself tends to add to its Sound Archives only those broadcasts which it expects to be able to use for future transmissions, whereas the Institute's standard of selection as a national reference archive is not necessarily the same.

Under an agreement negotiated with the theatres concerned and with Equity and the Musicians' Union, the Institute – which owns equipment of professional standard – itself records each production of the National Theatre and the Royal Shakespeare companies, during a public performance; most of the foreign companies' productions arranged in collaboration with these two organisations have also been recorded in recent years and it is hoped that the recording programme – which has the support of the Arts Council – may be extended to outstanding productions in other British theatres.

For obvious reasons the Institute cannot lend records: they are far more vulnerable than books and – unlike written matter – they are affected by the rights of performers. Thus many of the Institute's unpublished recordings – including those of broadcasts and of the theatre – have been made subject to the condition that they are to be available only for private study within the Institute.

In addition to its collection of sound recordings the Institute is building up as comprehensive a library as possible of written matter, including books and magazines in many languages, record catalogues, catalogues of other record libraries, texts and other documents relating to recordings, and copies of the internal documents of the record industry. About eighty periodicals are regularly taken and the collection of record catalogues, recording sheets and other industry documents on microfilm is a large one. As an indication of its scale, it includes 500,000 pages of microfilmed Indian record catalogues alone, and the library is probably already – in spite of lack of the necessary resources to develop its full potential – the largest and most comprehensive in its field.

Other activities, in addition to the organisation of many hundreds of lectures, have included the publication of a duplicated *Bulletin*, which was superseded in 1961 by a printed quarterly journal, *Recorded Sound*. This contains the texts of lectures promoted by the Institute, discographies, articles relating to any aspect of recorded sound of a non-technical nature, and book reviews. It is sent automatically to any individual or organisation enrolled as a Friend of the Institute.

One or two occasional publications have also appeared including *London Musical Shows on Records 1894–1954*, by Brian Rust (out of print), *Vertical-cut Cylinders and Discs: a catalogue of all hill and dale recordings of serious worth made and issued between 1897–1932 circa*, by Victor Girard and Harold M. Barnes (reprinting) and *An Elgar Discography*, by Jerrold N. Moore.

The Institute is a registered educational charity; its President is Sir Edward Boyle and it is governed by sixteen Governors, whose Chairman is Professor D. B. Fry. Though an independent body it receives an annual Government grant, which does not however cover all its income needs. A direct Treasury grant-in-aid was first made in 1964 but responsibility for official financial assistance to it – and of course to other grant-aided bodies – was transferred to the Department of Education and Science in 1966. In that year the Institute bought a freehold building – a Victorian house of sufficient architectural merit for it to have been made the subject of a preservation order – to serve as a permanent home. The house – 29 Exhibition Road, London, SW7 – is well situated in the museum area close to Hyde Park and to the Royal Albert Hall, the Royal College of Music, the Royal College of Organists, and Imperial College. It provides damp-proofed storage space for 250–300,000 discs and a large quantity of tapes; a book library and reading room; a lecture room seating 100 with tape and disc playback and tape-recording facilities; a refreshment room; listening rooms; and technical facilities including the means of recording broadcasts and copying discs and tapes. There is also space for expansion at some future date.

The new premises were formally opened by the Rt. Hon. Jennie Lee, MP, Minister of State in the Department of Education and Science, on 22 May 1968.

The BBC Gramophone Library

by DEREK LEWIS

Gramophone Record Librarian, BBC

In the beginning, when the "C" in BBC stood for "Company" there was no gramophone library. Gramophone records were hardly, if ever, broadcast – partly because their programme potential had not then been fully realised, but also, I believe, due to a certain amount of opposition from the gramophone companies, who feared that the broadcasting of their products might detract from sales.

By 1933 (the BBC was a Corporation now) the position had changed somewhat. Record programmes introduced by Christopher Stone had proved immensely popular with listeners, and had encouraged sales rather than detracted from them. To get everything on an official footing, an agreement was signed in January that year with Phonographic Performances Ltd. that authorised the BBC to broadcast gramophone records regularly.

Some organisation was now obviously necessary. Up till now records had been purchased as needed or broadcasters brought along their own. A standing order was placed with every record company then operating in the UK, and a copy of every new release was purchased automatically. This arrangement is still in operation today, except that one copy is no longer enough in most instances. Some 25,000 discs of previously issued material were also obtained, and the business of cataloguing, storage, and devising a workable issuing system begun.

I think now is the time to scotch once and for all the legend that the BBC owns a copy of every record ever issued, anywhere in the world. How I wish it were true. But those who have read Roland Gelatt's amazingly detailed history of the haphazard growth of the record industry in his book *The Fabulous Phonograph* will realise the sheer practical and financial impossibility of ever attempting such a feat. Enough to say that our current stock figure of some 800,000 discs offers a mouth-watering choice and at least a fairly comprehensive survey of the history of the industry and the treasures it has produced. And this stock is expanding by some 30,000 discs each year.

An important point to make clear is that the gramophone library consists of commercially issued records only. It is a completely separate department from that dealing with the BBC's own recordings; and although items from both sections may on occasion be combined to make up a programme, for administrative purposes it has been found essential that the two should pursue their own course in practical organisation and administration.

Another thing to bear in mind is that the library exists to serve the needs of broadcasting: one of the conditions of our agreement with Phonographic Performances Ltd., is that the records purchased will be used for broadcasting purposes only. Regretfully, therefore, we have to refuse the considerable number of applications from outside the BBC to use our resources for research, lectures, gramophone societies and the like. Apart from the legal side, we just don't have the facilities to deal with this sort of thing, although we will do our best to answer any queries about records, provided they are reasonable. The person who writes in asking for a list of every record made by Bing Crosby, complete with matrix numbers and recording dates, will get a firm but polite refusal, as this sort of thing is right outside our scope. We would, however, direct such a person to an appropriate source of such information where such exists.

In the last few years the pace of life, and consequently broadcasting, has stepped up considerably. Nowadays, the initial copy of a disc that we purchase on release cannot possibly satisfy all potential users. In the case of a really popular item (i.e. a new title by the Beatles) we will have purchased a dozen or more extra copies in the first couple of days. To anyone who thinks this sounds wasteful, I can only say that it is much cheaper than trying to organise a shuttle service of a few discs from one studio to another, especially when these are spread not only across London, but all over the country as well. The reason becomes apparent when I explain the vast network of programmes that the library has to service. For not only do we supply records to those programme departments immediately concerned with sound broadcasting on the Domestic Services (including the Regions), but the Television Service, and the BBC World Services as well.

The library is housed in Egton House, just a stone's throw from Broadcasting House, and, in fact, linked to it by an underground passage (very useful in bad weather). Television Centre, Bush House (World Service), Aeolian Hall (Popular Music), and the main Regions (Birmingham, Manchester, Glasgow, Edinburgh, Cardiff, Bristol, Belfast etc.) all have small libraries acting as subsidiaries of the main one. Television and Bush House each need a staff of around a dozen, while the Regions can usually get along with one person in charge. Their function is to maintain a basic stock from which they can supply the more predictable needs of their particular producers immediately, drawing on the main library stock as required. They keep copies of discs from the vast "mood music" catalogues issued by music publishers (Chappell, Boosey and Hawkes, etc.) and which we regard as "commercials" even though they are not on sale to the general public. These are designed to fill a particular need, which they do admirably, and many a well known signature tune has been chosen from the publishers' catalogues. Standard classical and light music repertoire in steady demand, and the current "pops" also form part of these sub-libraries' stock. Even so, the bulk of material requested still has to come from Egton House, resulting in a daily total output of some 850 records from here.

The London centres can be serviced several times per day by van or messenger, while records to the Regions are sent by train, post, or air in the case of Northern Ireland. Despite the enormous traffic which ensues, we find this works very well, and catastrophes are few.

Stock Acquisition

Situated conveniently in Central London, we can obtain daily deliveries from the record manufacturers, enabling most records in the UK catalogues to come to hand within 24 hours of ordering and frequently less. In emergencies, there are a number of record shops in the immediate vicinity from whom we can make purchases.

The ordering of records from abroad is an increasingly important part of our routine. Keeping Bush House supplied with material from literally all over the world is a mammoth task, and in the popular field in particular this must be as up-to-date as we can make it. Many programmes on the domestic services now feature foreign records regularly, and there are always the specialised programmes such as the recently introduced series for Indian and Pakistani listeners to be catered for.

For more serious fare, the same urgency does not always prevail. Nevertheless most record collectors are well aware that much interesting material is issued abroad that never appears in domestic catalogues, and it is one of the librarian's tasks to be always on the look out for items that might prove of interest for future use. The specialist record dealers who concentrate on imported records always have enticing titles on their shelves, and in addition we obtain a large number of records direct from manufacturers in the country of issue. In this way we can scoop the cream of issues all over the world, which will be of value to the listeners of today and the future.

I think I should stress at this juncture that we do not spend recklessly. Like all departments we have an annual budget to keep to, and are at pains to make sure it is put to the best possible use.

Registering and Cataloguing

As soon as a new record arrives in the building its existence is noted in a numerical register. We now have ninety of these loose-leaf volumes, listing record companies in alphabetical order, and subdivided into label prefixes. This "anchors" the record and enables us to know that a particular number is officially "in" even though it may not yet have appeared in the racks. Extra copies of individual numbers are also marked in this register, giving the stock position at a glance.

From here the record is passed to the "bagging" section, where it will obtain its own manila "master-bag", and have its number, printed on dynotape, affixed to the top right-hand corner. If it is extra stock then it passes immediately to the racks. If new to the library then there is a diversion to the cataloguing section. Our system of cataloguing is explained elsewhere in this volume (see p.000), so I need say no more than that basically this entails full details of the record's content being entered on cards for filing under title, artist, and composer. Of course it is not as simple as that, but I can safely leave the complexities to my colleague to explain. Now the record can come down into the racks, ready for prospective borrowers – of whom there is almost certainly a waiting list.

Record Storage and Issue

Stock is housed in adjustable metal racking, spread over two floors. The LP storage room has a floor area of approximately 400 square yards, with shelves up to head height. Assuming the present rate of expansion (always a dangerous thing to do) we estimate we shall be full up in another five or six years.

Records are stored in alphabetical order of make. Then divided into alphabetical order of prefix, and thence into numerical sequence. In fact, virtually the same system followed by most record shops.

Expansion is a constant problem: gaps are left at regular intervals to allow for this, but a small amount of shifting back and forth to cope with the introduction of new labels is unavoidable. Unfortunately, the excellent system of sliding racking would not prove practicable in our case, as it is usual to find up to a dozen people in different parts of the racks at any one time: some filing away records and others getting them out.

The actual issue of records is undertaken by a team of clerks. They are at the receiving end of the requisitions sent through the BBC internal post, or delivered in person by the borrower. The requisition is a printed form, with space for borrower's name, location, and department, and we also require title and transmission date of the actual programme. If the borrower has already done some research and has provided record numbers so much the better, but if not, then of course it is up to the library clerk to consult the card index and find this important information – for only then can he find the records in the racks. Both the record and its master-bag are coded with details of the borrower, and a copy of the requisition is filed separately, to be destroyed when all the records on it have been returned safely.

Staff

I have always thought it important that, wherever possible, our library staff be "record people". Lots of persons are knowledgeable about music in one form or another, but the strange ways of the record industry remain a closed book to them. I am always on the lookout, therefore, for people who have had some dealings with gramophone records in their working life, be it on the retail side, in a record company, or a library. We don't, of course, necessarily insist on any of these qualifications, and whatever a person's past experience has been they would have to impress us with a feeling of versatility and adaptability. A library clerk must be prepared to deal competently with any request, be it for authentic sounding recordings of mediaeval dance music or the latest "pop". For our purposes it would be useless to have someone who could discourse with authority for hours on the recorded works of Monteverdi, but who would be completely non-plussed if asked to produce the name of the first song ever recorded by Frank Sinatra. If our clerks do have a special interest in a specialised field of repertoire, be it poetry records, traditional jazz, or ottocento opera, then so much the better, for their brains can then be picked by those not so knowledgeable – but a basic knowledge about a lot of things, plus a keen interest in the programmes to be served is the most useful attribute of a library clerk in a broadcasting company. To ease the daily grind somewhat, there is always the pleasure of personal contact with the many broadcasters, musicians, disc-jockeys and other eminent names who visit the Library in connection with programmes – be it a Hollywood film star for "Desert Island Discs" or a famous concert artist preparing an item for "Music Magazine".

Deletions

For the enormous number of records that the companies put on to the market each year, there are an equally large number that they decide to withdraw from sale. This always poses a thorny problem for a broadcasting station. A record may have ceased to justify its existence through actual volume of sales, but to us it may be standard broadcast material for years to come. As soon as deletions lists are issued, a quick stock check is taken, and where necessary extra copies are ordered — the quantity depending on what we assess will be a record's programme potential in years to come. In some cases we can determine that a cheap-label re-issue is imminent, so extra stock may not be necessary. The new copies are sealed, stored away separately and only opened for actual transmissions. In that way we can be sure to have mint copies for broadcasting for some years to come. Remaining copies in the racks are stamped 'Deleted' to ensure that both library clerks and borrowers know exactly how the situation stands.

The fixing of labels and other marks to records is a tiresome business, and we try to keep it to a minimum. However, one other distinguishing mark we have found useful is the word "Import" stamped clearly on all records obtained from companies outside the UK. Again this signifies to the clerk and borrower that the record may not necessarily be replaceable, or extra copies obtainable at short notice. Another essential label informs the user if the material on the record must be cleared with copyright department before broadcasting — most important with speech, poetry or any humorous material, where special fees have to be negotiated with the author and sometimes the performer. While on the subject of copyright, it is important to remember that the small print around the rim of every record concerning unauthorised reproduction, means exactly what it says. Payment has to be made to Phonographic Performances Ltd. for every second of broadcasting that counts as "needletime", and we have to adhere strictly to the number of hours per week of broadcasting "canned" music allowed by Phonographic Performances Ltd. and the Musicians' Union.

Archive

Not to be confused with the "Sound Archives", which consists of BBC recordings only, this section of the library comprises some 7,000 discs of historical or rarity value, many of which are single copies, and impossible to replace. Here are our "treasures" — many of them such as the records made by Mei-Figner, Irene Abendroth, Rudolph Valentino, Puccini, Marie Tempest, and Sir Charles Santley would command a small fortune if they appeared on the collector's market today. Besides records there is a collection of cylinders, with a large number of interesting items among them.

An archive must be selective — and there are no set rules for what it should contain. The emphasis tends to be on the personality or the event rather than the musical merit. Representative records of famous artists in all fields of entertainment, examples of composers performing or directing recordings of their own works, statesmen and politicians, poets and authors – and any of the gramophone "classics", such as Stanley Holloway's *Brown Boots*, Ernest Lough's *Hear My Prayer*, and Myra Hess playing *Jesu, Joy of Man's Desiring*. Looked at from this angle the selection of Lenin and Mae West, Benjamin Britten and Fats Waller ceases to be arbitrary, and makes a kind of sense. It is largely thanks to the tireless efforts of my predecessor, Miss Valentine Britten, that the BBC has as good a collection of these unique records as it does, which with the passing of every year becomes an increasingly valuable heritage of programme material. Nowadays the archive section is not restricted to 78 RPM discs. Many interesting LPs have already disappeared, presumably never to return, and we have to view each list of deletions with an eye to their possible archive value, and preservation.

Stereo

Ever since the introduction of stereo we have purchased selectively from the new issues. Stereo demonstration broadcasts have been a feature of radio for a number of years, and today a good percentage of broadcasts on Radio 3 (both Music Programme and Third Programme) are in stereo.

Nowadays we buy stereo issues automatically – in any case monaural issues are fast being dropped by the record companies, and frequently a recording is issued only in a stereo version.

The majority of BBC studios and cutting rooms are now equipped with "compatible" cartridges, so that stereo records can be played, even if the actual transmission is monaural.

Services

Although we are first and foremost a library of gramophone records, certain ancillary reference sources are inevitable and desirable. Biographies of performers are kept on file, complete discographies of certain artists (very useful for reference – we may not possess all the records listed), lists of "Top Tunes" from 1900 onwards – things of this sort, usually compiled by an enthusiast, can be invaluable for programme research and ideas.

Texts of song recitals, opera libretti, and other notes that are frequently supplied with LPs today are filed separately from the actual records. These are loaned out if requested, but not sent automatically. They are so easily mislaid or destroyed, that we prefer to treat them independently.

All production departments, and of course the subsidiary libraries, are supplied regularly with the release information, catalogues, and other publicity matter issued by the record companies. This enables them to keep up to date with releases as regards the UK companies. In addition we issue a monthly bulletin, quoting all additions to library stock from foreign sources, which receives the same distribution. This is particularly valuable for those for whom the main library is inaccessible through distance, allowing them to keep up to date with new acquisitions.

We are always on the lookout for new ideas, especially any simplifications in work-procedure. At the moment of writing we are experimenting with a method of speeding up the registering and bagging operations, and are also enquiring into the possibility of using a computer for our booking-out process. It will be seen that we share the same basic principles of working as any other library. Some of our problems are different because we exist to serve the needs of broadcasting. But at least life is never humdrum, and we have come to take the unexpected as a matter of course.

There follows a list of the catalogues, journals, and selected reference works in the library.

CATALOGUES
(a) Annual alphabetical and/or numerical catalogues of the main issuing companies (Decca, EMI, Philips, Pye, etc.)
(b) Weekly and monthly supplements to above plus any other lists and information supplied by smaller record companies in the UK.
(c) *The Gramophone* Classical, Popular, Speech, and Stereo catalogues.
(d) Foreign catalogues such as *Santandrea* (Italy), *Diapason* (France), *Bielefelder* (Germany) and *Schwann* (USA).
(e) Current release information from a variety of foreign sources (especially useful in the purchase of up-to-date material for the BBC World Service).

JOURNALS

*The Gramophone	*Records and Recording	*Audio and Record Review
*Jazz Monthly	*Hi-Fi News	*Record Retailer
*Melody Maker	*Disc	Musica e Dischi (Italy)
Billboard (USA)	Cashbox (USA)	High Fidelity (USA)
American Record Guide	Diapason (France)	Revue des Disques (Belgium)

*All UK

Most of these are kept for a full year and then discarded. *The Gramophone* and *Melody Maker* are retained and bound. Certain items of interest from the other journals are retrieved and kept on file.

SELECTED REFERENCE WORKS
Jazz Records 1897–1931 and *Jazz Records 1932–1942* (Brian Rust)
London Musical Shows on Record 1894–1954
Top Tunes 1912–1962
Liturgical and other Church Music on Records (R. G. Angel)
Daily Mail Book of Golden Discs
World's Encyclopaedia of Recorded Music (Clough & Cuming)
The Fabulous Phonograph
Journal of the British Institute of Recorded Sound
Complete Book of Light Opera (Lubbock)
Decca Book of Opera
Kobbé's Complete Opera Book
A Guide to Popular Music (Gammond and Clayton)
Complete Book of Ballet (Beaumont)
Everyman's Dictionary of Music

The above books are for general reference only. It is not the library's function to supply detailed information of music. This is readily available from the hundreds of volumes in the BBC Reference Library or the BBC Music Library.

In addition there are some 1,700 record catalogues of domestic and foreign origin from 1900 onwards, as well as copies of periodicals such as *The Record Collector*, *The Voice*, *Talking Machine News* and *Phono Trader*.

Separate files of artists' biographies have been built up from publicity handouts and magazine articles, where these might be thought to be of help to programme contributors. Also complete discographies of certain well-known artists (even though all the records may not actually be in the library).

The Gramophone Record Library, East Sussex County Library

by R. T. G. ROWSELL, FLA
County Librarian, East Sussex County Library

The Record Library in East Sussex was started in a very small way in 1956. The stock was limited to what are popularly known as classical recordings and they were made available only to music societies and bona-fide music students in the county library area. At first an assistant with an interest in music was put in charge, part-time, and additions to stock were recommended by the County Music Adviser. It soon became apparent however, that the restriction laid on the lending of these records was too narrow and so in 1958 the resources of the record library were made available to all residents in the county library area, i.e., over the age of 15, on payment of an annual subscription of 10/-. With the naturally increased use made of the library thereafter it was agreed that an appointment should be made of a qualified music librarian. He was appointed in 1959 and a subject department was then formed at county library headquarters consisting of records, music scores, and musical literature. This department also took over the Schools Record Library which is still maintained as a separate collection. At the same time the scope of the collection was widened to include recordings of English poetry and drama and some folk music. The following year (January 1960) the first printed catalogue was produced and was kept up to date with stencilled lists of additions from time to time.

With the demand increasing more and more, it became necessary (1961) to appoint another assistant to help in this department, and it was also unfortunately necessary to increase the subscription to £1 p.a. More recently it was decided to include recordings of jazz (both classic and modern), language courses, shows and musicals, a wider selection of folk-music and stereo records.

For the last eighteen months, records have been loaned from both headquarters and fifteen branch libraries. Although there are no stocks of records at the branch libraries, records sent from headquarters are delivered at branch libraries twice a week by County Library van. Owing to increased postal costs, very few borrowers now use the postal service.

235

The checking for damage of records which are borrowed through the branch libraries or by post, is one of our most difficult problems. As these borrowers are not able to check their own records, staff have to do it instead. This has to be done thoroughly, and an important part of the service is to build up goodwill between borrowers and staff, so that when the inevitable query about a damaged record arises, amicable agreement can be reached. A detailed description of the method used to check records is usually welcomed by a borrower at such a time, and he is consequently more willing to accept the fact that the library does its utmost to safeguard his interests.

The stock of records on March 31st, 1969 was 4,543 LPs in the adult record library, and 930 records (both LPs and extended-play) in the schools' record library. All records are subject to the "parastat" process of cleaning before issue. The total number of members at the end of March 1969 was 1,029, using 1,126 subscriptions between them. Issues of records during the year ending March 31st 1969 were 21,163.

The latest improvement to the service has been the transfer of the whole department of music books, scores and gramophone records to new premises. This has made it possible to have a complete open access system for gramophone records, resulting in a considerable saving of staff time, which used to be wasted on fetching records for borrowers. Also the very great increase in floor space allows many more borrowers to choose records at the same time. This extra space has come at a time when the demand for gramophone records is increasing steadily, and should provide enough room for the expansion which is likely to occur during the next few years.

British Commercial Record Libraries and the Independent European Discothèques

by IVAN MARCH

Director, the Long Playing Record Library, Ltd., Blackpool

In considering the British Commercial Record Libraries alongside the Independent European Discothèque movement (which is largely self-supporting and initially financed by private foundation, and not in conjunction with the local authority public library system) I must point out that this chapter is not intended to embrace the whole of the European record-library movement. Apart from the small but growing number of record collections administered by the Belgian and Dutch equivalents of our own Library Association there are also record libraries in Scandinavia and Germany. I hope to deal with these in depth as part of an all-embracing book on "Gramophone Record Librarianship" to be published in 1970/71.

The commercial record libraries within the UK and the non-profitmaking independent discothèques on the European Continent originated almost simultaneously in the early 50s. The initial stimulus was provided by the advent of the long-playing record. In England earlier attempts to provide a commercial loan service with 78 discs had met with shortlived or limited success. However, mention must be made here of Allen's Library, which advertised regularly in *The Gramophone* before the last war, and the Yorkshire Gramophone Library (operated by H. Dagnall), which took over the field at the end of the war when Allen's Library gradually ceased operations because of the proprietor's ill health.

In both cases these libraries were based on large personal collections of 78 RPM discs. The only restriction placed on borrowers was that fibre needles should be used, and records travelled through the post in cardboard or (in the case of the Yorkshire Library) aluminium sheet boxes, fitted with inner-protective sponge rubber. Each aluminium box held eleven shellac discs, and breakages were very rare. The Yorkshire Library was terminated in 1953 when it was obvious that the LP record was rendering 78 RPM discs obsolete, and the library's proprietor did not have the capital available for restocking. Both these libraries were inspired by their owner's personal love of music and had a membership running into hundreds – a large number indeed, in the pre-LP gramophone-record era. It was then only a year or two before the first of the large British commercial record libraries, the Long Playing Record Library began operations.

The chief difference between the English and the Continental experiments in this field (apart from their general attitude to profit) is that the English commercial operation has been primarily postal, whereas European practice has favoured personal access based on LP collections housed in the centres of the large towns. Whilst the reasons for this are partly geographical, it must also be remembered that even in the early 50s there were already in existence in England an appreciable number of record libraries sponsored by local authorities, many of which had been formed during the 78 RPM era. Admittedly most of these were in the Greater London area, but the provinces were not entirely neglected, and in fact the very first British record library was in Herefordshire.

The earlier local authority library service did not always promote a reputation for care of the records issued (indeed this is still a major criticism of many current local collections) and this was, and remains, the trump card of the British commercial services.

It was the need for a national postal library service with discs maintained in first-class condition that encouraged the formation of the Long Playing Record Library in 1954. In tracing the history of this organisation I am able to convey the ambience and, broadly speaking, the system of the other British commercial libraries. Like our own organisation the two most prominent ones, The Crotchet Record Library and The Wilson Stereo Record Library, are "husband and wife" affairs, with both husband and wife prepared to work long hours for relatively modest returns. It must be emphasised that size (although in terms of publicity it may impress the public) is by no means a criterion of excellence in the operation of a commercial record library. The decisions to be taken on stock control alone multiply with size. Without the use of a computer, only the combination of extreme skill and knowledge of records themselves, plus a determined finger persistently held on the public pulse, can prevent the accumulation of a disastrous proportion of "dead" stock. Thus to operate efficiently a commercial service must have a built-in system of turning over its stock quickly and regularly. Every point of this operation needs a high degree of commercial flair and business sense. Even the disposal of unwanted used records (usually in good condition) is a highly specialised exercise.

Let us look, then, at the beginning of a commercial library. For staff there is, initially, a husband and wife team. Capital is inevitably limited, and in fact the library service is likely to exist at first on paper only, until the first members join and their subscriptions start flowing in. Fortunately credit is (or was) not too difficult to obtain in the record trade. The new library needs an outside source of income during its formative period, so that capital is not drained away in day-to-day living expenses. Ideally one of the team should be able to continue with a previous job which leaves a fair amount of leisure time, at least during the first months of operation and until the library's initial stock has paid for itself.

In the case of one commercial library the proprietor was a school-master; in my own case I chose to be a tram conductor for the Blackpool Corporation and on permanent "late turn" I could do almost a full day's work in the library before reporting for duty at about 3.30 p.m. each day. Such a double-tiered existence was practical for only the first six months, then the growth of the business needed my full-time attention; by then it could also afford my salary.

What had finally decided my wife and myself on the feasibility of a high-quality record loan library was a visit in 1953 to the North Staffs. Record Library at Fenton, near Stoke-on-Trent, operated by a Mr. F. E. Toft. Mr. Toft is a "character", to say the least, and his library was, uniquely, a one-man operation! His stock was in quite good condition and the operation was commercially viable. (Indeed a recent letter from its proprietor shows the North Staffs. Library still in existence although Mr. Toft, sad to say, is doubtful about its future.)

Our library system, from the very beginning, protected the records on loan by very careful packaging, first with paper bags and later polythene. (In those days many records arrived from their manufacturers with no inner bag whatsoever.) We also devised a reversible semi-permanent plywood packing held together at the circumference by a single football-boot lace of convenient length. This packing proved so effective that when on one occasion a train ran over a GPO sack including one of our parcels, two out of the three LP's inside remained undamaged, although the boards were shattered. The very first LPRL parcel was despatched in September 1954 (an historic moment for us) and because of the non-arrival of the "Fragile – With Care" labels, these words, required by the GPO ruling, were hastily written on with the aid of my wife's lipstick!

We had no means of determining the issue life of a record at that time and we had rashly assumed that – bearing in mind the stringent conditions of loan and careful inspection we envisaged – our records would have a very long life indeed. In fact we were not too rudely disillusioned by subsequent experience, and many of our earlier records had lives of three or four years (meaning upwards of 40 issues), often remaining in really first-rate condition throughout this period. We found, generally speaking, that Decca records seemed to last longest. I could not provide controlled figures to support this claim, it was a tendency rather than a statistic, but I was interested to hear the Director of the National Discotheek in Holland recently make a similar claim. He also supported our finding that Deutsche Grammophon records had the shortest lives, mainly because of their propensity of retaining static. Also in musical terms, we found that operatic records were easily the worst cared-for of all types of serious music whilst chamber music was the best. Opera sets are certainly the least successful repertoire for commercial loan from all points of view, except perhaps stereo spoken-word records which are a complete liability, at the moment anyway.

Whilst willing to accept normal wear and tear, we protected ourselves as far as possible against actual physical damage to records in our initial set of rules and regulations, keyed of course to a rigorous inspection of records on their return from loan. Very great care was taken in devising and setting out these rules, and they incorporated all known refinements concerning record care, stylus life, etc. They were carefully kept up to date at each reprinting, and a testimony to their excellence is provided by their adoption and use (sometimes almost word for word), together with our packaging system, by other commercial enterprises. Imitation is *certainly* the sincerest form of flattery when it is done commercially.

But the LPRL cannot claim to have devised the basic kingpin on which the success of our enterprises was finally to rest. The credit for this must go to a member living in Malton, Yorks. (who, strangely enough, was personally introduced by the recipient of our very first parcel). One day shortly afterwards, this member failed to return one of his borrowed records, sending instead a cheque covering its full retail price. Henceforth all library records were marked for sale to members, at a slowly reducing price, and we had found the way to replace our stock *before* it had reached the end of its useful life. The ability to replace stock in this way is absolutely essential to the economic structure of any commercial record-library. A further source of income is provided by members who buy their new LPs from the library and various incentives are given to stimulate this commerce.

A postal library needs to have lists of records available from which members can choose; it is quite impracticable to suggest that members should make their own lists. One British commercial loan service offers the choice of "any record in the *Gramophone Classical Catalogue*". This has the advantage of evading the necessarily expensive production of the organisation's own catalogue, but in practice it means – apart from the eccentric few who in any case will be expensive to service – that members will mostly want to borrow new issues. To supply members' demands, therefore, extra copies of notable issues will be needed for very brief periods, and in due course these extra copies will become surplus to library requirements. Such a service can only be provided if it runs in conjunction with a highly organised sales operation for secondhand records, outside the library as well as within it. Indeed, for the scheme to be completely successful, the library must become for the consumer in essence a "try-buy" new issue retail operation, with the special facility of being able to do the "trying" at home.

The alternative to this is the production of the library's own selective catalogue, the choice of recordings being based on the opinions of the major British record critics. This catalogue must be supplemented by regular lists of new issues. Such a catalogue is expensive to produce, but this expense can be offset by offering it for sale outside the library service (as well as within it) as a useful selective list of desirable records, which in fact it is. Examples of this are the LPRL's *Classical Catalogue and Handbook* (Photo-litho) and the Wilson Library's *Stereo Index* (Letterpress).

Obviously in a commercial library it is necessary that members should select records for loan from the main catalogue as well as the new issue lists, or library stock is in danger of having too limited a life span (in terms of demand rather than wear and tear). However, the regular purchase of library copies by borrowers, and skilful replacement policy should together maintain a proper balance, remembering that some older issues have a long life as standard "best versions".

In its early days a small commercial organisation seldom has the time or the administration to record figures of each detail of its operations, and when later the analysis is made its most important features are confidential for obvious commercial reasons. Also in a commercial library "issue" figures, as such, are unimportant. What is important is firstly, that the overall operation should be making a profit, and secondly that the basic stock should be turning over satisfactorily without being a financial drain. Records are normally hired out on a day-to-day or weekly fee-paying basis. If a member keeps a record for a month it will probably suffer less wear than if four members each have had it for a week. Issue figures are not, therefore, a yardstick of any importance and membership figures are even more elusive. The constant high turnover in membership is in fact the greatest single problem of the commercial library, and in terms both of advertising and stationery the cost of attracting a member in the first place is considerable. But even after he has joined and commenced to borrow records (a remarkable number of new members join, pay a subscription and do not borrow *any* records) the wastage from the loss of former members is considerable.

In the course of the first decade of the existence of the LPRL the postal service must have shown a membership turnover running well into five figures, but the great majority of these thousands of members only borrowed for a brief period. Obviously membership of a commercial service has a great novelty appeal, and perhaps also a suggestion, soon dispelled by experience, that it offers something for nothing. Thus only a minority of members stay the course.

This fickleness of the general public was further demonstrated when during the late 50s we tried experimental "personal libraries" in Manchester, Bradford, and Bath. It was soon obvious that the high basic overheads (rent, rates, etc.) coupled with lack of public response, prevented the operation from being commercially worthwhile, and its main attraction to us was that it gave us an opportunity to spread a large basic reserve stock. Yet a similar branch situated in Central London in the Aldwych area has always been and still is a commercial success, even though free local authority collections are available within walking distance, in Holborn and Westminster.

A link between my own commercial library and the Continental discothèques is provided by the fact that M. Jean Salkin, the prime mover and originator of the discothèque movement in Europe, should begin his first loan collection in Brussels around the same time as the LPRL was beginning to take its first faltering steps in Blackpool. Also we are physically alike, and can be taken for brothers when seen together, by the uninformed. We are also similar in temperament and we are both ex-musicians, M. Salkin favouring the trombone and myself the French horn!

The reasons why M. Salkin found himself at the centre of a non-profit-making enterprise and myself a commercial organisation, are at least partly connected with the contrast in cultural and economic backgrounds presented by England and the rest of Western Europe. The non-profitmaking but self-supporting institution, capitalised privately, with little or no return expected on the capital, is quite a normal solution of the cultural problem in Europe. Here, to attempt a new cultural venture on a non-commercial basis outside the established institutions is a well-nigh impossible task. The purse-strings of private foundations and grants are no less tightly held that those of the Government, and are not easily loosened in favour of an unestablished individual or venture.

Thus it was as inconceivable for me to have considered setting up a non-profitmaking British record library, as it was natural for M. Salkin to use just this framework for his organisation. He was able to raise a substantial sum of private capital, and although he started modestly, when I visited him in Brussels for the first time at the end of the 50s the Central Discothèque had already a collection of more than 10,000 LPs, and had opened its first two branches. All were amply staffed; indeed all the continental discothèques are much better staffed (in terms of numbers of personnel) than most British record libraries. Today (in 1969) the central collection in Brussels totals over 25,000 discs. Eight full-time branches in the provinces, 30 further centres open one day a week, and a "Discobus" serving 18 smaller communities spending two hours one day a week at each, share between them a further collection of 80,000 discs. Brussels alone issues more than 300,000 records a year, the average issue each Saturday being well over 2,000 records.

As M. Salkin was first in the European field it is natural that the French National Discothèque and the Centrale Discotheek in Rotterdam, Holland, were largely modelled on Belgian systems and practice. M. Rouvet, the volatile instigator of the French record-library system, however, conceived

Fig. 31. *Exterior and interior of the "Discobus".*

his discothèque as part of a wider cultural centre for each French town, the record collection being located in the central cultural building. It may be that, whilst seeming a good plan, it has in fact, weakened the financial structure of the French discothèque, and possibly accounts for its slower growth. With this must be coupled the fact that the Gaullist administration of the time, like any right wing political administration, was not by nature likely to be a generous benefactor of the offshoots of the arts. The issue figures and size of the collection in Paris do not compare with those in Brussels and although the French pioneered the "Discobus" their experience was not too successful, mainly because of the great expense in relation to the number of records issued. Apparently it proved difficult to "train" the public to arrive at a given hour at a given place for a regular weekly call. Also the broader overall cultural plans seem to be losing ground, and M. Rouvet has handed over his Directorship to M. Daudrix, who is content to administer the National Discothèque as a separate entity.

The Central Dutch Discotheek, under the Directorship of M. Rob Maas has its headquarters in Rotterdam. There is also an independent Discotheek at Delft, situated, perhaps surprisingly, within the library of the Technical University. In Holland, however, the provision of record libraries under the auspices of the Dutch Library Association is stronger than in Belgium or France. Apart from a small public record-collection of about 2,000 LPs at Amsterdam (which cannot be borrowed, and are intended for the use – on the premises – by students from the University and Music Conservatoires), there are other record libraries, associated with the public libraries at Enschede, Zwolle, the Hague, and Deventer. The library at Deventer is in a magnificent new library building, comparable with the new library at Hampstead. The financial structure of the public library system in Holland is different from the British system and finance comes severally from national and local sources. There is no comparable tradition of a *free* book loan service in every town as we know it in England and the revelation of the size of the book funds of the average small British library makes Dutch librarians (who incidentally are 80 per cent women, and have in the past been notoriously underpaid) very envious.

This lack of money for buying books is the reason that the European Bibliothèques have been so slow generally to incorporate records, thus leaving the field wide open for the establishment of a separate discothèque system. However, in 1965 the Dutch Library Association instituted a study-centre for Music and Record Libraries and today, even in Belgium, where the Discothèque is powerfully entrenched, there is a growing pressure from the Flemish Library Association (which has recently opened record collections in public libraries at Mechelen and Hasselt) towards some kind of integration.

In April 1966 the independent Rotterdam Discotheek moved to new premises which are part of the magnificent new Concert Hall building. M. Maas hopes that the success of the Discotheek at its new site will help him gain the finance for his planned central collection in Amsterdam. Like M. Salkin he wants co-operation with the Central Association for Public Libraries, but he feels that book libraries tend to approach the problems of record loan with experience and practice gained from books and because of this he considers wrong administrative decisions are made. M. Salkin expresses the independent Discothèque viewpoint as follows: "The fundamental problem is that book librarians think that a record-lending service should be in the hands of a trained librarian and not a musician with a supplementary training in librarianship. We feel that lending records is in every case a matter of enthusiasm and love for music without which a record library is just a dead weight, if not a dead loss. This seems to us a real danger in so far as 99 out of 100 libraries cannot afford to have a musician on the staff to cater for the record-borrowing public".

It is in cataloguing records that the main practical differences between public library procedures and those of the independent discothèques are most sharply defined. The libraries naturally favour, for their record collections, a basic card index system with extensive crossindexing. In Holland, besides title, artist, and subject indexes, a numerical index is also maintained. Alternatively, the independent discothèques have – broadly speaking – abandoned the card index for a printed catalogue which members can buy and take away. All records held in the library are listed in the catalogue (reprinted annually), the location of records at the different branches being shown. All the classical music is kept in closed access and there is no indicator. The member arrives at the library, returns the records he has had on loan (which are subjected to a rigorous and even intimidating inspection) and then takes his pre-prepared list to the issue counter, or alternatively chooses from one of the catalogues kept for members' use at the library. The assistant then looks to see if the required records are "in" and if they are not, the member chooses again.

This may seem incredibly "hit and miss" to the British reader but the chances are that with a stock of say, 10,000 LPs actually available on the premises (with many duplications among popular records) it works very well. Also it is held that because the member makes his request in person to the staff a strong personal contact is soon developed and this helps the staff not only to supply what the member came in to borrow (or perhaps an alternative version of it) but also to assist him in the exploration of the catalogue. In terms of staff time this system is incredibly wasteful, but in terms of public service it is strongly advocated as the best possible way of expanding members' musical interests.

The scheme has also a secondary advantage (as with the British commercial postal libraries) in that because most members purchase a catalogue for their own use this in itself helps to finance the cataloguing of the library's stock. Its limitation is that new issues not in the catalogue are not widely borrowed, even though they may be put out on open access in Browser boxes, simply because members become trained to borrow *via* the catalogue. Non-classical categories of records – jazz, folk, etc. – are, however, put out in Browser boxes and are successfully administered in this way*.

*As we go to press we understand the Belgium Discothèque is currently moving more and more over to open access – subject to available space – for serious as well as popular music.

Records themselves are not packaged, i.e. there is no outer protective sleeves, and furthermore many records I saw had their actual surfaces inadequately protected by the type of inner bag used. There are, however, plans to alter this by the adoption of the polythene-lined paper bag as standard. Records are not parastated, and obviously the main deterrent to damage due to careless handling is the extremely rigorous inspection on return from loan. The Dutch borrower is apparently phlegmatic about this but I understand that in Belgium a certain tension can sometimes exist between members and the library staff, members trying to pass any damaged records through the inspection undetected and the library staff determined to make sure that this will not happen.

The condition of discs I inspected was of a lower standard than is usual in the British commercial library, but distinctly higher than the average standard of the British local authority library. The number of issues expected from the loan of a record before it is withdrawn is lower than the similar figure given by many British libraries; on the other hand records are sold off to members and thus recover about a quarter of their original cost. The European record borrower will expect to pay an annual subscription of around 30/- for his record service and an issue charge of about 1/6 per record for a weekly hiring period. These charges are, however, offset by the fact that to buy records in Europe tends to cost half as much again as it does here and there are fewer bargain labels.

Whatever the differences in procedure and standards between the independent European discothèques and our own public record libraries the most interesting thing about them is that they provide a successful example of a self-supporting record library system, with cultural rather than commercial aims, which has developed as a separate entity with no roots whatsoever in practices devised for the loan of books. As such the operational procedure is fully worthy of study and attention by all British record librarians, who always, it seems to me, work with the initial disadvantage that (quite properly) books are so much a part of their training and thinking that there is always the danger of referring to a record library borrower as a "reader".

Gramophone Record Libraries in the United States of America

by ERIC COOPER
Music Librarian, Enfield Public Libraries

One reviewer of the first edition of *Gramophone Record Libraries* made the point that no reference was made to the extent of gramophone record provision in public libraries in the United States of America. I think that readers should be made aware that this was no accident. The contributors felt the scope of the work to be wide enough and the problems they were dealing with were of such a universal nature, that to examine the information on a national basis would have involved more work that could have been managed at that time. Since then, public and university libraries throughout the world have become more and more committed to providing audio materials and to exploiting the rapidly expanding wealth of recordings on disc and tape. Schools, universities, and colleges of further education are pressing ahead in using recordings as teaching aids and in so doing are assisting coming generations to regard gramophones and tape-recorders as more than mere electronic musical boxes.

Librarians have, albeit too often with reluctance, followed the trend. Consequently, observant readers of professional journals can discover information on developments in countries as far apart as Norway and New Zealand. In the case of Denmark, for instance, attempts are being made at quite revolutionary methods of provision in the sphere of general availability throughout the country which, if attended with success, will exceed the scope of any existing public lending service anywhere in the world. So it may well be that other reviewers will take us to task in the present book when they read a short dissertation on the work of our colleagues in the USA. With so much happening throughout the world, useful articles could be written about the differing methods employed in many lands. To these critics there is one simple defence – the first gramophone record libraries were started in America and there has been nearly sixty years of continuous work in that country since the beginning. No better justification can be offered than this, and I can only hope that it will be accepted as a valid reason.

The foregoing point is a matter of history, but it is not the intention here to write a potted history sprinkled with dates, places, and statistics, but rather to offer some factual information and a few observations. Most important of all, no comparisons will be made with other countries except where possible without risking offence to national pride anywhere. The history of American public-library phono-record loan collections, university, and Library of Congress collections has yet to be written. It will be a mammoth undertaking for whoever attempts it, but it will make fascinating reading if it ever becomes a reality. This is a task for an American librarian. As an Englishman writing at a distance of several thousands of miles I will not dare to get my feet wet, let alone take the plunge. To the American student of librarianship there will be no blinding revelations in the following lines.

The first collection of gramophone records in any library in America came about through a bequest of a collection of vocal and operatic records to a university library, before the First World War. Although this was not open to the general public, the discs were available to the students on the campus and so the claim of sixty years can safely be made out. The first public collection appeared in St. Paul's Public Library, Minnesota, in 1913. No doubt, but for the interruption to the American way of life caused by the hostilities in Europe, there would have been rapid developments springing from this beginning. As it was, there was no further activity until the early 1920s, when other public libraries began loan collections of phonograph records. I am deliberately refraining from naming names or giving dates since I have to rely on information sources that I cannot verify and I have no wish to find myself encircled by claimants who all sincerely believe their library was the first to follow St. Paul's lead. Suffice it to say various American journals have provided me with information over the years that contains the incontestable fact that public libraries there started to lend records to the public fifteen years before any other country. Within the space of a short time several record collections were formed and to their founders goes our gratitude for their initiative and foresight. Some libraries formed collections that could only be listened to on library premises. Others lent to the public only language records whilst some ventured not only into "classical" music but also into jazz. In 1939 there were twenty-five public collections, and by 1940 several universities had growing libraries and some fifty public libraries had collections of varying types. In that year the second public collection was opened here in the United Kingdom, and no significant activity was apparent in our universities. In the States the Library of Congress Music Division had already done several years work on building a recorded sound archive, whilst elsewhere in the world there was little activity in building national sound archives. Here and there in Europe were priceless collections of special materials but few attempts had yet been made to incorporate these into national sound libraries.

In the United Kingdom no work had been done, although the British Broadcasting Corporation and *The Gramophone* magazine both possessed, and still do, the largest collections of discs in the world. It was apt that the country that produced Edison and nurtured Emil Berliner should lead in the field of gramophone record lending libraries.

The Second World War, like the First, inhibited progress for all American libraries, but in 1945 the number of libraries offering phono-record lending services to the public or collections of recorded material for use on library premises began to increase in number at a tremendous speed. Microgroove recordings arrived in 1948 and only served to add impetus to the trend. So that by 1968 an examination of the American Library Directory would have revealed that over 40 per cent of general public libraries listed have phonorecords available either for loan or for listening to on library equipment. As in other countries today, the provision is very patchy. One can find small communities of a few thousand people with quite a reasonable little library at their disposal, while a large town with a population of hundreds of thousands or more just a few miles away has nothing at all to offer and no obvious intention of doing so. But it must be said that most of the libraries that have no record collections are in smaller communities and townships that have insufficient finance for extra services.

During the years some remarkable collections have grown up. The most obvious one of course is the collection to be found in the New York Public Libraries. Here exists one of the largest public loan collections, consisting of all types of recorded material in conjunction with very large and excellent archive and reference collections. The departments are staffed by a number of very experienced and well qualified people that make it the envy of many understaffed libraries in other States and other countries. Broadcasting and television facilities are available to the library along with recording and replay studios. Conditions such as these are the dream of all music and gramophone record librarians and no doubt endless plans for the use of such resources will never see the light of day for the want of such favourable conditions to put them into practice. But of course the USA provides a rather unusual situation in that its radio broadcasting and television services are nearly all commercial. The public library system is a keen and vital movement that is quite ready to use any reasonable channel to publicise its services and it is not unusual to find libraries buying time from their local radio station for giving book and record reviews and for providing programmes of recorded music. The fact that they do not own such facilities themselves in no way acts as a deterrent. Such opportunities for publicity are peculiar to the USA and commercial broadcasting, providing as they do enviable channels to publicise and extend library services.

The problems of administering gramophone record collections seem to be the same all the world over and a close study of articles and correspondence in American and Canadian professional journals only serves to confirm this view. Arguments for and against open access were being discussed in articles and correspondence columns in the 1940s and, as might be expected gramophone record collections in the USA were up to ten years ahead of European libraries in converting record collections to open access. The two main factors at work in this instance were (a) the earlier commencement of public loan collections, and (b) the earlier arrival of long-playing records that were far more suited to open stacks or Browsers than 78 RPM discs. By 1963 a questionnaire sent out by the Art and Music Department of the Kansas City, Missouri, Public Library showed that out of 392 libraries only 90 operated a closed stack system. As to methods of operation, etc., this same questionnaire revealed that, as in other countries, less than 10 per cent of the libraries that replied had modelled their system on that of another library. The vast majority had, in all aspects of the work, devised their own methods and found their own answers to the problems that revealed themselves day by day and year by year. In the fields of accessioning, classification, and shelf-arrangement, the variety of methods employed was quite amazing. Such a variety of individual thought and ingenuity in one profession is quite commendable, but one cannot help feeling that some combined effort through the preceding years might have produced answers that would have contributed to building the ideal method of operating a phonorecord lending service. But visits to libraries in the United Kingdom and on the continent have shown me that the history of libraries and the problems encountered are the same wherever one may look.

One point worthy of mention perhaps, is that a percentage of libraries in America and Europe have recognised the need for more detailed classification in shelf-arrangement and cataloguing. Too often, though, collections have been hurriedly assembled with only a rudimentary classified order and merely supplemented with a composer/author catalogue. As the individual library has grown, difficulties have been encountered in location and retrieval that could only be solved by attention to classification. But the exigencies of the service and its maintenance prevent the library staff from retracing their steps and effecting a cure. It would seem to be that, as elsewhere, the music and recorded-sound services operated in the western world are often the Cinderella of the library service. Schools and colleges of librarianship do not, as yet, give enough attention to producing courses for librarians who wish to specialise in operating gramophone record collections. The result is the usual one – the music library staffs have to develop their own techniques and skills in an area where, until recent years, little helpful information was in print. Hence the diversity of organisation and varying standards of public service. One or two libraries in the USA have already reached the ultimate, in that recorded material is no longer the prime responsibility of the music department. Recordings of plays are shelved with their printed counterparts, as are records of poetry. Instructional discs and documentary materials are all shelved along with books in the correct classified order. Only recorded music remains in the music department. This, to me at any rate, should be the final aim. But until all staff have adequate training in handling audio materials, both disc and tape, I cannot see that such far-seeing methods can provide any worthwhile level of service to the public. Provided training comes first, then the progressive method in question is the obvious way to handle recorded sound in the future.

A proportion of American gramophone record libraries is to be found in quite small libraries serving small communities. These have stocks ranging from 1,000–2,500 discs. To this group can be added a number of large libraries which, for unstated reasons (possibly financial), have small collections within this range. Many of these appear to have no specialist on the staff to cope with the administration. The responsibility falls on the inexperienced staff of the book-lending department. This is common wherever one may go and experience shows that, even if the staff are interested or even enthusiastic, results will fall below those libraries that employ specialists, or trained staff. Which brings us to the question I touched on above, of education and training for librarianship. Overall, the standard is very high, with a considerable degree of specialisation. Music librarianship is given more attention than in many parts of the world, and music posts in the public libraries appear to offer considerable scope. In larger libraries the music librarian would seem to have equal status and salary with other departmental chiefs and specialists. This is not always the case in European countries. However, when one looks at audio specialists the position, with notable exceptions, compares equally unfavourably with library posts throughout the world. The schools and colleges offer very little training in the area of sound recordings and staff employed in phonorecord lending libraries are forced to improvise and learn from experience. This is costly, and provides poor standards of public service. Consequently, gramophone record librarians lack qualifications or status and so are often regarded as inferior to specialists in charge of other departments. The gramophone librarian learns his profession as he goes along, and he keeps on doing it because he loves the job, and who knows, he may one day land one of the major posts, as and when one becomes vacant.

The two American professional bodies that interest themselves in the affairs of phonorecord librarians seem to be somewhat at variance in views and aims with regard to this minority. One section appears to understand the problem of this branch of the profession but could be more active on behalf of its members. The other body, whilst being more active, seems to be more interested in the specialised areas of university libraries, special collections, and national archives. This position is not only found in America. Doubtless there are reasons why this occurs, but this is not the place to discuss them. That such divisions exist is a pity, since they do harm to the common goal of promoting the use of audio materials for education and leisure. Readers may feel that I have been too general in my comments on this point. This is quite deliberate, as I have no wish to take sides or become involved in the course of writing these pages.

In concluding the section on public libraries it is clear that American gramophone record libraries have been in existence longer than anywhere else in the world. A great deal of work has been done by individual libraries throughout the fifty states. Much of this magnificent effort needs investigation and the information gained from it to be whittled down to all the best methods, etc. The results might well produce the best set of criteria for operating a public phonorecord library that ingenuity could devise. Here is a sizeable task for some ambitious person. Might this not provide the basis for a thesis for an examination, a thesis that would have a value beyond its purely academic one? I fear we shall never see it, and if we did, would libraries follow its recommendations? I think not. American record libraries are the same as elsewhere. Librarians on the whole possess a curious combination of conservatism and ingenuity that leads them into individual courses of action from which they are reluctant to deviate. A perusal of the correspondence columns of the *American Library Journal* will prove this to be a valid contention. It is reasonable to say that the contents of the whole of this book have worldwide relevance, and are not a product of conditions peculiar to Great Britain.

Where our American colleagues gain over the rest of the world is certainly in the cost of records. Records are cheaper than anywhere else and can be bought from discount houses at 50 per cent off the current price. Records are offered at reduced prices in many shops as the discs are superseded by newer and (sometimes) better versions. Remaindering and rack-jobbing are normal sales activities. Few of these opportunities occur outside America. These conditions may partly account for the rapid growth and size of libraries in recent times. Companies marketing records, library furniture, and equipment are well in advance of commercial organisations in Europe and the rest of the world. They offer a range of products for protecting record sleeves and presenting the stock that is varied and progressive. Special record-library furniture and equipment are available from a number of organisations. Few companies elsewhere have thought it worthwhile to venture into any comparable production ranges.

All in all, despite lack of co-operation in ideas and methods, the climate on the American continent is a healthy one. Progress is being made all the time. One library in Canada has already installed a video-tape camera and replay equipment in their building, and others have the use of such equipment when required. Certainly video-tape recordings are the next big step in the audio visual field. Once commercial recording organisations and equipment manufacturers break into the open market, libraries will follow with lending services for audio visual recordings. The American continent will certainly see the opening moves in this sphere as it did for sound recording libraries.

At this point it should be made clear that in discussing the public library sector I have limited myself to comment on the best work done by those public libraries in the estimated 40 per cent holding stocks of sound recordings. My American colleagues may well take me to task if I report only the credit side and, by so doing, inadvertently make their road to progress somewhat more difficult as a result. It would be quite wrong to overlook the fact that more than six in every ten library services do not lend recordings. According to the *Bowker Annual* for 1965 (the last year to provides statistics in this form) 18,000,000 Americans have no library service of any kind and 110,000,000 have an inadequate service. In that year the per capita annual expenditure, based on 1963 figures, was $2·05. The recommended figure was $3·85. This made the overall financial gap $310,000,000. By 1966 the amount fell by approximately $50,000,000; but the gap for 1967 showed little improvement. These figures are built upon a set standard, which, as far as one can tell, have not been adjusted during 1966 and 1967 to take into account steady worldwide increases in costs.

Library buildings set serious limits to the development of all types of library services. According to figures given in *Bowker* for 1963, of the 800 largest public library systems, nearly 50 per cent are housed in buildings erected before 1921. Of those, 75 per cent were erected between 1865 and 1910. Figures for smaller systems are not given, but information gleaned from other sources indicates that the pattern is a similar one. To implement new services under such conditions is very difficult indeed and in view of the progress made in providing sound recording services a warm tribute to the determination and organisation of library staff must be paid. In setting down these facts simply to keep the subject in proper perspective it becomes even more apparent that professional staff must work with enthusiasm to make new services a success.

The second part of this chapter is devoted to a brief look at the collections of sound recordings in university libraries and "national" archives and I propose to deal with them in that order.

Only American universities have realised, to any great extent, the need to build archives of recorded sound for the use of future generations. It is a matter for concern that so few educational organisations in the world have recognised their duty in this area. In the USA a few of the university collections of phonorecords rival the national archives of some countries in size and scope. This is a sobering thought. Most of the libraries have sound-recording collections compiled for reference purposes, though there are often lending services available as a separate activity. The point has already been made that the first phonorecord lending service began in a university library about fifteen years prior to the opening of the first public library department. It is not possible to examine all of these special collections, but to give readers some idea of the size and variety of the best of them I have singled out three or four for special mention. Limitations of space are the only reasons for this. If it were possible to compile a list of such libraries I would gladly have provided one, but no reference book in my possession provides sufficient information. Detailed mention of more than an arbitrary selection is out of the question.

The Rodgers and Hammerstein Archives of Recorded Sound

It will seem odd perhaps to place this library in the section on special libraries, university and "national" archives, since it is part of the New York Public Library system. But the fact that it is a reference collection of the highest possible standard puts it outside the scope of the foregoing material about public lending services. It differs from university libraries, in that it is open to the general public. But its aims are not so different from those other libraries. The brochure for the service makes it clear that the library at the Lincoln Center is open to all "who have a serious interest in the performing arts – the artist, advanced student and writer – they are welcome, as are the research worker and scholar in the various other fields represented in the Archives"

The library contains more than 135,000 recordings. The main emphasis is on the performing arts. The whole field of classical music is covered and jazz and folk music are well represented. Apart from this, a large number of recordings of "popular" music are included in the library to compensate for the lack of such holdings in other institutions. This is most unusual and provides evidence of advanced thought and planning. Original-cast recordings of plays and film soundtracks are also included. Outside the performing arts is a growing collection of discs and tapes of political speeches, interviews, debates, and Congressional hearings.

Language study forms part of the collection. A wide variety of recordings including such diverse subjects as bird calls, and medical recordings can also be referred to. The recordings are in all forms, from the earliest cylinders and piano rolls to the latest stereo discs and tapes.

Special mention must be made of the many unique recordings both private and commercial that are to be found in the collection. The Mapleson cylinders, recorded in the Metropolitan Opera House during 1901–03, are known to everyone even if they have not heard them. The only complete collection of the Columbia Grand Opera Records of 1903 is to be found here. There is also a fine collection of commercial catalogues of records and playing equipment with considerable quantities of other printed material covering all aspects of the history of records and recording. The collection is well documented and catalogued and housed in a specially designed building containing all the necessary replay equipment with relay facilities to a listening area on the third floor. So short a description offers only a general outline of the scope of the library which has flourished in recent years with generous help from the Rodgers and Hammerstein Foundation, from which it takes its name.

Yale University

The next library I have selected is that of Yale University and what it calls its Historical Sound Recordings Program. The aim of the Library is to collect, preserve, and study sound recordings which document the history of performance-practice in artistic media since the invention of the phonograph. There are four defined areas of significance for the Library: (1) performances by composers and other important musicians, (2) the musical theatre, (3) dramatic recitations, and (4) literary readings. Two other fields are represented by special collections. These are the James Welson Johnson Collection of Negro Arts, and Yale Memorabilia. Folk and light "popular" music are not included.

Recordings of distinguished composers, musicians, authors, and actors, document not only the mannerisms of the individual performer, but the styles and attitudes of his time and place. The collection is a truly comprehensive one and it contains many rare and unique items for study. One of the main objectives is to provide material to help in the study and reconstruction of past styles of performance. In this sense the recordings are regarded as primary research material for students and researchers at Yale. These recordings, a large part of which are very early examples of the art, are regarded as an essential complement to the University's collection of musical scores and documents, both printed and in manuscript. The library serves not only the music department of the graduate school and the music school, but also, with its non-music material, the school of drama, the history, literature and allied faculties of Yale College and Graduate School. This huge collection is all the more successful for its well defined subject areas. The Program at Yale is one of the most important collections of recorded material in the world, and no one doing research would have adequately covered his subject if he failed to take into account its unique contents. An interesting indication of these riches is contained in the *Yale University Library Gazette* for January 1964.

Stanford Archive of Recorded Sound

My third example is maintained by Stanford University. Its objective is the preservation and scholarly use of historically and artistically significant recordings. The scope of acquisition is quite wide and covers music, literature, drama, interviews and public addresses, and radio and television broadcasts. The library is open to all qualified students and scholars.

In common with other libraries, the Stanford Archive contains all types of recordings, including cylinders, discs, films, tapes, and pianola rolls. Original recordings are of prime importance in the archive. Allied to the recordings are other related materials, such as record catalogues, discographies, books, commercial periodicals, record trade publications, biographies, and much other material.

As at Yale, apart from music, students of literature and the social sciences are able to study recordings of hundreds of literary and political figures of the past seventy years. The library also collects recordings of social events, institutional procedures, legislative sessions, labour — management negotiations, and many other activities of present-day society. The collection also contains radio and television recordings. The archive seeks to provide now, and increasingly in the future, materials of interest to the philologist, anthropologist, sociologist, and political scientist. Archives of sound recordings will be invaluable in time to come and be of at least equal importance as printed documents. I believe that sound recording archives of this kind will eventually surpass the value of much printed material. In the past seventy years the techniques of preservation and storage of sound recordings have been developed to a high degree in America. At Stanford, as at other major recorded sound libraries, these techniques have been put into practice. The library is housed in specially designed fireproof accommodation and is supervised by an archivist and experienced staff.

Library of Congress Recorded Sound Section

No group of examples that failed to include this library could be considered as representative. Though it has not had the status of a national archive during the thirty years of its existence it has become the outstanding library within its field. Though not the largest recorded-sound library in the world, it is certainly one of the most efficient. It can certainly be said to be the largest and best organised collection of phonorecords that forms an integral part of a very fine and extensive reference library. I know of no other library so situated as to offer such excellent overall facilities to the student and research worker. With over 500,000 recorded examples it is the largest reference collection in America with a worldwide reputation.

The Library of Congress began asking record companies to donate records to the Recorded Sound Section during the latter half of the 1930s. Despite the many difficulties involved in keeping contact with record manufacturers, good results have been obtained over the years. With this method of voluntary deposit and through gifts and bequests of record collections, the library now has around 200,000 commercially produced recordings. The latter form of acquisition has enabled the library to get together a reasonable amount of "vintage" material. To this must be added the recordings of the Archive of Folk Song and the unique collection of cylinders of the Smithsonian Bureau of Ethnology. These are not commercial recordings but were specially produced, many by the staff and by researchers who handed their material to the library. Apart from the non-musical material contained in commercial discs, the section has extended its recording work into the area of spoken word. This is a vast and varied field and the Library of Congress was greatly helped in this when it received an enormous quantity of material from the armed forces along with the complete reference holdings of the office of War Information. This collection of recorded history consisted of some 200,000 items.

Through a grant from the Carnegie Corporation in 1940, a recording laboratory and studios were established. The library's policy of recording its own material requirements was made possible from this time. Many of these recordings are duplicated for the public on payment of a fee, as there are not the copyright restrictions that exist on commercial material. The recordings are numerous and varied, covering music, folk music, plays, poetry, etc. Catalogues can be obtained at little cost from The Superintendent of Documents, Government Printing Office, Washington DC, 20402.

The laboratory has done a great deal of research work into the collection and preservation of sound recordings. One has only to look at one of its publications, *The Preservation and Storage of Sound Recordings*, by A. G. Pickett and M. M. Lemcoe, to recognise what all libraries throughout the world owe to the laboratory and the Library of Congress for its own research and publication of this particular piece of research. Pickett and Lemcoe's work will be the standard reference book on the subject for the foreseeable future.

But the Library of Congress has rendered many services in other fields. One of the major problems of gramophone record librarians is cataloguing. In Europe there is no catalogue card service for gramophone records, apart from two small commercial organisations that offer cards with records they sell. This essential but time-consuming work has to be done by staff. But for the past fifteen years the Library of Congress has been printing catalogue cards. This is the only service of its kind that I know of. I only wish I could report that most librarians on the American continent availed themselves of the service. Most of them still seem to prefer to devise and use their own methods. This is another form of conservatism that seems to afflict all sound recordings librarians in America as well as throughout the world. Finally one must mention the cataloguing code for sound recordings developed by the Library of Congress and the constant interest it has in the development of the documentation of sound recordings. Indeed, one is constantly gratified to see how interested and active the library is in the whole field of recorded sound with special regard to the development of library services and archives anywhere.

The staff of the Library of Congress will doubtless know of facets of their work that I should have referred to and have omitted, and, conversely, may feel that too much emphasis has been placed on some points at the expense of others. I hope they will overlook these points when it is understood that I was limited in the information available to me. I would have much preferred to have visited the library before committing myself to print, but this was impossible. These comments refer to all the other libraries that I have mentioned. To those I have not referred to, I apologise. I could have referred, in considerable detail, to the University of Washington and its collection of Second World War material, but limits had to be set. America provides such vast library resources in this field that I could only indicate the nature and size of a few of them.

Much remains to be done in the public recorded sound libraries, and the university and other institutional reference and archive libraries. There are tremendous areas for development and co-operation between them all. America has led the way in the past and will continue to do so if progressive attention is paid to the possible role that these libraries can play in the lives of people in the future.

I would like to thank Donald L. Leavitt, Head of the Recorded Sound Section of the Library of Congress for help and information. Also David Hall, Head of the Rodgers and Hammerstein Archives of Recorded Sound and Brooks Shepard Jr., Formerly Music Librarian at Yale University. Thanks must also be extended to the American Music Library Association and to Miss E. Puckette for tracing numerous references in the *Library Journal* and other periodicals.

The Record Library of the Music Department of the Musée de l'Homme

by GILBERT ROUGET
Head of the Music Department, Musée de l'Homme.
Translated by Christiane Keane
Commonwealth Institute Library

The Musée de l'Homme is both a museum and a laboratory. In its public galleries, the collections of ethnography, of physical anthropology, and prehistory are exhibited so as to show the close connection which exists between all these studies. Most of its departments are thus devoted both to the conservation of collections and the scientific research connected with it. Such is the case of the music department, where musical instruments and archives of recorded music are considered as objects for preservation, study, and publication. The record library which we are going to study is within this framework. We must add that the Musée de l'Homme and, consequently, its record library, are mainly concerned with the ethnography of the whole world, excluding France which is the prerogative of the Musée des Arts et Traditions Populaires. This has also a department of ethnomusicology set up, like the Musée de l'Homme, at the suggestion of Georges-Henri Rivière.

In 1929, André Schaeffner grouped all musical instruments to create a department of "organology" in the institution then known as the Musée d'Ethnologie du Trocadero which was directed by P. Rivet. In 1932, a record library was added to this department. The museum having been called in 1937, "Musée de l'Homme", the department took the name of Department of Musical Ethnology. It became in 1956 the Department of Ethnomusicology.

During the last twenty years, the record library of this department has developed considerably. The new techniques which, since the last war, have caused a revolution in recording and sound reproduction had important consequences for ethnomusicological research. Portable and lightweight tape-recorders which are in use nowadays have made recording "on the spot" a relatively simple and safe operation. More and more of it is done. Furthermore, the quality of documents so obtained has boosted their publication on disc and thus considerably increased their circulation amongst the general public. The expansion of the record library of the

Musée de l'Homme is closely connected with this general trend to which it had in any case largely contributed. We shall return to it below.

Organisation: Buildings, Equipment, Staff, Funds

The Department of Music and consequently the record library, which is a part of it, make up one of the "internal services" of the museum. Therefore, they are not opened to the public but only to research workers and specialists. The premises are situated on the third floor of the Palais de Chaillot (Passy Wing) (1). Out of a total area of 250 square metres, only 35, divided in two rooms, are exclusively reserved to the record library. The first room, which for a long time was the only one, has 20 square metres and housed until spring 1966 the recording apparatus, the re-recording and listening apparatus, as well as half of the record and tape archives. The rest was housed in other rooms of the department.

The second room, built recently when Professor Jacques Millot was director of the museum, is a soundproof studio. It is air-conditioned and protected by a special lining against interference caused by broadcasts from the Eiffel Tower nearby. It communicates by a double glazed bay with another room of 20 square metres in which the tape-recorders will be placed in such a way as to make the whole setup work as a professional recording studio. In this technical room will also be put laboratory machinery. A plan for the reorganisation of the Palais de Chaillot, to be put into effect in, it is hoped, the very near future, will allow the addition on the floor above of an area equal to the three rooms. Also, sound recordings made by relatively important musical groups will eventually be made in the cinema (250 seats), which is on the first floor and which has a podium.

The permanent installations (turntables, tape-recorders, amplifiers, soundproofing) consist of equipment according to the specifications required by the Radiodiffusion Télévision Française: record-players manufactured by P. Clément, tape-recorders by Tolana and Lie-Belin, which provide speeds of 76, 38, 19 and 9·5 cm/s, full-track, half-track, double-track and stereo. To these professional tape-recorders is also added a Nagra 111 BH.

The portable tape-recorders are either Nagra (some of which are equipped with the "Piloton" system and with quartz control for synchronised turning) or Uher. A number of tape-recorders which can be used by amateurs (portable and specialised) and running off the mains supply, provide slow playing speeds. Some have four tracks. They are mainly for listening, listing, and eventually transcribing recordings. Also they are put at the disposition of research workers, on their return, to replace portable tape-recorders lent to them during their assignments.

The equipment of this laboratory, intended to provide acoustical facilities for musicological research, consists of a "Sonagraph", a frequency analyser, a Bruel and Kjaer level recorder, a stroboscope (Stroboconn), a frequency generator, and an oscilloscope. For re-recordings and the eventual correction of badly recorded documents, we have a Klein-Hummel universal correcting filter which also, owing to its sharp filter cuts and ample choice of controls, makes it possible to listen to selected parts of the sound pattern whilst eliminating others (i.e. to listen to the treble, whilst eliminating the bass and middle, etc.).

Apart from a sound engineer, who has been specially chosen for the job, in recent times the record library has had no other staff apart from the staff controlling the general administration of the music department: a departmental head, belonging to the Centre National de la Recherche Scientifique, an assistant, belonging to the Musée National d'Histoire Naturelle and occasional consultants – scientific, technical, or admini-strative – obtaining their funds from different sources. There is for the time being, no post of librarian.

The funds of the record library come from many varied sources and represent a rather complex organisation. Apart from the grant from the general budget of the museum, an important share of the library's funds comes from the Centre National de la Recherche Scientifique, and its record sales, which we shall mention later, were financed at first by the Office de la Recherche Scientifique Outre Mer (Office of Scientific Research Overseas). These recording activities functioned later, partially by being self-supporting, and thanks also partly to grants coming from the CNRS.

Archives of Recorded Music
Master Copies

CYLINDERS AND DISCS. A catalogue of cylinders and discs, "direct recordings" (acetate), which constitute the stock of "originals", has been published (2). We shall, therefore, not refer to it again. We must, however, mention, because of its historical value, the collection of cylinders cut by Dr. Azoulay for the Anthropological Society during the Exposition Universelle of 1900 in Paris, and deposited at the Musée de l'Homme: 375 items of which 95 are concerned with the peoples of Europe, 195 of Asia, 20 of North Africa, 35 of West Africa, and 30 from Madagascar and the Comoro Islands. One of the major projects of the department is to transfer the contents of the cylinders (which are in excellent condition) on to tapes and publish the best on long-playing records.

TAPES. When they have returned from their travels, the ethnologists, ethnomusicologists, film-makers, etc. very often present to or deposit with the library of the Musée de l'Homme the recordings which they made "on the spot" These gifts or deposits, already considerable in number, are bound to become more numerous henceforth as the re-recording laboratory is now able to give donors and depositors copies of good quality, technically speaking, which they rightly expect in exchange. It is hardly necessary to add that scientific rights in the documents remain wholly with them.

We shall not list, even briefly, these recordings. Let us simply mention that they come from the most diverse sources, but mainly from White Africa, West Africa, Central and Equatorial Africa, South-East Asia and India, America (Central and South). As for Europe, and the Near and Middle East, we can foresee that substantial contributions will soon fill important gaps. Polynesia and Melanesia remain, up to now, less well represented, at least as far as "originals" are concerned.

It is precisely this stock of originals, on discs or tape which has supplied the content of the recorded editions which will be spoken of below.

Later Recordings

DISC RECORDINGS.   The record library of the Musée de l'Homme, dating only from 1932, does not include very old records. Among the most important collections of 78 RPM records, we must mention the collection recorded in 1931 in Paris, for the Colonial Exhibition of Vincennes and of which only a very few copies were issued by the Musée de la Parole et du Geste (Museum of Speech and Motion), and by Pathé (174 records, concerning White Africa and the Levant, 25 communities of Black Africa, Madagascar, India, Indochina, Bali, and Java); the records of C. Brailoiu (Society of Roumanian Composers); the relatively important collection of Spanish popular music acquired by André Schaeffner under the guidance of Curt Sachs; two little series on Java, the gift of Jaap Kunst; two others from Tibet by J. Bacot; one from Japan by M. and Mme Hackin; a certain number of records brought from India by different people; collections bought in Paris from export companies (mainly North Africa, Near East, Indochina); then, of course, the famous series "Musik des Orients".

In the field of 78 RPM discs, the accessions of the post-war period have been mainly those of records issued by the Discoteca Municipal de São Paulo, by the Library of Congress of Washington, the Ethnography Museum of Budapest, and the Institute of Musicology of Japan, all obtained by exchange; and also the Navajo records of the Peabody Museum.

As for long-playing records, the lists of what has been published since 1952 are known well enough to make it unnecessary to enter into details. Without asserting that these archives contain everything put out in this form, we can, however, assume that there are no important gaps — or, if there are, that they are in the process of being closed. Let us mention, however, because of its size and its special scientific value (increased further by the articles and analyses assembled in a special number of *Oceania*) the collection of aboriginal music of Australia and New Guinea, issued under the guidance of Professor Elkin.

TAPE RECORDINGS. Among tape-recordings, we must note those from Leningrad (music of various peoples of Central Asia and the Arctic regions), the collection of recordings made by Audrey Butt in British Guiana, (a collection which should inaugurate a series of exchanges between the British Institute of Recorded Sound and the Musée de l'Homme), and finally a number of tapes from Finland, also received as exchanges.

LANGUAGE SPECIMENS. Among the recordings of which we have just read a summary description, we of course find documents which it would be inaccurate to call "linguistic" but which hold nevertheless a certain interest for linguists. They are recordings of spoken languages gathered by ethnographers during their work. They are, of course, of all kinds, from a few fragments of vocabulary to complete texts, from spoken texts having no written form to those which are already elaborately transcribed. At present, there is no separate inventory of this stock. The creation of recorded archives of specimens of language connected more or less closely with the musical archives is being considered.

Disc Recording Issues

Whether they are in 78 RPM or long-playing (33 RPM and 45 RPM), we must distinguish those issues which have been the subject of special agreements with commercial concerns from those made under the label of the Musée de l'Homme. In the first category some records have been pressed in limited editions under the label of the Musée de l'Homme and at the same time without restriction on a commercial label. Others have only been issued under various commercial labels with the description "Collection of the Musée de l'Homme". The records issued exclusively under the label of the Musée de l'Homme have mostly been pressed in small editions — the minimum, however, being 25 — and have been severely restricted in circulation. Two records have been issued in small format (17 cm, 33 RPM or 45 RPM) to be inserted in scientific reviews, and to be complementary to musicological studies. Some records have been published in collaboration with other institutions: the Peabody Museum, l'Institut Français de l'Afrique noire (of Dakar and Saint-Louis in Senegal), and finally, the French broadcasting overseas service (now the OCORA).

In spring 1966 the total number of records issued under the label of the Musée de l'Homme was 104 of 78 RPM and 27 long-playing records of various sizes. To these should be added 20 records issued in co-production or with the acknowledgement "Collection of the Musée de l'Homme" (3).

The records issued by the Musée de l'Homme have three main objectives: to give the widest possible access to original documents in stock, to allow study of them, to ensure their conservation. This is doubly guaranteed, by the multiplication and dissemination of specimens on the one hand, and on the other, by the existence of the master-pressings which correspond to them. With very few exceptions, the complete materials — "father" copy, "mother" copy, and matrix — are deposited in the music department, when the records are issued by the museum. In the case of records issued with the description "Collection of the Musée de l'Homme", only the "mother" copy is deposited. These copies form a special stock, adequate care being taken to ensure their preservation.

Film Archives

The activities of the cinema of the Musée de l'Homme are entirely independent from the music department. It is nevertheless the fact that the Committee of Ethnographic Films constitutes — to the extent that it produces films and, therefore, houses documents — a source of music recorded "on the spot" which becomes more important as the desire for authenticity becomes more pressing. Moreover, this kind of sound is mostly recorded during filming on magnetic tape (6·35 mm H) and when synchronisation is aimed at, on Nagra or Stellavox. After having been transferred for the purposes of the film on to 16 mm perforated magnetic tapes, with the help of the equipment devised by J. Rouch, these documents, being no longer required, constitute the archives which should gradually be amalgamated with those of the music department. Only financial difficulties and the lack of space and staff have hitherto prevented the commencement of this process, which will make a considerable contribution to the stock of original recordings.

This account would be incomplete if mention were not made of the archive of synchronised music and film which has only just begun to be formed. Of the music which concerns us here, this offers the only documentation which is really "total" and, therefore, satisfactory. The close collaboration between the music department, the Committee of Ethnographic Films and the audio visual laboratory of the Ecole Pratique des Hautes Etudes (Dpt of Religious Studies — Sorbonne) which has not long been formed under the direction of J. Rouch and the present writer, has just recently made possible the making of a film of this nature. Musicological study of it remains to be completed and, further, poses technical problems on the solution of which we are still working. But it has indicated a path which from now on will be followed more and more at the Musée de l'Homme to establish an archive of non-classical musicology.

REFERENCES

(1) Housed in the Palais de Chaillot, the Musée de l'Homme is, however, only one of its occupants. It is under the control of the Museum National d'Histoire Naturelle which is situated a long way away at the Jardin des Plantes. This association, which may seem unexpected, can be explained by the fact that the Director of the Musée de l'Homme is the holder of the Chair of Anthropology of the Museum. In its turn the Museum is under the control of the "Direction of University Studies" of the Ministry of National Education.
(2) Collection "Musée d'Homme". *Archives of Recorded Music, series C, Ethnographic and Folkloric Music.* UNESCO, Paris 1952, 74 pages. Catalogue compiled by Simone Roche; introduction by Laszlo Lajtha. English and French text.
(3) A general catalogue published in 1956 is now out of print. Roneotyped supplements covering available records only can be sent on request.

La Phonotèque Nationale

by ROGER DECOLLOGNE
Director of the Phonothéque Nationale and the Musée de la Parole.
Translated by Christiane Keane
Commonwealth Institute Library

History: from the Musée de la Parole to the Phonothèque Nationale

Many of our visitors are surprised to notice that a part of the Phonothèque nationale is housed in a university building. One has to go back in time to explain this situation.

It was following the setting up of the first sound archives, those of Austria (1899) and Germany, that public opinion began to favour the preservation of such a new medium as sound documentation. In France, the Pathé Brothers made a proposition to the Académie de Paris in 1911 to supply the material and technical staff necessary for the making of sound recordings which would be mainly used for the study and preservation of languages and dialects. They therefore proposed to associate this laboratory with the chair of phonetics. The University of Paris agreed and so the Archives de la Parole were born.

Although this new organisation seemed to have at first a limited scope, it in fact developed in several directions, under the guidance of Professor Ferdinand Brunot. As well as dialects, popular melodies, voices of literary figures and voices from the past were also recorded. At the same time, commercial recordings, in the form of donations, of great singers found their way into the Archives de la Parole.

This is the reason why, under the direction of Professor Pernot, the Archives de la Parole were changed, in 1928, into Musée de la Parole et du Geste with the help of the Municipality of Paris.

Meanwhile, by the law of May 19th 1925, the system of legal deposit was modified by the French legislature so as to make it compulsory to deposit phonographic and cinematographic works also. Following the passing of this law, a group of well disposed men formed a commission to study the problems caused by this reorganisation and to investigate the extent to which the Bibliothèque Nationale would be able to deal with these extra commitments. But that institution was suffering from growing pains and the shortage of space did not allow it to house new collections.

At the request of the Minister of Education, the University of Paris agreed to undertake the administration of the legal deposit of recorded works. It was by the decree of April 8th 1938, which had been proposed by Jean Zay, then Minister of Education, that a national record library was created "where recorded documents of all types will be deposited for preservation". The same regulation stipulated that this record library, for the purposes of legal deposit, constituted a branch of the Bibliothèque Nationale and that it would be housed in the premises put at its disposal by the University of Paris at the Musée de la Parole 19 rue des Bernardins.

There came about then a kind of symbiosis between the Musée de la Parole and the Phonothèque Nationale which was broken between 1953 and 1963 and was re-established at the later date. At first, it was the Musée de la Parole which supported the Phonothèque Nationale; today, the opposite is true. But the link between the University of Paris and the Phonothèque Nationale has grown steadily stronger during the last twenty-six years in which the latter has been regarded as an institute of the former and treated as such. Thus it would not be inaccurate to call the synthesis of these two institutions the Phonothèque Nationale et Universitaire.

The Organisational Framework

The Phonothèque Nationale took some time to find its feet. During the period of its existence alongside the Musée de la Parole, it was sometimes difficult to make a clear distinction between the commitments of each institution. On the one hand that legal deposit material had to go to the Phonothèque Nationale, and gifts of commercial recordings to the Musée de la Parole ceased; on the other hand, the Phonothèque Nationale having more adequate resources than the Musée de la Parole was better equipped to further its recording aims.

Furthermore, as the Phonothèque Nationale had to preserve all types of relevant materials and all technical varieties of sound recordings, it was necessary that it should be supplied with adequate mechanical means of reproduction of these various forms of recordings. The Musée du Phonographe was a natural development from this.

All these technical activities have also compelled the Phonothèque Nationale to organise a service where all the necessary documentary material could be consulted when needed: recorded biographies, works of reference on music etc. Where there was no proper treatise written on the subject, as was the case in the cataloguing of sound recordings, the Phonothèque Nationale had to decide itself on the rules to be used. But in order to prevent these from being too different from the rules used in similar institutions, the library arranged international meetings where problems common to record libraries could be discussed.

The constant development of the various services of the Phonothèque Nationale has caused the transformation of what was originally just the librarian's office to a proper administrative department. The framework set up for the carrying out of the various functions ennumerated can be summed up in the form of an organisational diagram:

ORGANIZATION DIAGRAM OF THE NATIONAL RECORD LIBRARY

HEAD LIBRARIAN

General Secretariat

Reception of visitors
and listeners

| Administration Financial and Establishment Dpt | Historical Museum of Recording and Sound Reproduction | Record Documentation | Recording and Sound Reproduction Laboratory |

Accessions

| Research Dpt Accessions of Archive Records | Legal Deposit | Queries Recording requests |

Stock checking and Cataloguing Dpt
Statistics — Catalogues.

"Conservation"
Technical Studies — Reserve Stock.

The Collections

LEGAL DEPOSIT. Even though it was set up in 1938, the Phonothèque Nationale only commenced work in January 1940, when it received its first financial allocation and the first deposit of records as required by law. But the long years of the Second World War were not propitious to the development of this new organisation and the legal requirements were not properly observed by publishers faced with all sorts of difficulties. The law of June 21st 1943, which revised the requirements on deposit of the law of May 19th 1925, was also somewhat lacking in precision with respect to recorded works; that is why it proved necessary to clarify it by means of regulations. The regulation of August 1st 1963 left no means of evasion to manufacturers, publishers, and importers of recorded works; besides this it specified that recorded works should include sound recording in all its aspects, whatever the mechanical means and techniques used. This definition applied equally to records and to magnetic tapes, it can also apply to reproductions of old cylinders, or to all other kinds of recording which may be invented in the future. The regulation specifies, in addition, that the specimens deposited should be of normal type and that special care should be taken to include sleeves, boxing, binding, and blurbs. Further, all re-publication, even although only in part, of a recorded work must be deposited in the same manner as a new work. This deposit must be made 48 hours before commercial publication.

Another decree, dated June 17th 1964, extends deposit requirements to the overseas departments.

The statistics of accessions of records received as legal deposit reflect the main stages of its development:

> 1940–44: 2,854 records
> 1945–49: 5,908 records
> 1950–54: 12,173 records
> 1955–59: 25,887 records
> 1960–64: 34,255 records

The year 1965, by bringing 7,436 records to the Phonothèque Nationale, shows that the annual production of records in France seems likely to stay at an average of 7,500.

So, in the form of legal deposit, the Phonothèque Nationale has received 86,958 different records, and it has in fact housed more than 170,000 records, since two copies of each work are deposited. To these records have been added, since 1962, 162 pre-recorded tapes which are also deposited in duplicate.

PURCHASES AND GIFTS.   We shall pass over acquisitions of recent records from abroad, and instead, we shall deal with the building up of the archive stock, either by purchase or by the gift of private collections, including cylinders, sapphire-needle records (vertical groove), and steel-needle records (lateral groove).

When I first took up my duties at the Phonothèque Nationale Library in 1954, this archive stock only numbered 1,471 items. Because of a shortage of funds, it had only reached 2,858 items by December 31st 1960; from 1961, a special provision in our budget enabled us to intensify our efforts. At the same time, donations became more important, so much so that within the five years, from 1961 to 1965, more than 25,000 records or cylinders were added to the archive stock.

RECORDINGS MADE BY THE PHONOTHÈQUE NATIONALE.   Record librarians are aware of the wide field of action left unexplored by commercial recordings. This is why the Phonothèque Nationale itself makes a certain number of recordings of philosophers, scientists, prominent barristers, poets, writers, playwrights, composers, etc.

Care is also taken to collaborate with explorers who bring back from their travels on the five continents various sound recordings, some of which are of the highest quality.

THE HISTORICAL MUSEUM OF RECORDING AND SOUND REPRODUCTION. As well as sound recordings, the Phonothèque Nationale formed an important collection of mechanical musical instruments and old phonographs. The Musée de la Parole took the initiative in 1935 to show a small collection of old phonographs, mainly from the Pathé factories, but it is to the Phonothèque Nationale that the credit must be given for having built it up from 1959 into a "Musée historique du Phonographe". The prehistory of the phonograph is represented by mechanical music.

It is not possible to give a list of phonographs as there are now more than 300 of them. Mention, however, must be made of the first jukebox, the first apparatus with grooved tracks, the first speaking clock, the first system of sound correspondence (with a grooved postcard or with a record), the first attempts at stereophony, the first audio-visual machines for the teaching of languages, and the first dictating machines.

Other Activities

The Phonothèque Nationale does not limit itself simply to preservation. From its beginning, its first director had wanted to give it a living interest by excursions into the record world of yesterday, and some talks illustrated with records dealing essentially with folklore. Today, the Phonothèque Nationale receives constant visits from groups (schools, artistic or cultural societies). These visits with guide and commentary are always followed by the performance of selected documents of all kinds: music, history, literature, theatre, folklore.

The Phonothèque Nationale also organises regular lectures, the theme of which is selected to illustrate a specific sound. For this, it makes use of speakers with specialised knowledge. Among the topics dealt with have been:

Debussy and the record
Manuel de Falla and the record
Homage to Francis Poulenc
French song in 1925

Famous voices of the heroic age of the phonograph
The film musician
Fifty years of history illustrated by sound documents

The average number of visitors to the Phonothèque Nationale is about 1,800 a year. But quite a few outside activities make it possible to reach a very large proportion of the public, as there are exhibitions organised within the framework of the International Festival of Sound, newspaper articles, and radio or television programmes.

We must consider particularly all those who are conducting record research, musical or literary; not only have they available a card catalogue with four entries for each work – author or composer, speaker or performer, title and form – but, furthermore, they can use cubicles which enable them to listen to recordings needed for their particular studies.

On the other hand, the Phonothèque Nationale has made an important contribution to the various studies of sound recording and an information bulletin on its activities is published by the library, although in a very limited way.

Finally, we must mention another function that has been assigned to the Phonothèque Nationale by the decree of October 16th 1953. Indeed, at the end of the Second World War it became apparent that the delay in the developing of record libraries plus the terrible destruction suffered by the whole of Europe because of war made information concerning sound recording difficult to obtain. This is why the decree previously mentioned stipulated that a centre of phonographic information should be set up at the Phonothèque Nationale. Because of the lack of staff and funds, the application of that decree was postponed. But from the time the library moved to new premises, although still very small, in 1959, patient research on various documents has been undertaken. The results already obtained show that the method chosen is efficacious. Henceforth it would be appropriate to allocate specialised staff to the development of this service. After having completed a survey of all the basic material still available under the national plan, they could make inquiries abroad to gather together widely scattered information, the existence of which we already know.

The activities of the Phonothèque Nationale go far beyond the border of France. Indeed, it was France who took the initiative by creating in 1963 the "Fédération Internationale des Phonothèques", after having taken part very actively in several congresses of international organisations of various kinds. There is no doubt that this new body after having undergone the necessary trial period will be recognised by UNESCO. Then record libraries, which up to now have been too often considered unimportant, will have attained their legitimate place among all the other cultural organisations of the world.

The Central Gramophone Record Library of the Office de Radiodiffusion-Television Française

by ODETTE MANINGE
Head of the Services of Information Storage and Documentation
of La Radiodiffusion-Television Francaise,
Translated by Christiane Keane
Commonwealth Institute Library

The Central Gramophone Record Library of the Office de Radio-diffusion-Television Française is one of the most important departments of the Services of Information Storage and Documentation. The main departments have now been regrouped under the authority of one official, as follows:

1. Central Administration.
2. Central Catalogue.
3. Arts Reference Library. Includes Music, Light music, Literature and Theatre.
4. General Reference Department (printed and recorded material).
5. Circulation Department:

   The Central Recording Library which holds the recordings made by the ORTF (L'Office de Radiodiffusion-Television Française).

   The Central Music Library where music scores and materials as well as works on music are held.

   The Central Drama Library which holds literary works as well as unpublished works broadcast by radio or television.

   The Central Gramophone Record Library where commercial records are bought, stocked, classified, and stored for use.

The Central Gramophone Record Library holds at the moment 500,000 records for current use and 100,000 records for archives (i.e. now deleted). It buys 90,000 records a year, almost everything which is recorded in France or sold there. An average of 1,500 records *a day* is lent for broadcasting (either on radio, TV, or broadcasts to foreign countries); if one considers the processes involved in the choice and selection of these records by the users of the library, this, in fact, implies a daily handing out of 8,000 records, and as many will have to be put back. In addition, the Central Record Library serves the needs of the nine regional broadcasting stations and of the nine overseas stations.

A staff of 35, working under a chief record librarian, runs this department. The various members of the staff are grouped into different sections according to the work to be done.

Accessions

Two clerks, one typist, one porter, under a qualified record librarian.

The records purchased are either new ones or re-issues. Four copies of each new record are bought automatically. Orders for re-issues have first to be authorised by the head record librarian who receives requests from his staff and also from the provincial, overseas, and foreign broadcasting stations. Those responsible for the purchase of records:

Order them, receive them, and check them against the orders and invoices.

Write an entry for each new record bought in the appropriate registers which are arranged under labels of the issuing companies: for each record number, one can check at a glance how many copies have been bought.

Example: Deutsche-Grammophon register:

Numbers :	:	:	:	:	:	:	:	:
619.141	: 1	: 2	: 3	: 4	: 5	: 6	: 7	: 8 :
619.142	: 1	: 2	: 3	: 4 :	:	:	:	
619.143	: 1	: 2	: 3	: 4	: 5	: 6 :	:	

Mark all the records with an electric pen (the only permanent process).

Number each copy 1–2–3–etc., the class number of a record being in fact the label number and copy number.

Send copies of each record to various departments:

Re-issues are put in the general stock.

New records: 1 copy to the Arts Reference Library,
1 copy to the reserve stock,
1 copy to the general stock.

Post to the regional, overseas, and foreign broadcasting stations records which they have requested.

Send the invoices to the general administration department which pays the accounts.

The General Stock

A staff of six: one record librarian, five unqualified assistants.

The stock includes the general current lending stock as well as reserve stock. One copy of each new record purchased (the first) is sent to reserve stock. The reserve stock is only used in two instances:

1. When there are no copies of a record left in the general lending stock.
2. When a new record has to be used as an emergency measure.

No record can be taken out of the reserve stock unless it has been decided to buy new copies or to send it to the archives.

Reserve stock and general lending stock are classified in the same way: By size: 45 RPM and 33 RPM. Within each size, by alphabetical order of manufacturer and then by the record number.

The staff shelve and issue records under the supervision of the librarian in charge. The record librarian is also responsible for the withdrawal of used and worn copies. He will, if necessary, suggest their replacement to the chief librarian.

The Request-Programmes Section

Four record librarians supervised by a senior librarian prepare the programmes to be presented to the disc-jockeys. It is their duty to see that the orders given by the producers and the commercial department are carried out efficiently.

The Programmes Advisory Service

A supervising record librarian and four qualified assistants deal with the radio and television producers who come to consult them in planning programmes of all kinds. They give them advice and help in choosing suitable music.

The Archives

One librarian and three professional assistants. They consist of the following.

Records which are no longer available commercially.

Purchases from private collections of old records.

The archive is composed of about 100,000 items. There are old 78 RPM records (pre-electric and electric) as well as quite a number of cylinders. Archives are shelved under the names of performers. This is different from the practice adopted in cataloguing the general stock. Only tape-recordings of originals are lent out by the archives department. When a record is transferred to the archives, a note of the new location is put on the catalogue cards (composers, performers, genre) as well as in the accessions register. The title entry is taken out of the title catalogue and inserted in the archives catalogue (which is arranged in title order). This work is done by the record archivists. They also make a rough copy of accession entries of old recordings.

When a copy of a recording is made, a note is entered on the archives catalogue card indicating the number of the copy.

Copies of recordings are numbered in an unbroken chronological sequence and are shelved in that order.

SOUND EFFECTS are classified separately by types. All sound effects are the responsibility of a record librarian who first makes a tape-recording of the sounds on each record, track by track, to facilitate its use, and who is then available to help borrowers in making their choice.

The Issue Desk

Six assistants. An average of 1,500 records is lent daily, and as many will be returned to the library. The number of records on loan is between 30,000 and 40,000, making it necessary to use ORTF's computer to count the number of records issued and returned. When a borrower has made his selection, he presents the records to the issue desk. There a record of the make and number is made in triplicate: one copy is given to the borrower, another to the computer, and the third is kept at the issue desk for a week. The same process is followed when records are returned.

1. Every week the computer supplies the following lists of issues, which are always up to date:
   (a) By alphabetical order of make, with the label number, the name of the borrower and date of issue. This acts as an exact guide as to what is actually on the shelves and makes it easy for the librarian to ensure the quick return of overdue records.
   (b) By alphabetical order of borrowers' names, and, for each borrower the date when the record was issued, also its make and number. This list provides a means of controlling abuse of the library.
2. Each month the computer gives statistics of issues for each broadcasting service: number of records by type (33, 45, and 78 RPM), together with a list for the preceding month and a cumulative list dating form January 1st of the current year.
3. Also each month, the computer supplies overdue notices for borrowers who have retained records for more than one month. It does this by extracting these from the monthly loan lists. This system has been working for 8 months, has proved entirely satisfactory and ensures a very brisk and efficient turnover of the stock.

We have seen already that a copy of each record was sent to the Arts Reference Library. There it is thoroughly examined by specialists who also deal with other types of material (printed music, dramatic works, ORTF recordings, periodical reviews, etc.). The reference librarians make out rough catalogue cards which are sent to the central catalogue. Catalogue cards are then produced on machines with a perforated ribbon technique and printed automatically; thus making it possible after one set has been processed to issue as many copies as necessary.

Catalogues
The Gramophone Record Library catalogues, like all other catalogues of the Services of Information Storage and Documentation, are part of the Central Catalogue; they consist of the following entries:-

AUTHOR CATALOGUE
Alphabetical sequence of authors' names.
Subdivisions — by title of the work,
            by performer,
            by speed.

TITLE CATALOGUE
Alphabetical sequence of titles.
Subdivisions — by name of author,
            by performer,
            by speed.

PERFORMER CATALOGUE
Alphabetical sequence of performers' names.
Subdivisions — by title,
            by author
            by speed.

SUBJECT CATALOGUE
I. INSTRUMENTAL MUSIC
1. Solo Instruments: Alphabetical arrangement by instruments.
                Subdivision by title.
        Organ: Double arrangement: (a) by title,
                                (b) By location of the instrument.
2. Chamber Music: By title.
3. Early Music: By title.

II. SYMPHONIC MUSIC

1. Orchestras with solo instruments: arranged under instruments,
                        Subdivision by title.
2. Orchestras: by title.

III. RELIGIOUS MUSIC

1. Liturgy   : (a) by title,
                        : (b) by rite.
2. Oratorios   : by title.
3   Cantatas   : by title.
4. Motets   : by title.
5. Gregorian Chant   : by title.
6. Christmas Carols   : arrangement: (a) vocal,
                                        (b) instrumental.

7. Early Music   : by title.

IV. STAGE AND SCREEN MUSIC

1. Theatre Music   : (a) operas and comic operas.
                          (b) operettas — in French,
                                         — in English,
                                         — in German,
                                         — etc.
                        Arranged by titles of works.

                        Subdivisions:
                        (1) Complete recordings of performances:
                            in order of the principal performer.
                        (2) Excerpts: in order of the principal performer.
                        (3) Arias: the arrangement follows the order
                            of appearamce in the work.
                        (c) Musical comedies — in French.
                                              — in English.
                                              — in German.
                                              — etc.

2. Film Music   : arrangement by titles.
3. Ballet Music   : arrangement by titles.

V. VOCAL MUSIC

1. Solo Songs   : (a) in French: by title.
                          (b) in foreign languages: by language, sub-
                                                    division by title.

                          (c) early songs: by title.
2. Choral Music   : (a) by title.
                          (b) early works: by title.
3. Secular Canatas and Oratorios : by title.

VI. LIGHT MUSIC

1. Light Music
2. Various Types of: (a) music for brass band,
                       (b) military music,
                       (c) tavern music,
                       (d) fairground music,
                       (e) circus music,
                       (f) various.

VII. MISCELLANEOUS

1. Songs   : (a) in French : by title.
                    (b) in English : by title.
                    (c) In German : by title.
                    (d) in Italian : by title.
                    (e) various   : by title.
                    (f) special types of song: drinking,
                                             early,
                                             student,
                                           sea shanties,
                                           work,
                                           marching,
                                         nursery rhymes,
                                         ribald,
                                         patriotic,
                                         scout.

2. Dances   : alphabetical order of dances
                                      subdivision
                                        by title.

3. Arrangements : in alphabetical order under the original title.

VIII. JAZZ

Alphabetical arrangement under title.

IX. FOLKLORE

1. France   : alphabetical arrangement under provinces
                    subdivision by title.
2. Abroad   : arrangement under continent and country.
                    Some countries will have subheadings under
                    their characteristic types of music, e.g.
                    Germany: Beer-house music.

case by discovering passages missed out of the pressing by careless editing.

As most people think they can write a book or play, so many record enthusiasts are confident that they could review records; but writing ability is just as essential as knowledge of music, a critical ear, and balanced judgement. Even with experienced reviewers, severe editing is often necessary before the reviews are printed and some have to be rejected altogether. As in the book-reviewing world there are reviewers who want to write about everything and anything but the record in question. There are critics with particular aversions to certain composers, performers, and styles of performance, and there are others with overwhelming enthusiasms. All this must be allowed for in reading the reviews. There is pretentiousness in some reviews of classical music and in rather more reviews of jazz records. In sum, though, the standard of record-reviewing is higher than that of book-reviewing and over 100,000 copies of the three monthly magazines are sold each issue while the readership of the other reviews must be very much greater.

The Gramophone

379, Kenton Road, Kenton, Harrow, Middlesex (3/-)

The largest circulation (in Europe, too, it is claimed) is enjoyed by *The Gramophone*, founded by Compton Mackenzie and Christopher Stone in 1923. Issues vary somewhat in size according to the amount of advertising booked for a particular month (all three journals rely on advertising to help meet costs of publishing) but might run to fifty pages of editorial and eighty of advertisements. Most of the text pages are devoted to reviews, but there are also one or two general articles and a quarterly retrospect. Technical notes and equipment tests are also included. The reviews are by a panel of experienced reviewers among whom are some well known names in music and record journalism and writing. The feature, described in the first edition of this book as "unique and valuable", whereby alternative recordings of the same work were listed and compared with the present version, still appears, and is still most valuable.

An annual index makes the journal into a useful reference work when it is bound up and *The Gramophone Classical Record Catalogue* refers to the reviews also. As many as 140 reviews of classical records plus those of jazz and popular and miscellaneous works are included in each issue. The format is solid rather than exciting and the colourful advertisements contrast with the sober typography of the review columns. Regular features include Federation and Society Notes; small advertisements of records and equipment for sale and wanted; correspondence and book reviews.

Audio and Record Review*

Audio and Record Review incorporates *The Gramophone Record,* founded in 1933, *Record Review,* and *Gramophone Record Review.* A larger proportion of the editorial pages is devoted to articles about music and records than *The Gramophone,* and there are some very useful features such as a series of complete catalogues and guides to recordings of individual composers, and another series of "Music on Record", which is a selective guide to the field appearing in advance of a new edition of the book of this title edited by Peter Gammond, and Burnett James.

Again fluctuating in size, this journal may run to 100 or so editorial and advertising pages and the reviews cover the whole range of recordings, classical music, jazz and blues, folk, popular albums and stage and screen. Tape-recordings are also reviewed. The format is attractive and the journal well printed, while the reviews and articles are in the hands of a panel of approximately equal strength to that of *The Gramophone,* with some well known names among them. The index has not appeared for some years but apparently it is hoped to resume this most useful feature.

The equipment reviews and technical articles are particularly well regarded in this journal.

Records and Recording

Hansom Books Ltd., 75, Victoria St., Artillery Mansions, London, S.W.1. (3/- or 42/- per annum)
Unlike the previous two journals, *Records and Recording* is one of several related periodicals concerned with the arts of which one, *Music and Musicians,* also contains record reviews in some quantity. Reviews are confined to classical music, jazz, folk, country and western, and speech, but with no attempt at coverage of popular music, stage and screen, etc. There are general musical articles and equipment reviews and, again, the format and printing are attractive. If the reviewers are slightly less weighty than their colleagues on the other journals, they compensate by a livelier style. Two special features are listings of new releases (irrespective of whether reviews appear) and "last month's best sellers" although the latter is rather less useful than the former. There is also a short list entitled "Pick of the Month".

*Now called *Record Review.* Published by Link House Publications, Ltd., Editorial Office: Pembroke House, P.O. Box 200, Croydon, CR9 2DY (3/6 or 42/- per annum). Incorporates *Audio and Record Review.* Editor, April 1970.

The Monthly Letter

EMG Handmade Gramophones Ltd., 26, Soho Square, London, W.1. (30/- per annum)

The Monthly Letter is a dealer production widely consulted, and enjoyed, for its anonymous reviews which are concise and penetrating, having not so much space available to hedge their criticisms or praise. A series of symbols is used to sum up recommendations and this system also applies to the same publisher's *The Art of Record Buying*, so that in effect the two publications comprise a current and a retrospective service. *The Art of Record Buying* is published annually (25/-).

The Consensus and Review

Henry Stave and Co., 8, Dean Street, London, W.1. (2/6 or 30/- per annum)

The Consensus and Review combines similar concise and anonymous reviews by the staff of this firm with a review of opinions from the other leading reviewing journals so that comparisons can be made. This acts rather as a guide to the other reviews than as a final arbiter and performs a similar function to that of *Notes*, the quarterly review of the Music Library Association (of the United States). These are both very useful publications.

Newspapers and Other Journals

The record librarian needs, in most cases, a comprehensive or nearly complete review service. Often, however, the reviews in *The Times, Daily Telegraph*, and *The Guardian* will throw further (and perhaps more confusing?) light on the qualities of a recording, while the *Sunday Times* and the *Observer* from time to time deal with recent records in their colour supplements. Other general magazines also carry regular or occasional record reviews but particular mention must be made of *Library World* in which E. T. Bryant writes a quarterly survey "Discographia" from the librarian's point of view. *Recorded Sound*, the quarterly journal of the British Institute of Recorded Sound, and *The Record Collector*, although rather outside the scope of this article, must be mentioned as of considerable value in the field of historical recording.

Gramophone Record Librarianship: a Selective Bibliography

MIRIAM H. MILLER, LRAM, FLA

Lecturer, School of Librarianship, North-Western Polytechnic

This bibliography covers material published up to the end of 1967 but is not meant to be exhaustive. Discographies have been excluded, as have technical manuals and selection guides which do not relate primarily to the library context.

The majority of books and articles included are in English. Material written in other languages has been included only where an abstract in English is known to exist, in which case a translation of the title and details of the abstract are given immediately after the original reference.

ADREASSEN, A. Audio-visuelle Hjelpemidler i Bibliotekene. *Bok og bib* **31** (3) May, 1964. Pp. 179–180. [Audio-visual Aids in Libraries. L.S.A. 14811.]

AKKERMAN, O., *et al.* Bibliotheewerk voor blinden. *Bibliotheek* **6** (4) May, 1963. Pp. 125–45. [Libraries for the Blind. L.S.A. 13438.]

ALDOUS, D. Two Famous Libraries; the Danish National Record Library Jubilee and the BBC Record Library. *Audio and Record Review* **2** (11) August, 1963. Pp. 8–9.

ALLISON, M. Workshops for Librarians having Audio-visual Responsibility. *California School Libraries* **36** (4) May, 1965. Pp. 33–7.

ALVIN, M. *and* MICHELLE, M. La Roche College Classification System for Phonorecords. *Library Resources and Technical Services* **9** (4) 1965. Pp. 443–5.

AMERICAN LIBRARY ASSOCIATION. Library Technology Project. The Testing and Evaluation of Record Players for Libraries. Chicago, American Library Association, 1962. Series II. Chicago, American Library Association, 1964. (*LTP Publications no. 8*)

ANDERSON, E. L. Recordings in Public Libraries. (*In* HOULE, C.O., *ed.* Libraries in Adult and Fundamental Education. Paris, UNESCO, 1951, Pp. 93–100.)

ANDERSON, J. The Auckland University College Gramophone Library. *New Zealand Libraries* **13** (11) December, 1950. Pp. 64–9.

Gramophone Record Librarianship: a Selective Bibliography

by MIRIAM H. MILLER, LRAM, FLA

Lecturer, School of Librarianship, North-Western Polytechnic

This bibliography covers material published up to the end of 1967 but is not meant to be exhaustive. Discographies have been excluded, as have technical manuals and selection guides which do not relate primarily to the library context.

The majority of books and articles included are in English. Material written in other languages has been included only where an abstract in English is known to exist, in which case a translation of the title and details of the abstract are given immediately after the original reference.

ADREASSEN, A. Audio-visuelle Hjelpemidler i Bibliotekene. *Bok og bib* **31** (3) May, 1964. Pp. 179–180. [Audio-visual Aids in Libraries. L.S.A. 14811.]

AKKERMAN, O., *et al.* Bibliotheewerk voor blinden. *Bibliotheek* **6** (4) May, 1963. Pp. 125–45. [Libraries for the Blind. L.S.A. 13438.]

ALDOUS, D. Two Famous Libraries; the Danish National Record Library Jubilee and the BBC Record Library. *Audio and Record Review* **2** (11) August, 1963. Pp. 8–9.

ALLISON, M. Workshops for Librarians having Audio-visual Responsibility. *California School Libraries* **36** (4) May, 1965. Pp. 33–7.

ALVIN, M. *and* MICHELLE, M. La Roche College Classification System for Phonorecords. *Library Resources and Technical Services* **9** (4) 1965. Pp. 443–5.

AMERICAN LIBRARY ASSOCIATION. Library Technology Project. The Testing and Evaluation of Record Players for Libraries. Chicago, American Library Association, 1962. Series II. Chicago, American Library Association, 1964. (*LTP Publications no. 8*)

ANDERSON, E. L. Recordings in Public Libraries. (*In* HOULE, C.O., *ed.* Libraries in Adult and Fundamental Education. Paris, UNESCO, 1951, Pp. 93–100.)

ANDERSON, J. The Auckland University College Gramophone Library. *New Zealand Libraries* **13** (11) December, 1950. Pp. 64–9.

ANDERSON, S. Cataloging of "Folk Music" on Records. *Library Resources and Technical Services* 3 (1) Winter, 1959. Pp. 64–9.

BENISON, S. Reflections on Oral History. *American Archivist* 28 (1) January, 1965. Pp. 71–7.

BESCOBY-CHAMBERS, J. The Archives of Sound. Lingfield, Surrey, Oakwood Press, 1966.

BIENEMAN, D. Mighty Oaks. *Illinois Libraries* 38 (10) December, 1956. Pp. 300–301.

BLAUENFELDT, A. Musikbiblioteket i Lyngby-Taarboek Kommune. *REOL: Nordisk Biblioteks Tidsskrift* 4 (1) January/April, 1965. Pp. 3–15. [The Music Library in the Borough of Lyngby-Taarboek, Denmark. L.S.A. 15606.]

BOULTON, L. I search for Ancient Music. *Columbia Library columns* 12 (2) February, 1963. Pp. 13–22.

BØRRESEN, A. Musikbiblioteket i Lyngby-Taarboek Kommune. *Bogens verden* 45 (4) 1963. Pp. 221–224. [The Music Library in Lyngby-Taarboek. L.S.A. 13740.]

BRITISH INSTITUTE OF RECORDED SOUND The Institute's Library of Written Matter. *Recorded Sound* (18) April, 1965. Pp. 342–3.

BRITTEN, V. The BBC Gramophone Library. *Recorded Sound* 1 (1) May, 1961. Pp. 13–21.

BRITTEN, V. The Formation and Administration of a Gramophone Library. London, Library Association, 1946.

BRITTEN, V. Recordings. (*In* BURKETT, J. *and* MORGAN, T. S. Special Materials in the Library. London, Library Association, 1963, Chapter 10, Pp. 110–16.)

BROBURG, J. The Poetry Room of Harvard University. *Recorded Sound* (27) July, 1967. Pp. 214–18.

BROWNING, J. The American Music Center. *Notes* 21 (4) Fall, 1964. Pp. 511–12.

BRYANT, E. T. Collecting Gramophone Records. London, Focal Press, 1962.

BRYANT, E. T. Gramophone Records in the Public Library. *Audio and Record Review* 2 (9) May, 1963. P. 23.

BRYANT, E. T. Indexing Gramophone Records. *Indexer* 2 (3) Spring, 1961. Pp. 90–94.

BRYANT, E. T. Long playing Records and the Gramophone Library. *Library Association Record* 53 (3) March, 1951. Pp. 76–8.

BRYANT, E. T. Gramophone Record Libraries. (*In* BRYANT, E. T. *Music Librarianship; a Practical Guide.* London, Clarke, 1959. Chapter 5, Pp. 184–281.)

BULLING, B. Die Neue Bremer Musikbibliothek. *Bücherei und Bildung* 17 (10) October, 1965. Pp. 516–24. [The New Music Library in Bremen. L.S.A. 66/171.]

BURBRIDGE, E. *and* AUDSLEY, J. Gramophone Record Libraries: a review article. *Library Association Record* **66** (3) March, 1964. Pp. 100–104.

CHAILLEY, J. *et al.* Le Catalogage des Documents Ethnomusicologiques (disques et bandes) de l'Institut de Musicologie de Paris. *Fontes Artis Musicae* **9** (2) July/December, 1962. Pp. 76–8. [Cataloguing of Sound Reproductions of Ethnomusicology (on records and tapes) in the Institute of Musicology, Paris. L.S.A. 13285.]

CHASSE, J. La Bibliothèque et la Disque. *Bulletin des Bibliothèques de France* **1** (4) April, 1956. Pp. 249–67. [The Public Library and the Disc. L.S.A. 6089.]

CHRISTENSEN, R. M. The Junior College Library as an Audio-visual Center. *College and Research Libraries* **26** (2) March, 1965. Pp. 121–8.

CHRISTIANSEN, B. Plader i Biblioteket. Udvalgsprincipper – udlånspraksis. *Bogens verden* **49** (4) July, 1967. Pp. 287–91. [The Gramophone Record in the Library. Principles of Selection – Practice of Issuing. L.S.A. 67/705.]

CLARK, P. J. Public Library Records Collections. *News Notes of Californian Libraries* **49** (2) April, 1954. Pp. 308–10.

CLARKE, V. Non-book Library Materials; a handbook of procedures for a uniform and simplified system of handling audio-visual aids, vertical file and other non-book materials in the school library. Denton, North Texas State College, 1953.

COHEN, A. Classification of Four-track Tapes. *Library Resources and Technical Services* **6** (4) Fall, 1962. Pp. 360–61.

COLBY, E. E. Sound Recordings in the Music Library, with special reference to Record Archives. *Library Trends* **8** (4) April, 1960. Pp. 556–65.

COLBY, E. E. *and* JOHNSON, K. O. Sound Reproduction and Recording Equipment. (*In* BRADLEY, C. J. *ed.* Manual of Music Librarianship. Michigan, Music Library Association, 1966. Pp. 76–98.)

COLLISON, R. L. Libraries for Television. *Library World* **67** (781) July, 1965. Pp. 3–7.

COLLISON, R. L. Gramophone Records. (*In* COLLISON, R. L. The treatment of Special Materials in Libraries. London, ASLIB, 1955. Pp. 41–51.)

COLLISON, R. L. Recordings: Disc and Tape. (*In* COLLISON, R. L. *Commercial and Industrial Records Storage,* London, Benn, 1969. Pp. 141–5.)

COLMAN, G. P. Oral History – an Appeal for More Systematic Procedures. *American Archivist* **28** (1) January, 1965. Pp. 79–83.

COOPER, E. *and* WILLIAMS, D. G. Gramophone Record Libraries; a Short Survey. *Gramophone* **42** (3) August, 1964. Pp. 83–5.

COWAN, J. C. The Care and Treatment of Long playing Records in Public

Libraries. *Librarian and Book World* 47 (4) April/May, 1958, Pp. 76–9.

COWAN, J. C. Sound Recordings. (*In* MASON, D. *ed*. Primer of Nonbook materials in Libraries. London, Association of Assistant Librarians, 1958. Pp. 94–112.)

COX, C. T. The Cataloguing of Records. *Library Journal* 85 (17) December 15th., 1960. Pp. 4523–5.

CUMING, G. Problems of Record Cataloguing. *Recorded Sound* 1 (4) Autumn, 1961. Pp. 116–22.

CUNMON, T. Cataloguing and Classification of Phonograph Records. *Proceedings of the Catholic Library Association Conference, 1960*. Pp. 180–85.

CURRY, D. Building a Record Collection. *Ontario Library Review* 35 (3) August, 1954. Pp. 53–5.

CUSHMAN, J. Folk Music in the Library. *Library Journal* 88 (9) May 1st., 1963. Pp. 1833–4.

DACHS, D. The New Long-playing Libraries. *Saturday Review* 49 January 29th., 1966. Pp. 49–51.

DANIELS, E. Music to Borrow: Recordings Service of Illinois State Library. *Illinois Libraries* 33 (10) December, 1951. Pp. 449–52.

DAVIS, C. K. Record Collections, 1960: LJ's survey of fact and opinion. *Library Journal* 85 (17) October 1st., 1960. Pp. 3375–80.

DAY, D. L. Audio-visual Services on a Community-wide Basis. (*In* STROHECKER, E. D., *ed*. Allies of Books. Louisville, Kentucky, Catherine Spalding College, 1964. Pp. 23–30.)

DEAN-SMITH, M. Proposals towards the Cataloguing of Gramophone Records in a Library of National Scope. *Journal of Documentation* 8 (3) September, 1952, Pp. 141–56.

DÉCOLLOGNE, R. Un bel example de Cohésion: le Groupe Francais des Phonothèques. *Fontes Artis Musicae* (1) 1961. Pp. 24–6. [A Fine Example of Co-operation: the French Record Libraries group. L.S.A. 11673.]

DÉCOLLOGNE, R. The French National Archive of Recordings: twenty Years of Evolution, 1940–1960. [Abstract in *Recorded Sound* 1 (8) Autumn, 1962. Pp. 277–8].

DÉCOLLOGNE, R. La Phonothèque Nationale. *Bulletin des Bibliothèques de France* 12 (2) February, 1967. Pp. 35–60. [National Library of Sound Recordings. L.S.A. 67/355.]

DEWEY, H. Music and Phonorecord Code Criticised. *Library Journal* 83 (11) June 1st., 1958. pp. 1665–8.

DE YOUNG, C. D. Proposed Record Collection for a Medium Sized Library. Ann Arbor, University of Michigan Department of Library Science, 1950.

DIXON, E. I. Oral History: a New Horizon. *Library Journal* 87 (7) April 1st., 1962. Pp. 1363–1365.

DIXON, M. V. Music Library service. *New Zealand Libraries* **14** (7) August, 1951, Pp. 165—71.

DOUGLAS, J. R. The Composer and his Music on Record. *Library Journal* **92** (6) March 15th., 1967. Pp. 1117—21.

ECKERSLEY, T. The Recorded Programmes Libraries of the BBC. *Recorded Sound* **1** (6) Spring, 1962. Pp. 181—5.

EDMUND, M. Techniques for Handling Phonograph Records. *Catholic Library World* **27** (3) December, 1955. Pp. 107—10.

ENGSTRÖM, A. Grammofonsteivan och Biblioteken. *Biblioteket och vi* **10** 1956—7. Pp. 46—59. [Gramophone Records and Libraries. L.S.A. 8389.]

FOSTER, D. L. Notes used on Music and Phonorecord catalog Cards. *University of Illinois Graduate School of Library Science Occasional Papers,* no. 66, 1962.

FREY, J. E. Recorded Reviews. *Wilson Library Bulletin* **39** (4) December, 1964, Pp. 333—4.

GEISER, C. Selecting and Using Story Recordings. *Library Journal* **85** (17) December 15th., 1960. Pp. 4521—3.

GILBRIN, C. La Discothèque Municipale de Neuilly-sur-Seine. *Bulletin d'information de L'Association des Bibliothèques Français* **39** November, 1962. Pp. 179—80. [The Public Record Library at Neuilly-sur-Seine. Abstract in *Recorded Sound* (13) January, 1964. P. 190.]

GOTTLIEB, B. Lincoln Center's New Sound Library: a Trend. *Music Journal* **24** April, 1966. Pp. 58—9.

GREENHALL, M. P. Young Adults as Record Borrowers. *Top of the News* **19** (4) May, 1963. P. 52.

GUNTER, S. Coventry Public Libraries. *Open Access* **12** (N.S.1.) October, 1963. Pp. 4—5; 10—11.

HAGEN, C. B. Proposals Presented to the 1966 meeting of the Association for Recorded Sound Collections held at Washington, D.C., U.S.A. *Recorded Sound* **26** April, 1967. Pp. 181—92.

HAGEN, C. B. A Proposed Information Retrieval System for Sound Recordings. *Special Libraries* **56** (4) April, 1965. Pp. 223—8.

HAMMACK, M. C. A Review of the Discussions of the Workshop Groups. (*In* STROHECKER, E. C., *ed.* Allies of Books. Louisville, Kentucky, Catherine Spalding College, 1964. Pp. 31—52.)

HANNA, E. F. First Steps towards a Record Collection. *Illinois Libraries* **44** (2) February, 1962. Pp. 134—50.

HANNA, E. F. Strictly for the Record. *Illinois Libraries* **39** (4) April, 1957. Pp. 129—31.

HARRISON, K. C. The Gramophone Record Library. *Unesco Bulletin for Libraries* **14** (5) September/October, 1960. Pp. 197—201.

HART, R. *and* BURNETTE, F. Non-musical Collections. *Library Journal* **83** (4) February 1st., 1958. Pp. 536—43.

HASKELL, P. T. The Library of Recorded Animal Sounds. *Recorded Sound* 1 (2) June, 1961. P. 99.

HIRSCH, F. Schallplattensammlungen in öffentlichen Bibliotheken. *Der Bibliothekar* 15 (7) July, 1961. Pp. 687–98. [Record Collections in Public Libraries. Abstract in *Recorded Sound* 1 (6) Spring, 1962. P. 194.]

HOOD, B. Gramophone Records, Art Prints and Films. *South African Libraries* 24 (4) April, 1957. Pp. 132–5.

HOOD, B. G. Music and Gramophone Records in Public Libraries. *New Zealand Libraries* 14 (7) August, 1951. Pp. 172–83.

HOWES, J. Gramophone Record Library Procedure. *Library Association Record* 61 (11) November, 1959. Pp. 289–94.

HOWES, J. The History of Music on Gramophone Records. *Librarian and Book World* 41 (4) April, 1952. Pp. 81–5.

HOWES, J. W. Long playing records. *Librarian and Book World*. 41 (10) October, 1952. Pp. 195–6.

HUS, S. H. Uitleen – Discotheek – Zwolle. *Openbare Bibliotheek* 6 (7) September, 1963. Pp. 205–6. [Record Lending Library in Zwolle. Abstract in *Recorded Sound* (16) October, 1964. P. 280.]

INTERNATIONAL FOLK MUSIC COUNCIL International Directory of Folk Music Record Archive. *Recorded Sound* 2 (10/11) April/July, 1963. Pp. 103–14.

JARVIS, S. M. They've got it taped. *Library World* 53 (743) May, 1962. Pp. 290–91.

JENSEN, H. Folkebiblioteket og Grammofonpladerne. *Bogens Verden* 36 (7) October, 1954. Pp. 297–304. [Public Libraries and Gramophone Records. L.S.A. 4103.]

JENSEN, H. Grammofonpladendlån. Ergaringer fra en studierejse. *Bibliotekaren* 19 (5) 1957. Pp. 149–65. [Gramophone Record Lending. L.S.A. 7869.]

JIRECKOVA, O. Mestska Knihovna ve Varsave: Vyuziti Magnetofonu. *Ctenar* 15 (11) 1963. P. 374. [Magnetic Tapes in the Public Library of Warsaw. Abstract in *Recorded Sound* (16) October, 1964. Pp. 280–81.]

JUGE, M. Création et Entretien d'un Discothèque. *Bulletin D'Information de l'Association des Bibliothèques Français* 39 November, 1962. Pp. 171–8. [Establishment and Organisation of a Record Library. Abstract in *Recorded Sound* (13) January, 1964. P. 190.]

J.W.P. The Phonograph Record Collection. Part 2: Technical Notes. *Edmonton Public Library News Notes* 7 (1) January, 1962.

KALLAI, S. A Music Critic Looks at Basic L.P. Collections. *Library Journal* 88 (18) October 15th., 1963. Pp. 3802–3.

KELLOG, P. P. Problems of Storing Natural Sounds on Tape. *Bioacoustics Bulletin* 1 (1) January/March, 1961.

KENNEDY, W. S. The Record Collection. *Books at Brown* **18** (3) March, 1958. Pp. 125–8.

KLEIN, A. L. The Spoken Recordings: an Innovation. *Library Journal* **83** (4) February 15th., 1958. Pp. 533–5.

KUMARI, S. Use of Sound Recordings in the Libraries. *Indian Association of Special Libraries and Information Centres Bulletin* **11** (2) June, 1966. Pp. 107–18.

KWIATKOWSKI, J. Plytoteka w Bibliotece. *Nanki Humanistyizno Spoleczne* (7) 1962. Pp. 199–224. [Gramophone Records in the Library. L.S.A. 13775.]

LANG, P. H. The L.P. and the well-appointed Library. *Library Journal* **88** (9) May 1st., 1963. Pp. 1809–12.

LEDVINKA, F. Význam Audiovizuálních Prostředků činnosti Knihovny. *Techniká Knihovna* (1) 1964. Pp. 2–7. [Audio-visual Materials in Libraries. L.S.A. 14519.]

LECOMPTE, Y. Comment Nous utilisons l'électro-mécanographie. *Fontes Artis Musicae* (1) 1957. Pp. 18–24. [How we use Electro-mechanical Methods. L.S.A. 7308.]

LEPPANEN, R. Kielistudio Kirjastossa. *Kirjastolehti* **59** (7) 1966. Pp. 210–211. [Language Laboratory at the Public Library. L.S.A. 66/994.]

LIBRARY AND INFORMATION BULLETIN Gramophone Records. *Library and Information Bulletin* **1** (1) 1967, Pp. 6–13.

LIBRARY ASSOCIATION Phonorecords. (*In* Anglo-American cataloguing rules. London, Library Association, 1967. Chapter 14, Pp. 247–53.)

LIBRARY OF CONGRESS Rules for Descriptive Cataloguing: Phono-records. Preliminary edition. Washington D.C., Library of Congress, 1952.

LIBRARY JOURNAL A Report from 100 Libraries on Current Practices regarding Records in Libraries. *Library Journal* **85** (17) December, 1960. Pp. 4516–17.

LIBRARY JOURNAL A Roundup of Experiences in Programming with Records. *Library Journal* **85** (17) December 15th., 1960. Pp. 4511–15.

LIMBACHER, J. L. Recordings for Young People. *Library Journal* **91** (18) October 15th., 1966. Pp. 5139–41.

LINDBERG, F. Broadcasting Libraries and Archives as Music Research Centres. *Fontes Artis Musicae* (1) January/April, 1966. Pp. 76–9.

LIST, G. Archiving Sound Recordings. *Phonetica* **6** 1931. Pp. 18–31.

LIST, G. The Indiana University Archives of Folk and Primitive Music. *British Institute of Recorded Sound Bulletin* 15/16, Spring, 1960. Pp. 3–7.

LOVELL, L. G. Gramophone Record Provision in Public Libraries. *Library Association Record* **56** (7) July, 1954. Pp. 251–9.

LUENING, O. Music Materials and the Public Library: a Report to the Director of the Public Library Inquiry. New York, Social Science

25 (4) December 1960. Pp. 310–11.

REDFERN, B. R. Arranging and Cataloguing Gramophone Records. (*In* REDFERN, B. R. *Organizing Music in Libraries.* London, Bingley, 1966. Chapter 6, Pp. 67–73.)

REINHARD, K. The Berlin Phonogramm-Archiv. *Recorded Sound* **1** (2) June, 1961. Pp. 44–5.

ROBINSON, A. J. Gramophone Record Library Co-operation. *Library World* **65** (764) February, 1964. Pp. 272–5.

RUFSVOLD, M. L. Recordings, Transcriptions and Recorders. (*In* RUFSVOLD, M. L. Audio-visual School Library Service. Chicago, American Library Association, 1949. Pp. 42–9.)

RYAN, M. History in Sound: a Descriptive Listing of the KIRO-CBS Collection of Broadcasts of the World War II years and After, in the Phonoarchive of the University of Washington. Seattle, University of Washington Press, 1963.

SAFFI, *Count* The Italian State Record Library. *British Institute of Recorded Sound Bulletin* (1) Summer, 1956. Pp. 8–11.

SAGE, J. P. Notes on a Record Lending Library: Wellington Public Library. *New Zealand Libraries* **19** (9) November/December, 1956. Pp. 209–10.

SAUL, P. The British Institute of Recorded Sound. *Fontes Artis Musicae* (2) 1956. Pp. 171–3.

SAUL, P. Museums of Sound – History and Principles of Operation. (*In* BEREDAY, G. Z. F. *and* LAUWERYS, J. A., *eds.* The Yearbook of Education, 1960; Communications Media and the School. London, Evans brothers Ltd., 1960. Pp. 183–91.)

SAUL, P. Preserving Recorded Sound. (*In* SHERRINGTON, U. *and* OLDHAM, G., *eds.* Music, Libraries and Instruments. London, Hinrichsen, 1961. *Hinrichsen's Eleventh Music Book.* Pp. 110–16.)

SAUL, P. Some Problems in the Preservation of Valuable Sounds. *British Institute of Recorded Sound Bulletin* (13) Summer, 1959. Pp. 24–30.

SCHERMALL, H. Schallplatte und Tonband in der Musikbibliothek. *Bücherei und Bildung* **14** (18/19) August/September, 1962. Pp. 425–7. [Record and Tape in the Music Library. L.S.A. 12955.]

SCHOLZ, D. D. A Manual for the Cataloguing of Recordings in Public Libraries. Louisiana, Louisiana Library Association, 1964.

SCHUURSMA, R. L. The Sound Archives of the University of Utrecht. *Recorded Sound* (15) July, 1964, Pp. 246–50.

SCOTTISH LIBRARY ASSOCIATION New Record Library at Airdrie. *Scottish Library Association News* November/December, 1962. P. 4.

SHANK, W. *and* ENGELBRECHT, L. C. Records and Tapes (*In* BRADLEY, C. J., *ed.* Manual of Music Librarianship. Chicago, American Library Association, 1966. Pp. 65–75.)

SHORES, L. The Dimensions of Oral History. *Library Journal* **95** (2)

March 1st., 1967. Pp. 979—83.

SILBER, I. A Basic Library of U.S. Folk Music. *Library Journal* 88 (19) May 1st., 1963. Pp. 1835—8.

SIMMONS, M. L. The New York Public Library. *Bookmark* 24 (2) November, 1964. Pp. 35—42.

SIMPSON, D. J. Some London Gramophone Record Libraries: Impressions of Visits to the Collections of Six Public Libraries. *Library World* 60 (704) February, 1959. Pp. 137—40.

SIMPSON, V. Books for the Blind. *News Notes of Californian Libraries* 58 (4) Fall, 1963. Pp. 387—94.

SINIFF, H. A Rental Record Library. *Illinois Libraries* 38 (10) December, 1956. Pp. 303—4.

SJOBLOM, C. Bibliotekarier till Grammofonarkivet — Kom! *Biblioteksbladet* 49 (4/5) 1964. Pp. 228—231. [Librarians to the Gramophone Archive — Come! L.S.A. 14755.]

SOFFKE, G. Anlage und Verwaltung von Schallplattensammlungen in Wissenschaftlichen Bibliotheken. (*Arbeiten aus dem Bibliothekar-Lehrinstitut des Landes Nordheim-Westfalen, Hft. 19, 1961.*) [Layout and Operation of a Record Library Collection in a Scientific Library. L.S.A. 14523.]

SPIVACKE, H. A National Archives of Sound Recording. *Library Journal* 88 (18) October 15th., 1963. Pp. 3738—88.

SPIVACKE, H. The Preservation and Reference Services of Sound Recordings in a Research Library. (*In* SHERRINGTON, U. *and* OLDHAM, G., *eds*. Music, Libraries and Instruments. London, Hinrichsen, 1961. *Hinrichsen's Eleventh Music Book.* Pp. 99—110.)

STEVENSON, G. Classification Chaos. *Library Journal* 88 (18) October 15th., 1963. Pp. 3789—94.

STEVENSON, G. Don't Ignore the Gifted Listener. *Library Journal* 88 (3) February 1st., 1963. Pp. 519—22.

STEVENSON, G. Echoes of Bugle and Drum. *Wilson Library Bulletin* 37 (6) February, 1963. Pp. 479—82.

STEVENSON, G. The Practical Record Selector: a "plaine and easie" Introduction. *Library Journal* 88 (9) May 1st., 1963. Pp. 1819—22.

STEVENSON, G. Reports from the Field on the Magic Dragon; or, Life with Stereo. *Library Journal* 88 (18) October 15th., 1963. Pp. 3799—3801.

STILES, H. J. Phonograph Record Classification at the United States Air Force Academy Library. *Library Resources and Technical Services* 9 (4) 1965. Pp. 446—8.

STRANDBYGAARD, E. Musikbiblioteker og Musiksamlinger i Polske Biblioteker. *Bogens Verden* 48 (5) September, 1966. Pp. 345—50. [Music Libraries and Music Collections in Polish Libraries. L.S.A. 66/968.]

SYKES, H. Sutton Coldfield Public Library. *Open Access* 12 (N.S.1.) October, 1963. Pp. 14–15.

SWAIN, D. C. Problems for Practitioners of Oral History. *American Archivist* 28 (1) January, 1965. Pp. 63–9.

TAINSH, K. B. Radio Foretagens Ljudarkiv. *Biblioteksbladet* 45 (1) 1960. Pp. 21–30. [The Collections of Recorded Sound of Broadcasting Companies. Abstract in *Recorded Sound* 1 (6) Spring, 1962. Pp. 193–4.]

THOMSON, E. W. Records in the Child's Life. *Library Journal* 85 (22) December 15th., 1960. Pp. 4505–7

TILIN, M. Treat Records like Books. *Library Journal* 85 (22) December 15th., 1960. Pp. 4518–21.

TILLY, D. You and Your Music: Maintenance Costs. *Library Journal* 76 (19) November 1st., 1951. Pp. 1774–5.

VAN DER WOLK, L. J. De Stichting Discotheek Delft. *Openbare Bibliotheek* 7 (6) July/August, 1964. Pp. 173–179. [The Record Library Foundation at Delft. L.S.A. 14714.]

VAUGHAN, E. L. Cataloguing Recordings in the Illinois State Library. *Illinois Libraries* 35 February 1953. Pp. 79–85.

WEDGEWORTH, R. Jazz. *Library Journal* 88 (9) May 1st., 1963. Pp. 1830–32.

WILMOT, L. *and* SKILLING, B. Gramophone Record Libraries – the Second Phase: an Examination of Some Factors affecting the Cost of Maintaining a Collection of Long playing Records in a Public Library. *Library World* 60 (705) March, 1959. Pp. 176–8.

WILSON, A. Dudley Public Libraries. *Open Access* 12 (N.S.1.) October, 1963. Pp. 11–13.

WYLIE, D. M. Library Record Collections. *New Zealand Libraries* 24 (11) December, 1961. Pp. 245–60.

YOUNG, W. Music and the Librarian. *Australian School Librarian* 4 (1) March 1967. Pp. 3–13.

YURCHENKO, H. Folk Music around the World: a Basic Library Collection. *Library Journal* 88 (9) May 1st., 1963. Pp. 1838–40.

Index

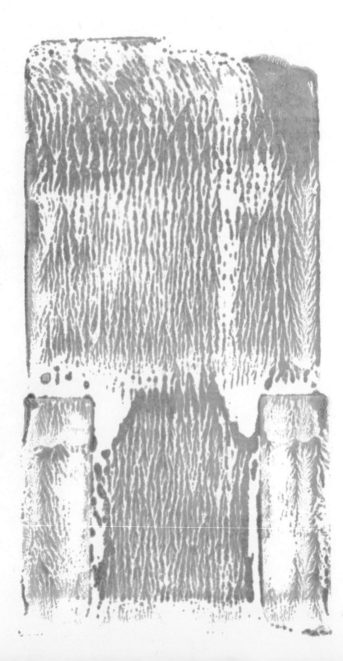